OTHE

How Highly Effective People

Eloquence

How Legendary Leaders Speak

Influential Leadership

Public Speaking Mastery

The 7 Keys to Confidence

Trust is Power

Influence

Decoding Human Nature

The Psychology of Persuasion

How Visionaries Speak

The Eloquent Leader

The Language of Leadership

The Psychology of Communication

The Charisma Code

Available on Amazon

Claim These Free Resources that Will Help You Unleash the Power of Your Words and Speak with Confidence. Visit www.speakforsuccesshub.com/toolkit for Access.

18 Free PDF Resources

30 Free Video Lessons

2 Free Workbooks

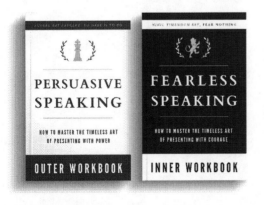

Claim These Free Resources that Will Help You Unleash the Power of Your Words and Speak with Confidence. Visit www.speakforsuccesshub.com/toolkit for Access.

18 Free PDF Resources

12 Iron Rules for Captivating Story, 21 Speeches that Changed the World, 341-Point Influence Checklist, 143 Persuasive Cognitive Biases, 17 Ways to Think On Your Feet, 18 Lies About Speaking Well, 137 Deadly Logical Fallacies, 12 Iron Rules For Captivating Slides, 371 Words that Persuade, 63 Truths of Speaking Well, 27 Laws of Empathy, 21 Secrets of Legendary Speeches, 19 Scripts that Persuade, 12 Iron Rules For Captivating Speech, 33 Laws of Charisma, 11 Influence Formulas, 219-Point Speech-Writing Checklist, 21 Eloquence Formulas

30 Free Video Lessons

We'll send you one free video lesson every day for 30 days, written and recorded by Peter D. Andrei. Days 1-10 cover authenticity, the prerequisite to confidence and persuasive power. Days 11-20 cover building self-belief and defeating communication anxiety. Days 21-30 cover how to speak with impact and influence, ensuring your words change minds instead of falling flat. Authenticity, self-belief, and impact – this course helps you master three components of confidence, turning even the most high-stakes presentations from obstacles into opportunities.

2 Free Workbooks

We'll send you two free workbooks, including long-lost excerpts by Dale Carnegie, the mega-bestselling author of *How to Win Friends and Influence People* (5,000,000 copies sold). *Fearless Speaking* guides you in the proven principles of mastering your inner game as a speaker. *Persuasive Speaking* guides you in the time-tested tactics of mastering your outer game by maximizing the power of your words. All of these resources complement the Speak for Success collection.

PUBLIC

SPEAKING

MASTERY

HOW TO SPEAK WITH CONFIDENCE, IMPACT, AND INFLUENCE

Peter Andrei

PUBLIC SPEAKING MASTERY

SPEAK FOR SUCCESS COLLECTION BOOK

V

SPEAK
TRUTH
WELL
PRESS

A SUBSIDIARY OF SPEAK TRUTH WELL LLC
800 Boylston Street
Boston, MA 02199

**SPEAK
TRUTH
WELL LLC**

Copyright © 2021 Peter Andrei
All rights reserved. No part of this publication may be reproduced, distributed, or transmitted in any form or by any means, including photocopying, recording, or other electronic or mechanical methods, without the prior written permission of the publisher, except in the case of brief quotations embodied in critical reviews and certain other noncommercial uses permitted by copyright law. For permission requests, write to the publisher, addressed "Attention: Permissions Coordinator," at the email address pandreibusiness@gmail.com.

SPEAK FOR SUCCESS COLLECTION

Printed in the United States of America
40 39 38 37 36 35 34 33 32 31

While the author has made every effort to provide accurate internet addresses at the time of publication, neither the publisher nor the author assumes any responsibility for errors, or for changes that occur after publication. Further, the publisher does not have any control over and does not assume any responsibility for author or third-party websites or their content.

www.speakforsuccesshub.com/toolkit

FREE RESOURCES FOR OUR READERS

We believe in using the power of the internet to go above and beyond for our readers. That's why we created the free communication toolkit: 18 free PDF resources, 30 free video lessons, and even 2 free workbooks, including long-lost excerpts by Dale Carnegie, the mega-bestselling author of *How to Win Friends and Influence People*. (The workbooks help you put the most powerful strategies into action).

We know you're busy. That's why we designed these resources to be accessible, easy, and quick. Each PDF resource takes just 5 minutes to read or use. Each video lesson is only 5 minutes long. And in the workbooks, we bolded the key ideas throughout, so skimming them takes only 10 minutes each.

Why give so much away? For three reasons: we're grateful for you, it's useful content, and we want to go above and beyond. Questions? Feel free to email Peter directly at pandreibusiness@gmail.com.

www.speakforsuccesshub.com/toolkit

WHY DOES THIS HELP YOU?

I

The PDF resources cover topics like storytelling, logic, cognitive biases, empathy, charisma, and more. You can dig deeper into the specific topics that interest you most.

II

Many of the PDF resources are checklists, scripts, example-compilations, and formula-books. With these practical, step-by-step tools, you can quickly create messages that work.

III

With these free resources, you can supplement your reading of this book. You can find more specific guidance on the areas of communication you need to improve the most.

IV

The two workbooks offer practical and actionable guidance for speaking with complete confidence (*Fearless Speaking*) and irresistible persuasive power (*Persuasive Speaking*).

V

You can even learn from your phone with the free PDFs and the free video lessons, to develop your skills faster. The 30-lesson course reveals the secrets of building confidence.

VI

You are reading this because you want to improve your communication. These resources take you to the next level, helping you learn how to speak with power, impact, and confidence. We hope these resources make a difference. They are available here:

www.speakforsuccesshub.com/toolkit

From the desk of Peter Andrei
Speak Truth Well LLC
800 Boylston Street
Boston, MA 02199
pandreibusiness@gmail.com

May 15, 2021

What is Our Mission?

To whom it may concern:

The Wall Street Journal reports that public speaking is the world's biggest fear – bigger than being hit by a car. According to Columbia University, this pervasive, powerful, common phobia can reduce someone's salary by 10% or more. It can reduce someone's chances of graduating college by 10% and cut their chances of attaining a managerial or leadership position at work by 15%.

If weak presentation kills your good ideas, it kills your career. If weak communication turns every negotiation, meeting, pitch, speech, presentation, discussion, and interview into an obstacle (instead of an opportunity), it slows your progress. And if weak communication slows your progress, it tears a gaping hole in your confidence – which halts your progress.

Words can change the world. They can improve your station in life, lifting you forward and upward to higher and higher successes. But they have to be strong words spoken well: rarities in a world where most people fail to connect, engage, and persuade; fail to answer the question "why should we care about this?"; fail to impact, inspire, and influence; and, in doing so, fail to be all they could be.

Now zoom out. Multiply this dynamic by one thousand; one million; one billion. The individual struggle morphs into a problem for our communities, our countries, our world. Imagine the many millions of paradigm-shattering, life-changing, life-saving ideas that never saw the light of day. Imagine how many brilliant convictions were sunk in the shipyard. Imagine all that could have been that failed to be.

Speak Truth Well LLC solves this problem by teaching ambitious professionals how to turn communication from an obstacle into an engine: a tool for converting "what could be" into "what is." There is no upper limit: inexperienced speakers can become self-assured and impactful; veteran speakers can master the skill by learning advanced strategies; masters can learn how to outperform their former selves.

We achieve our mission by producing the best publications, articles, books, video courses, and coaching programs available on public speaking and communication, and at non-prohibitive prices. This combination of quality and accessibility has allowed Speak Truth Well to serve over 70,000 customers in its year of launch alone (2021). Grateful as we are, we hope to one day serve millions.

Dedicated to your success,

Peter Andrei
President of Speak Truth Well LLC
pandreibusiness@gmail.com

PROLOGUE:

This three-part prologue reveals my story, my work, and the practical and ethical principles of communication. It is not a mere introduction. It will help you get more out of the book. It is a preface to the entire 15-book Speak for Success collection. It will show you how to use the information with ease, confidence, and fluency, and how to get better results faster. If you want to skip this, flip to page 42, or read only the parts of interest.

I

page XIII

MY STORY AND THE STORY OF THIS COLLECTION

how I discovered the hidden key to successful communication, public speaking, influence, and persuasion

page XXI

THE 15-BOOK SPEAK FOR SUCCESS COLLECTION

confidence, leadership, charisma, influence, public speaking, eloquence, human nature, credibility - it's all here

II

III

page XXIV

THE PRACTICAL TACTICS AND ETHICAL PRINCIPLES

how to easily put complex strategies into action and how to use the power of words to improve the world

I

MY STORY AND THE STORY OF THIS COLLECTION

how I discovered the hidden key to successful communication, public speaking, influence, and persuasion (by reflecting on a painful failure)

HOW TO GAIN AN UNFAIR ADVANTAGE IN YOUR CAREER, BUSINESS, AND LIFE BY MASTERING THE POWER OF YOUR WORDS

I WAS SITTING IN MY OFFICE, TAPPING A PEN against my small wooden desk. My breaths were jagged, shallow, and rapid. My hands were shaking. I glanced at the clock: 11:31 PM. "I'm not ready." Have you ever had that thought?

I had to speak in front of 200 people the next morning. I had to convince them to put faith in my idea. But I was terrified, attacked by nameless, unreasoning, and unjustified terror which killed my ability to think straight, believe in myself, and get the job done.

Do you know the feeling?

After a sleepless night, the day came. I rose, wobbling on my tired legs. My head felt like it was filled with cotton candy. I couldn't direct my train of thoughts. A rushing waterfall of unhinged, self-destructive, and meaningless musings filled my head with an uncompromising cacophony of anxious, ricocheting nonsense.

"Call in sick."

"You're going to embarrass yourself."

"You're not ready."

I put on my favorite blue suit – my "lucky suit" – and my oversized blue-gold wristwatch; my "lucky" wristwatch.

"You're definitely not ready."

"That tie is ugly."

"You can't do this."

The rest went how you would expect. I drank coffee. Got in my car. Drove. Arrived. Waited. Waited. Waited. Spoke. Did poorly. Rushed back to my seat. Waited. Waited.

Waited. Got in my car. Drove. Arrived home. Sat back in my wooden seat where I accurately predicted "I'm not ready" the night before.

Relieved it was over but disappointed with my performance, I placed a sheet of paper on the desk. I wrote "MY PROBLEMS" at the top, and under that, my prompt for the evening: "What did I do so badly? Why did everything feel so off? Why did the speech fail?"

"You stood in front of 200 people and looked at... a piece of paper, not unlike this one. What the hell were you thinking? You're not fooling anyone by reading a sentence and then looking up at them as you say it out loud. They know you're reading a manuscript, and they know what that means. You are unsure of yourself. You are unsure of your message. You are unprepared. Next: Why did you speak in that odd, low, monotone voice? That sounded like nails on a chalkboard. And it was inauthentic. Next: Why did you open by talking about yourself? Also, you're not particularly funny. No more jokes. And what was the structure of the speech? It had no structure. That, I feel, is probably a pretty big problem."

I believed in my idea, and I wanted to get it across. Of course, I wanted the tangible markers of a successful speech. I wanted action. I wanted the speech to change something in the real world. But my motivations were deeper than that. I wanted to see people "click" and come on board my way of thinking. I wanted to captivate the audience. I wanted to speak with an engaging, impactful voice, drawing the audience in, not repelling them. I wanted them to remember my message and to remember me. I wanted to feel, for just a moment, the thrill of power. But not the petty, forceful power of tyrants and dictators; the justified power – the earned power – of having a good idea and conveying it well; the power of Martin Luther King and John F. Kennedy; a power harnessed in service of a valuable idea, not the personal privilege of the speaker. And I wanted confidence: the quiet strength that comes from knowing your words don't stand in your way, but propel you and the ideas you care about to glorious new mountaintops.

Instead, I stood before the audience, essentially powerless. I spoke for 20 painful minutes – painful for them and for me – and then sat down. I barely made a dent in anyone's consciousness. I generated no excitement. Self-doubt draped its cold embrace over me. Anxiety built a wall between "what I am" and "what I could be."

I had tried so many different solutions. I read countless books on effective communication, asked countless effective communicators for their advice, and consumed countless courses on powerful public speaking. Nothing worked. All the "solutions" that didn't really solve my problem had one thing in common: they treated communication as an abstract art form. They were filled with vague, abstract pieces of advice like "think positive thoughts" and "be yourself." They confused me more than anything else. Instead of illuminating the secrets I had been looking for, they shrouded the elusive but indispensable skill of powerful speaking in uncertainty.

I knew I had to master communication. I knew that the world's most successful people are all great communicators. I knew that effective communication is the bridge between "what I have" and "what I want," or at least an essential part of that bridge. I knew that without effective communication – without the ability to influence, inspire, captivate, and move – I would be all but powerless.

I knew that the person who can speak up but doesn't is no better off than the person who can't speak at all. I heard a wise man say "If you can think and speak and write, you are absolutely deadly. Nothing can get in your way." I heard another wise man say "Speech is power: speech is to persuade, to convert, to compel. It is to bring another out of his bad sense into your good sense." I heard a renowned psychologist say "If you look at people who are remarkably successful across life, there's various reasons. But one of them is that they're unbelievably good at articulating what they're aiming at and strategizing and negotiating and enticing people with a vision forward. Get your words together... that makes you unstoppable. If you are an effective writer and speaker and communicator, you have all the authority and competence that there is."

When I worked in the Massachusetts State House for the Department of Public Safety and Homeland Security, I had the opportunity to speak with countless senators, state representatives, CEOs, and other successful people. In our conversations, however brief, I always asked the same question: "What are the ingredients of your success? What got you where you are?" 100% of them said effective communication. There was not one who said anything else. No matter their field – whether they were entrepreneurs, FBI agents, political leaders, business leaders, or multimillionaire donors – they all pointed to one skill: the ability to convey powerful words in powerful ways. Zero exceptions.

Can you believe it? It still astonishes me.

My problem, and I bet this may be your obstacle as well, was that most of the advice I consumed on this critical skill barely scratched the surface. Sure, it didn't make matters worse, and it certainly offered some improvement, but only in inches when I needed progress in miles. If I stuck with the mainstream public speaking advice, I knew I wouldn't unleash the power of my words. And if I didn't do that, I knew I would always accomplish much less than I could. I knew I would suffocate my own potential. I knew I would feel a rush of crippling anxiety every time I was asked to give a presentation. I knew I would live a life of less fulfillment, less success, less achievement, more frustration, more difficulty, and more anxiety. I knew my words would never become all they could be, which means that I would never become all I could be.

To make matters worse, the mainstream advice – which is not wrong, but simply not deep enough – is everywhere. Almost every article, book, or course published on this subject falls into the mainstream category. And to make matters worse, it's almost impossible to know that until you've spent your hard-earned money and scarce time with the resource. And even then, you might just shrug, and assume that shallow, abstract advice is all there is to the "art" of public speaking. As far as I'm concerned, this is a travesty.

I kept writing. "It felt like there was no real motive; no real impulse to action. Why did they need to act? You didn't tell them. What would happen if they didn't? You didn't tell them that either. Also, you tried too hard to put on a formal façade; you spoke in strange, twisted ways. It didn't sound sophisticated. And your mental game was totally off. You let your mind fill with destructive, doubtful, self-defeating thoughts. And your preparation was totally backward. It did more to set bad habits in stone than it did to set you up for success. And you tried to build suspense at one point but revealed the final point way too early, ruining the effect."

I went on and on until I had a stack of papers filled with problems. "That's no good," I thought. I needed solutions. Everything else I tried failed. But I had one more idea: "I remember reading a great speech. What was it? Oh yeah, that's right: JFK's inaugural address. Let me go pull it up and see why it was so powerful." And that's when everything changed.

I grabbed another sheet of paper. I opened JFK's inaugural address on my laptop. I started reading. Observing. Analyzing. Reverse-engineering. I started writing down what I saw. Why did it work? Why was it powerful? I was like an archaeologist, digging through his speech for the secrets of powerful communication. I got more and more excited as I kept going. It was late at night, but the shocking and invaluable discoveries I was making gave me a burst of energy. It felt like JFK – one of the most powerful and effective speakers of all time – was coaching me in his rhetorical secrets, showing me how to influence an audience, draw them into my narrative, and find words that get results.

"Oh, so that's how you grab attention."

"Aha! So, if I tell them this, they will see why it matters."

"Fascinating – I can apply this same structure to my speech."

Around 3:00 in the morning, an epiphany hit me like a ton of bricks. That night, a new paradigm was born. A new opportunity emerged for all those who want to unleash the unstoppable power of their words. This new opportunity changed everything for me and eventually, tens of thousands of others. It is now my mission to bring it to millions, so that good people know what they need to know to use their words to achieve their dreams and improve the world.

Want to hear the epiphany?

The mainstream approach: Communication is an art form. It is unlike those dry, boring, "academic" subjects. There are no formulas. There are no patterns. It's all about thinking positive thoughts, faking confidence, and making eye contact. Some people are naturally gifted speakers. For others, the highest skill level they can attain is "not horrible."

The consequences of the mainstream approach: Advice that barely scratches the surface of the power of words. Advice that touches only the tip of the tip of the iceberg. A limited body of knowledge that blinds itself to thousands of hidden, little-known communication strategies that carry immense power; that blinds itself to 95% of what great communication really is. Self-limiting dogmas about who can do what, and how great communicators become great. Half the progress in twice the time, and everything that entails: missed opportunities, unnecessary and preventable frustration and anxiety, and confusion about what to say and how to say it. How do I know? Because I've been there. It's not pretty.

My epiphany, the new Speak for Success paradigm: Communication is as much a science as it is an art. You can study words that changed the world, uncover the hidden secrets of their power, and apply these proven principles to your own message. You can discover precisely what made great communicators great and adopt the same strategies. You can do this without being untrue to yourself or flatly imitating others. In fact, you can do this while being truer to yourself and more original than you ever have been before. Communication is not unpredictable, wishy-washy, or abstract. You can apply predictable processes and principles to reach your goals and get results. You can pick and choose from thousands of little-known speaking strategies, combining your favorite to create a unique communication approach that suits you perfectly. You can effortlessly use the same tactics of the world's most transformational leaders and speakers, and do so automatically, by default, without even thinking about it, as a matter of effortless habit. That's power.

The benefits of the Speak for Success paradigm: Less confusion. More confidence. Less frustration. More clarity. Less anxiety. More courage. You understand the whole iceberg of effective communication. As a result, your words captivate others. You draw them into a persuasive narrative, effortlessly linking your desires and their motives. You know exactly what to say. You know exactly how to say it. You know exactly how to keep your head clear; you are a master of the mental game. Your words can move mountains. Your words are the most powerful tools in your arsenal, and you use them to seize opportunities, move your mission forward, and make the world a better place. Simply put, you speak for success.

Fast forward a few years.

I was sitting in my office at my small wooden desk. My breaths were deep, slow, and steady. My entire being – mind, body, soul – was poised and focused. I set my speech manuscript to the side. I glanced at the clock: 12:01 AM. "Let's go. I'm ready."

I had to speak in front of 200 people the next morning. I had to convince them to put faith in my idea. And I was thrilled, filled with genuine gratitude at the opportunity to do what I love: get up in front of a crowd, think clearly, speak well, and get the job done.

I slept deeply. I dreamt vividly. I saw myself giving the speech. I saw myself victorious, in every sense of the word. I heard applause. I saw their facial expressions. I rose. My head was clear. My mental game was pristine. My mind was an ally, not an obstacle.

"This is going to be fun."

"I'll do my best, and whatever happens, happens."

"I'm so lucky that I get to do this again."

I put on my lucky outfit: the blue suit and the blue-gold watch.

"Remember the principles. They work."

"You developed a great plan last night. It's a winner."

"I can't wait."

The rest went how you would expect. I ate breakfast. Got in my car. Drove. Arrived. Waited. Waited. Waited. Spoke. Succeeded. Walked back to my seat. Waited. Waited. Waited. Got in my car. Drove. Arrived home. Sat back in my wooden seat where I accurately predicted "I'm ready" the night before.

I got my idea across perfectly. My message succeeded: it motivated action and created real-world change. I saw people "click" when I hit the rhetorical peak of my speech. I saw them leaning forward, totally hushed, completely absorbed. I applied the proven principles of engaging and impactful vocal modulation. I knew they would remember me and my message; I engineered my words to be memorable. I felt the thrilling power of giving a great speech. I felt the quiet confidence of knowing that my words carried weight; that they could win hearts, change minds, and help me reach the heights of my potential. I tore off the cold embrace of self-doubt. I defeated communication anxiety and broke down the wall between "what I am" and "what I could be."

Disappointed it was over but pleased with my performance, I placed a sheet of paper on the desk. I wrote "Speak Truth Well" and started planning what would become my business.

To date, we have helped tens of thousands of people gain an unfair advantage in their career, business, and life by unleashing the power of their words. And they experienced the exact same transformation I experienced when they applied the system.

If you tried to master communication before but haven't gotten the results you wanted, it's because of the mainstream approach; an approach that tells you "smiling at the audience" and "making eye contact" is all you need to know to speak well. That's not exactly a malicious lie – they don't know any better – but it is completely incorrect and severely harmful.

If you've been concerned that you won't be able to become a vastly more effective and confident communicator, I want to put those fears to rest. I felt the same way. The people I work with felt the same way. We just needed the right system. One public speaking book written by the director of a popular public speaking forum – I won't name names – wants you to believe that there are "nine public speaking secrets of the world's top minds." Wrong: There are many more than nine. If you feel that anyone who would boil down communication to just nine secrets is either missing something or holding it back, you're right. And the alternative is a much more comprehensive and powerful system. It's a system that gave me and everyone I worked with the transformation we were looking for.

Want to Talk? Email Me:

PANDREIBUSINESS@GMAIL.COM

This is My Personal Email.
I Read Every Message and
Respond in Under 12 Hours.

Visit Our Digital Headquarters:

WWW.SPEAKFORSUCCESSHUB.COM

See All Our Free Resources, Books, Courses, and Services.

THE 15-BOOK SPEAK FOR SUCCESS COLLECTION

confidence, leadership, charisma, influence, public speaking, eloquence, human nature, credibility - it's all here, in a unified collection

....A Brief Overview...

- I wrote *How Highly Effective People Speak* to reveal the hidden patterns in the words of the world's most successful and powerful communicators, so that you can adopt the same tactics and speak with the same impact and influence.

- I wrote *Eloquence* to uncover the formulas of beautiful, moving, captivating, and powerful words, so that you can use these exact same step-by-step structures to quickly make your language electrifying, charismatic, and eloquent.

- I wrote *How Legendary Leaders Speak* to illuminate the little-known five-step communication process the top leaders of the past 500 years all used to spread their message, so that you can use it to empower your ideas and get results.

- I wrote *Influential Leadership* to expose the differences between force and power and to show how great leaders use the secrets of irresistible influence to develop gentle power, so that you can move forward and lead with ease.

- I wrote *Public Speaking Mastery* to shatter the myths and expose the harmful advice about public speaking, and to offer a proven, step-by-step framework for speaking well, so that you can always speak with certainty and confidence.

- I wrote *The 7 Keys to Confidence* to bring to light the ancient 4,000-year-old secrets I used to master the mental game and speak in front of hundreds without a second of self-doubt or anxiety, so that you can feel the same freedom.

- I wrote *Trust is Power* to divulge how popular leaders and career communicators earn our trust, speak with credibility, and use this to rise to new heights of power, so that you can do the same thing to advance your purpose and mission.

- I wrote *Decoding Human Nature* to answer the critical question "what do people want?" and reveal how to use this knowledge to develop unparalleled influence, so that people adopt your idea, agree with your position, and support you.

- I wrote *Influence* to unearth another little-known five-step process for winning hearts and changing minds, so that you can know with certainty that your message will persuade people, draw support, and motivate enthusiastic action.

- I wrote *The Psychology of Persuasion* to completely and fully unveil everything about the psychology behind "Yes, I love it! What's the next step?" so that you can use easy step-by-step speaking formulas that get people to say exactly that.

- I wrote *How Visionaries Speak* to debunk common lies about effective communication that hold you back and weaken your words, so that you can boldly share your ideas without accidentally sabotaging your own message.

- I wrote *The Eloquent Leader* to disclose the ten steps to communicating with power and persuasion, so that you don't miss any of the steps and fail to connect, captivate, influence, and inspire in a crucial high-stakes moment.

- I wrote *The Language of Leadership* to unpack the unique, hidden-in-plain-sight secrets of how presidents and world-leaders build movements with the laws of powerful language, so that you use them to propel yourself forward.

- I wrote *The Psychology of Communication* to break the news that most presentations succeed or fail in the first thirty seconds and to reveal proven, step-by-step formulas that grab, hold, and direct attention, so that yours succeeds.

- I wrote *The Charisma Code* to shatter the myths and lies about charisma and reveal its nature as a concrete skill you can master with proven strategies, so that people remember you, your message, and how you electrified the room.

You Can Learn More Here:
www.speakforsuccesshub.com/series

HOW HIGHLY EFFECTIVE PEOPLE SPEAK

HOW HIGH PERFORMERS USE PSYCHOLOGY TO INFLUENCE WITH EASE

PETER D. ANDREI

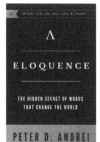

ELOQUENCE

THE HIDDEN SECRET OF WORDS THAT CHANGE THE WORLD

PETER D. ANDREI

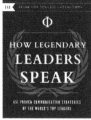

HOW LEGENDARY LEADERS SPEAK

451 PROVEN COMMUNICATION STRATEGIES OF THE WORLD'S TOP LEADERS

PETER D. ANDREI

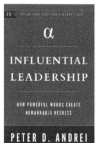

INFLUENTIAL LEADERSHIP

HOW POWERFUL WORDS CREATE REMARKABLE RESULTS

PETER D. ANDREI

PUBLIC SPEAKING MASTERY

HOW TO SPEAK WITH CONFIDENCE, IMPACT, AND INFLUENCE

PETER D. ANDREI

THE 7 KEYS TO CONFIDENCE

HOW TO LEAD, SPEAK, AND LIVE WITH COURAGE

PETER D. ANDREI

TRUST IS POWER

HOW TO COMMUNICATE IN A WORLD THAT DOUBTS EVERYTHING

PETER D. ANDREI

DECODING HUMAN NATURE

THE UNDERGROUND GUIDE TO EMOTIONAL INTELLIGENCE

PETER D. ANDREI

INFLUENCE

THE PSYCHOLOGY OF WORDS THAT WIN HEARTS AND CHANGE MINDS

PETER D. ANDREI

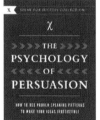

THE PSYCHOLOGY OF PERSUASION

HOW TO USE PROVEN SPEAKING PATTERNS TO MAKE YOUR IDEAS IRRESISTIBLE

PETER D. ANDREI

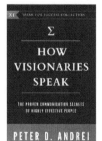

HOW VISIONARIES SPEAK

THE PROVEN COMMUNICATION SECRETS OF HIGHLY EFFECTIVE PEOPLE

PETER D. ANDREI

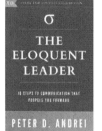

THE ELOQUENT LEADER

10 STEPS TO COMMUNICATION THAT PROPELS YOU FORWARD

PETER D. ANDREI

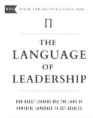

THE LANGUAGE OF LEADERSHIP

HOW GREAT LEADERS USE THE LAWS OF POWERFUL LANGUAGE TO GET RESULTS

PETER D. ANDREI

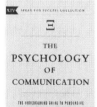

THE PSYCHOLOGY OF COMMUNICATION

THE UNDERGROUND GUIDE TO PERSUASIVE PRESENTATIONS AND EASY ELOQUENCE

PETER D. ANDREI

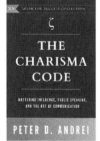

THE CHARISMA CODE

MASTERING INFLUENCE, PUBLIC SPEAKING, AND THE ART OF COMMUNICATION

PETER D. ANDREI

III

PRACTICAL TACTICS AND ETHICAL PRINCIPLES

how to easily put complex strategies into action and how to use the power of words to improve the world in an ethical and effective way

MOST COMMUNICATION BOOKS

H AVE YOU READ ANOTHER BOOK ON COMMUNICATION? If you have, let me remind you what you probably learned. And if you haven't, let me briefly spoil 95% of them. "Prepare. Smile. Dress to impress. Keep it simple. Overcome your fears. Speak from the heart. Be authentic. Show them why you care. Speak in terms of their interests. To defeat anxiety, know your stuff. Emotion persuades, not logic. Speak with confidence. Truth sells. And respect is returned."

There you have it. That is most of what you learn in most communication books. None of it is wrong. None of it is misleading. Those ideas are true and valuable. But they are not enough. They are only the absolute basics. And my job is to offer you much more.

Einstein said that "if you can't explain it in a sentence, you don't know it well enough." He also told us to "make it as simple as possible, but no simpler." You, as a communicator, must satisfy both of these maxims, one warning against the dangers of excess complexity, and one warning against the dangers of excess simplicity. And I, as someone who communicates about communication in my books, courses, and coaching, must do the same.

THE SPEAK FOR SUCCESS SYSTEM

The Speak for Success system makes communication as simple as possible. Other communication paradigms make it even simpler. Naturally, this means our system is more complex. This is an unavoidable consequence of treating communication as a deep and concrete science instead of a shallow and abstract art. If you don't dive into learning communication at all, you miss out. I'm sure you agree with that. But if you don't dive *deep*, you still miss out.

THE FOUR QUADRANTS OF COMMUNICATION

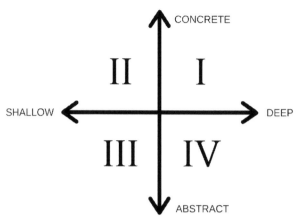

FIGURE VIII: There are four predominant views of communication (whether it takes the form of public speaking, negotiation, writing, or debating is irrelevant). The first view is that communication is concrete and deep. The second view is that communication is concrete and shallow. The third view is that communication is shallow and abstract. The fourth view is that communication is deep and abstract.

WHAT IS COMMUNICATION?

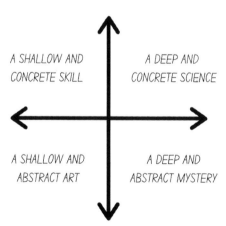

FIGURE VII: The first view treats communication as a science: "There are concrete formulas, rules, principles, and strategies, and they go very deep." The second view treats it as a skill: "Yes, there are concrete formulas, rules, and strategies, but they don't go very deep." The third view treats it as an art: "Rules? Formulas? It's not that complicated. Just smile and think positive thoughts." The fourth view treats it as a mystery: "How are some people such effective communicators? I will never know…"

WHERE WE STAND ON THE QUESTION

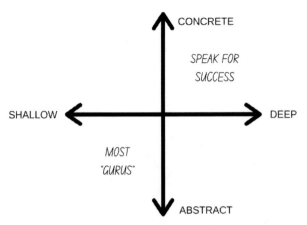

FIGURE VI: Speak for Success takes the view that communication is a deep and concrete science. (And by "takes the view," I mean "has discovered.") Most other writers, thought-leaders, public speaking coaches, and individuals and organizations in this niche treat communication as a shallow and abstract art.

This doesn't mean the Speak for Success system neglects the basics. It only means it goes far beyond the basics, and that it doesn't turn simple ideas into 200 pages of filler. It also doesn't mean that the Speak for Success system is unnecessarily complex. It is as simple as it can possibly be. In this book, and in the other books of the Speak for Success collection, you'll find simple pieces of advice, easy formulas, and straightforward rules. You'll find theories, strategies, tactics, mental models, and principles. None of this should pose a challenge. But you'll also find advanced, complicated tactics. These might.

What is the purpose of the guide on the top of the next page? To reveal the methods that make advanced strategies easy. When you use the tactics revealed in this guide, the difficulty of using the advanced strategies drops dramatically. If the 15-book Speak for Success collection is a complete encyclopedia of communication, to be used like a handbook, then this guide is a handbook for the handbook.

A SAMPLING OF EASY AND HARD STRATEGIES

Easy and Simple	Hard and Complicated
Use Four-Corner Eye Contact	The Fluency-Magnitude Matrix
Appeal to Their Values	The VPB Triad
Describe the Problem You Solve	The Illusory Truth Effect
Use Open Body Language	Percussive Rhythm
Tell a Quick Story	Alliterative Flow
Appeal to Emotion	Stacking and Layering Structures
Project Your Voice	The Declaratory Cascade
Keep it as Simple as Possible	Alternating Semantic Sentiments

THE PRACTICAL TACTICS

R ECOGNIZE THAT, WITH PRACTICE, YOU can use any strategy extemporaneously. Some people can instantly use even the most complex strategies in the Speak for Success collection after reading them just once. They are usually experienced communicators, often with competitive experience. This is not an expectation, but a possibility, and with practice, a probability.

CREATE A COMMUNICATION PLAN. Professional communication often follows a strategic plan. Put these techniques into your plan. Following an effective plan is not harder than following an ineffective one. Marshall your arguments. Marshall your rhetoric. Stack the deck. Know what you know, and how to say it.

DESIGN AN MVP. If you are speaking on short notice, you can create a "minimum viable plan." This can be a few sentences on a notecard jotted down five minutes before speaking. The same principle of formal communication plans applies: While advanced strategies may overburden you if you attempt them in an impromptu setting, putting them into a plan makes them easy.

MASTER YOUR RHETORICAL STACK. Master one difficult strategy. Master another one. Combine them. Master a third. Build out a "rhetorical stack" of ten strategies you can use fluently, in impromptu or extemporaneous communication. Pick strategies that come fluently to you and that complement each other.

PRACTICE THEM TO FLUENCY. I coach a client who approached me and said he wants to master every strategy I ever compiled. That's a lot. As of this writing, we're 90 one-hour sessions in. To warm up for one of our sessions, I gave him a challenge: "Give an impromptu speech on the state of the American economy, and after you stumble, hesitate, or falter four times, I'll cut you off. The challenge is to see how long you can go." He spoke for 20 minutes without a single mistake. After 20 minutes, he brought the impromptu speech to a perfect, persuasive, forceful, and eloquent conclusion. And he naturally and fluently used advanced strategies throughout his impromptu speech. After he closed the speech (which he did because he wanted to get on with the session), I asked him if he thought deeply about the strategies he used. He said no. He used them thoughtlessly. Why? Because he practiced them. You can too. You can practice them on your own. You don't need an audience. You don't need a coach. You don't even need to speak. Practice in your head. Practice ones that resonate with you. Practice with topics you care about.

KNOW TEN TIMES MORE THAN YOU INTEND TO SAY. And know what you do intend to say about ten times more fluently than you need to. This gives your mind room to relax, and frees up cognitive bandwidth to devote to strategy and rhetoric in real-time. Need to speak for five minutes? Be able to speak for 50. Need to read it three times to be able to deliver it smoothly? Read it 30 times.

INCORPORATE THEM IN SLIDES. You can use your slides or visual aids to help you ace complicated strategies. If you can't remember the five steps of a strategy, your slides can still follow them. Good slides aren't harder to use than bad slides.

USE THEM IN WRITTEN COMMUNICATION. You can read your speech. In some situations, this is more appropriate than impromptu or extemporaneous speaking. And if a strategy is difficult to remember in impromptu speaking, you can write it into your speech. And let's not forget about websites, emails, letters, etc.

PICK AND CHOOSE EASY ONES. Use strategies that come naturally and don't overload your mind. Those that do are counterproductive in fast-paced situations.

TAKE SMALL STEPS TO MASTERY. Practice one strategy. Practice it again. Keep going until you master it. Little by little, add to your base of strategies. But never take steps that overwhelm you. Pick a tactic. Practice it. Master it. Repeat.

MEMORIZE AN ENTIRE MESSAGE. Sometimes this is the right move. Is it a high-stakes message? Do you have the time? Do you have the energy? Given the situation, would a memorized delivery beat an impromptu, in-the-moment, spontaneous delivery? If you opt for memorizing, using advanced strategies is easy.

USE ONE AT A TIME. Pick an advanced strategy. Deliver it. Now what? Pick another advanced strategy. Deliver it. Now another. Have you been speaking for a while? Want to bring it to a close? Pick a closing strategy. For some people, using advanced strategies extemporaneously is easy, but only if they focus on one at a time.

MEMORIZE A KEY PHRASE. Deliver your impromptu message as planned, but add a few short, memorized key phrases throughout that include advanced strategies.

CREATE TALKING POINTS. Speak from a list of pre-written bullet-points; big-picture ideas you seek to convey. This is halfway between fully impromptu speaking and using a script. It's not harder to speak from a strategic and persuasively-advanced list of talking points than it is to speak from a persuasively weak list. You can either memorize your talking points, or have them in front of you as a guide.

TREAT IT LIKE A SCIENCE. At some point, you struggled with a skill that you now perform effortlessly. You mastered it. It's a habit. You do it easily, fluently, and thoughtlessly. You can do it while you daydream. Communication is the same. These tactics, methods, and strategies are not supposed to be stuck in the back of your mind as you speak. They are supposed to be ingrained in your habits.

RELY ON FLOW. In fast-paced and high-stakes situations, you usually don't plan every word, sentence, and idea consciously and deliberately. Rather, you let your subconscious mind take over. You speak from a flow state. In flow, you may flawlessly execute strategies that would have overwhelmed your conscious mind.

LISTEN TO THE PROMPTS. You read a strategy and found it difficult to use extemporaneously. But as you speak, your subconscious mind gives you a prompt: "this strategy would work great here." Your subconscious mind saw the opportunity and surfaced the prompt. You execute it, and you do so fluently and effortlessly.

FOLLOW THE FIVE-STEP CYCLE. First, find truth. Research. Prepare. Learn. Second, define your message. Figure out what you believe about what you learned. Third, polish your message with rhetorical strategies, without distorting the precision with which it conveys the truth. Fourth, practice the polished ideas. Fifth, deliver them. The endeavor of finding truth comes before the rhetorical endeavor. First, find the right message. Then, find the best way to convey it.

CREATE YOUR OWN STRATEGY. As you learn new theories, mental models, and principles of psychology and communication, you may think of a new strategy built around the theories, models, and principles. Practice it, test it, and codify it.

STACK GOOD HABITS. An effective communicator is the product of his habits. If you want to be an effective communicator, stack good communication habits (and break bad ones). This is a gradual process. It doesn't happen overnight.

DON'T TRY TO USE THEM. Don't force it. If a strategy seems too difficult, don't try to use it. You might find yourself using it anyway when the time is right.

KNOW ONLY ONE. If you master one compelling communication strategy, like one of the many powerful three-part structures that map out a persuasive speech, that can often be enough to drastically and dramatically improve your impact.

REMEMBER THE SHORTCOMING OF MODELS. All models are wrong, but some are useful. Many of these complex strategies and theories are models. They represent reality, but they are not reality. They help you navigate the territory, but they are not the territory. They are a map, to be used if it helps you navigate, and to be discarded the moment it prevents you from navigating.

DON'T LET THEM INHIBIT YOU. Language flows from thought. You've got to have something to say. And *then* you make it as compelling as possible. And *then* you shape it into something poised and precise; persuasive and powerful; compelling and convincing. Meaning and message come first. Rhetoric comes second. Don't take all this discussion of "advanced communication strategies," "complex communication tactics," and "the deep and concrete science of communication" to suggest that the basics don't matter. They do. Tell the truth as precisely and boldly as you can. Know your subject-matter like the back of your hand. Clear your mind and focus on precisely articulating exactly what you believe to be true. Be authentic. The advanced strategies are not supposed to stand between you and your audience. They are not supposed to stand between you and your authentic and spontaneous self – they are supposed to be integrated with it. They are not an end in themselves, but a means to the end of persuading the maximum number of people to adopt truth. Trust your instinct. Trust your intuition. It won't fail you.

MASTERING ONE COMMUNICATION SKILL

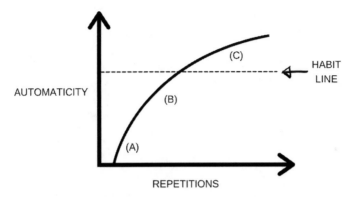

FIGURE V: Automaticity is the extent to which you do something automatically, without thinking about it. At the start of building a communication habit, it has low automaticity. You need to think about it consciously (A). After more repetitions, it gets easier and more automatic (B). Eventually, the behavior becomes more automatic than deliberate. At this point, it becomes a habit (C).

MASTERING COMMUNICATION

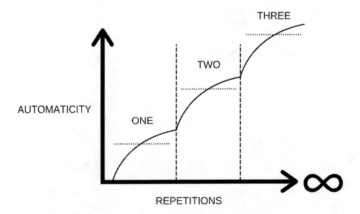

FIGURE IV: Layer good communication habits on top of each other. Go through the learning curve over and over again. When you master the first good habit, jump to the second. This pattern will take you to mastery.

THE FOUR LEVELS OF KNOWING

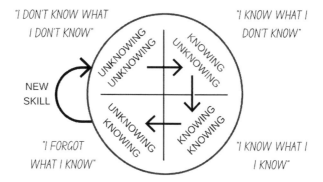

FIGURE III: First, you don't know you don't know it. Then, you discover it and know you don't know it. Then, you practice it and know you know it. Then, it becomes a habit. You forget you know it. It's ingrained in your habits.

REVISITING THE LEARNING CURVE

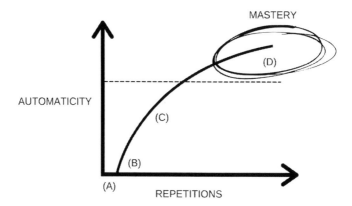

FIGURE II: Note the stages of knowing on the learning curve: unknowing unknowing (A), knowing unknowing (B), knowing knowing (C), unknowing knowing (D).

WHAT'S REALLY HAPPENING?

Have you ever thought deeply about what happens when you communicate? Let's run through the mile-high view.

At some point in your life, you bumped into an experience. You observed. You learned. The experience changed you. Your neural networks connected in new ways. New rivers of neurons began to flow through them.

The experience etched a pattern into your neurobiology representing information about the moral landscape of the universe; a map of *where we are, where we should go, and how we should make the journey.* This is meaning. This is your message.

Now, you take the floor before a crowd. Whether you realize it or not, you want to copy the neural pattern from your mind to their minds. You want to show them where we are, where we should go, and how we should make the journey.

So, you speak. You gesture. You intone. Your words convey meaning. Your body language conveys meaning. Your voice conveys meaning. You flood them with a thousand different inputs, some as subtle as the contraction of a single facial muscle, some as obvious as your opening line. Your character, your intentions, and your goals seep into your speech. Everyone can see them. Everyone can see you.

Let's step into the mind of one of your audience members. Based on all of this, based on a thousand different inputs, based on complex interactions between their conscious and nonconscious minds, the ghost in the machine steps in, and by a dint of free will, acts as the final arbiter and makes a choice. A mind is changed. You changed it. And changing it changed you. You became more confident, more articulate, and deeper; more capable, more impactful, and stronger.

Communication is connection. One mind, with a consciousness at its base, seeks to use ink or pixels or airwaves to connect to another. Through this connection, it seeks to copy neural patterns about the present, the future, and the moral landscape. Whatever your message is, the underlying connection is identical. How could it not be?

IS IT ETHICAL?

By "it," I mean deliberately using language to get someone to do or think something. Let's call this rhetoric. We could just as well call it persuasion, influence, communication, or even leadership itself.

The answer is yes. The answer is no. Rhetoric is a helping hand. It is an iron fist. It is Martin Luther King's dream. It is Stalin's nightmare. It is the "shining city on the hill." It is the iron curtain. It is "the pursuit of happiness." It is the trail of tears. It is "liberty, equality, and brotherhood." It is the reign of terror. Rhetoric is a tool. It is neither good nor evil. It is a reflection of our nature.

Rhetoric can motivate love, peace, charity, strength, patience, progress, prosperity, common sense, common purpose, courage, hope, generosity, and unity. It can also sow the seeds of division, fan the flames of tribalism, and beat back the better angels of our nature.

Rhetoric is the best of us and the worst of us. It is as good as you are. It is as evil as you are. It is as peace-loving as you are. It is as hate-mongering as you are. And I know what you are. I know my readers are generous, hardworking people who want to build a better future for themselves, for their families, and for all humankind. I know that if you have these tools in your hands, you will use them to achieve a moral mission. That's why putting them in your hands is my mission.

Joseph Chatfield said "[rhetoric] is the power to talk people out of their sober and natural opinions." I agree. But it is also the power to talk people out of their wrong and harmful opinions. And if you're using rhetoric to talk people out of their sober opinions, the problem isn't rhetoric, it's you.

In the *Institutes of Rhetoric*, Roman rhetorician Quintilian wrote the following: "The orator then, whom I am concerned to form, shall be the orator as defined by Marcus Cato, a good man, skilled in speaking. But above all he must possess the quality which Cato places first and which is in the very nature of things the greatest and most important, that is, he must be a good man. This is essential not merely on account of the fact that, if the powers of eloquence serve only to lend arms to crime, there can be nothing more pernicious than eloquence to public and private welfare alike, while I myself, who have labored to the best of my ability to contribute something of the value to oratory, shall have rendered the worst of services to mankind, if I forge these weapons not for a soldier, but for a robber."

Saint Augustine, who was trained in the classical schools of rhetoric in the 3rd century, summed it up well: "Rhetoric, after all, being the art of persuading people to accept something, whether it is true or false, would anyone dare to maintain that truth should stand there without any weapons in the hands of its defenders against falsehood; that those speakers, that is to say, who are trying to convince their hearers of what is untrue, should know how to get them on their side, to gain their attention and have them eating out of their hands by their opening remarks, while these who are defending the truth should not? That those should utter their lies briefly, clearly, plausibly, and these should state their truths in a manner too boring to listen to, too obscure to understand, and finally too repellent to believe? That those should attack the truth with specious arguments, and assert falsehoods, while these should be incapable of either defending the truth or refuting falsehood? That those, to move and force the minds of their hearers into error, should be able by their style to terrify them, move them to tears, make them laugh, give them rousing encouragement, while these on behalf of truth stumble along slow, cold and half asleep?"

THE ETHICS OF PERSUASION

R EFER BACK TO THIS ETHICAL GUIDE as needed. I created this in a spirit of humility, for my benefit as much as for the benefit of my readers. And you don't have to choose between efficacy and ethics. When I followed these principles, my words became more ethical *and* more powerful.

FOLLOW THESE TWELVE RULES. Do not use false, fabricated, misrepresented, distorted, or irrelevant evidence to support claims. Do not intentionally use specious, unsupported, or illogical reasoning. Do not represent yourself as informed or as an "expert" on a subject when you are not. Do not use irrelevant appeals to divert attention from the issue at hand. Do not cause intense but unreflective emotional reactions. Do not link your idea to emotion-laden values, motives, or goals to which it is not related. Do not hide your real purpose or self-interest, the group you represent, or your position as an advocate of a viewpoint. Do not distort, hide, or misrepresent the number, scope, or intensity of bad effects. Do not use emotional appeals that lack a basis of evidence or reasoning or that would fail if the audience examined the subject themselves. Do not oversimplify complex, gradation-laden situations into simplistic two-valued, either/or, polar views or choices. Do not pretend certainty where tentativeness and degrees of probability would be more accurate. Do not advocate something you do not believe (Johannesen et al., 2021).

APPLY THIS GOLDEN HEURISTIC. In a 500,000-word book, you might be able to tell your audience everything you know about a subject. In a five-minute persuasive speech, you can only select a small sampling of your knowledge. Would learning your entire body of knowledge result in a significantly different reaction than hearing the small sampling you selected? If the answer is yes, that's a problem.

SWING WITH THE GOOD EDGE. Rhetoric is a double-edged sword. It can express good ideas well. It can also express bad ideas well. Rhetoric makes ideas attractive; tempting; credible; persuasive. Don't use it to turn weakly-worded lies into well-worded lies. Use it to turn weakly-worded truths into well-worded truths.

TREAT TRUTH AS THE HIGHEST GOOD. Use any persuasive strategy, unless using it in your circumstances would distort the truth. The strategies should not come between you and truth, or compromise your honesty and authenticity.

AVOID THE SPIRIT OF DECEIT. Wrong statements are incorrect statements you genuinely believe. Lies are statements you know are wrong but convey anyway. Deceitful statements are not literally wrong, but you convey them with the intent to mislead, obscure, hide, or manipulate. Hiding relevant information is not literally lying (saying you conveyed all the information would be). Cherry-picking facts is not literally lying (saying there are no other facts would be). Using clever innuendo to twist reality without making any concrete claims is not literally lying (knowingly making a false accusation would be). And yet, these are all examples of deceit.

ONLY USE STRATEGIES IF THEY ARE ACCURATE. Motivate unified thinking. Inspire loving thinking. These strategies sound good. Use the victim-perpetrator-benevolence structure. Paint a common enemy. Appeal to tribal psychology. These strategies sound bad. But when reality lines up with the strategies that sound bad, they become good. They are only bad when they are inaccurate or move people down a bad path. *But the same is true for the ones that sound good.* Should Winston Churchill have motivated unified thinking? Not toward his enemy. Should he have avoided appealing to tribal psychology to strengthen the Allied war effort? Should he have avoided painting a common enemy? Should he have avoided portraying the victimization of true victims and the perpetration of a true perpetrator? Should he have avoided calling people to act as the benevolent force for good, protecting the victim and beating back the perpetrator? Don't use the victim-perpetrator-benevolence structure if there aren't clear victims and perpetrators. This is demagoguery. Painting false victims disempowers them. But if there are true victims and perpetrators, stand up for the victims and stand against the perpetrators, calling others to join you as a benevolent force for justice. Don't motivate unified thinking when standing against evil. Don't hold back from portraying a common enemy when there is one. Some strategies might sound morally suspect. Some might sound inherently good. But it depends on the situation. Every time I say "do X to achieve Y," remember the condition: "if it is accurate and moves people up a good path."

APPLY THE TARES TEST: truthfulness of message, authenticity of persuader, respect for audience, equity of persuasive appeal, and social impact (TARES).

REMEMBER THE THREE-PART VENN DIAGRAM: words that are authentic, effective, and true. Donald Miller once said "I'm the kind of person who wants to present my most honest, authentic self to the world, so I hide backstage and rehearse honest and authentic lines until the curtain opens." There's nothing dishonest or inauthentic about choosing your words carefully and making them more effective, as long as they remain just as true. Rhetoric takes a messy marble brick of truth and sculpts it into a poised, precise, and perfect statue. It takes weak truths and makes them strong. Unfortunately, it can do the same for weak lies. But preparing, strategizing, and sculpting is not inauthentic. Unskillfulness is no more authentic than skillfulness. Unpreparedness is no more authentic than preparedness.

APPLY FITZPATRICK AND GAUTHIER'S THREE-QUESTION ANALYSIS. For what purpose is persuasion being employed? Toward what choices and with what consequences for individual lives is it being used? Does the persuasion contribute to or interfere with the audience's decision-making process (Lumen, 2016)?

STRENGTHEN THE TRUTH. Rhetoric makes words strong. Use it to turn truths strong, not falsities strong. There are four categories of language: weak and wrong, strong and wrong, weak and true, strong and true. Turn weak and true language into strong and true language. Don't turn weak and wrong language into strong and wrong language, weak and true language into strong and wrong language, or strong and true language into weak and true language. Research. Question your assumptions. Strive for truth. Ensure your logic is impeccable. Defuse your biases.

START WITH FINDING TRUTH. The rhetorical endeavor starts with becoming as knowledgeable on your subject as possible and developing an impeccable logical argument. The more research you do, the more rhetoric you earn the right to use.

PUT TRUTH BEFORE STYLE. Rhetorical skill does not make you correct. Truth doesn't care about your rhetoric. If your rhetoric is brilliant, but you realize your arguments are simplistic, flawed, or biased, change course. Let logic lead style. Don't sacrifice logic to style. Don't express bad ideas well. Distinguish effective speaking from effective rational argument. Achieve both, but put reason and logic first.

AVOID THE POPULARITY VORTEX. As Plato suggested, avoid "giving the citizens what they want [in speech] with no thought to whether they will be better or worse as a result of what you are saying." Ignore the temptation to gain positive reinforcement and instant gratification from the audience with no merit to your message. Rhetoric is unethical if used solely to appeal rather than to help the world.

CONSIDER THE CONSEQUENCES. If you succeed to persuade people, will the world become better or worse? Will your audience benefit? Will you benefit? Moreover, is it the best action they could take? Or would an alternative help more? Is it an objectively worthwhile investment? Is it the best solution? Are you giving them all the facts they need to determine this on their own?

CONSIDER SECOND- AND THIRD-ORDER IMPACTS. Consider not only immediate consequences, but consequences across time. Consider the impact of the action you seek to persuade, as well as the tools you use to persuade it. Maybe the action is objectively positive, but in motivating the action, you resorted to instilling beliefs that will cause damage over time. Consider their long-term impact as well.

APPLY THE FIVE ETHICAL APPROACHES: seek the greatest good for the greatest number (utilitarian); protect the rights of those affected and treat people not as means but as ends (rights); treat equals equally and nonequals fairly (justice); set the good of humanity as the basis of your moral reasoning (common good); act consistently with the ideals that lead to your self-actualization and the highest potential of your character (virtue). Say and do what is right, not what is expedient, and be willing to suffer the consequences of doing so. Don't place self-gratification, acquisitiveness, social status, and power over the common good of all humanity.

APPLY THE FOUR ETHICAL DECISION-MAKING CRITERIA: respect for individual rights to make choices, hold views, and act based on personal beliefs and values (autonomy); the maximization of benefits and the minimization of harms, acting for the benefit of others, helping others further their legitimate interests; taking action to prevent or remove possible harms (beneficence); acting in ways that cause no harm, avoid the risk of harm, and assuring benefits outweigh costs (non-maleficence); treating others according to a defensible standard (justice).

USE ILLOGICAL PROCESSES TO GET ETHICAL RESULTS. Using flawed thinking processes to get good outcomes is not unethical. Someone who disagrees should stop speaking with conviction, clarity, authority, and effective paralanguage. All are irrelevant to the truth of their words, but impact the final judgment of the audience. You must use logic and evidence to figure out the truth. But this doesn't mean logic and evidence will persuade others. Humans have two broad categories of cognitive functions: system one is intuitive, emotional, fast, heuristic-driven, and generally illogical; system two is rational, deliberate, evidence-driven, and generally logical. The best-case scenario is to get people to believe right things for right reasons (through system two). The next best case is to get people to believe right things for wrong reasons (through system one). Both are far better than letting people believe wrong things for wrong reasons. If you don't use those processes, they still function, but lead people astray. You can reverse-engineer them. If you know the truth, have an abundance of reasons to be confident you know the truth, and can predict the disasters that will occur if people don't believe the truth, don't you have a responsibility to be as effective as possible in bringing people to the truth? Logic and evidence are essential, of course. They will persuade many. They should have persuaded you. But people can't always follow a long chain of reasoning or a complicated argument. Persuade by eloquence what you learned by reason.

HELP YOUR SELF-INTEREST. (But not at the expense of your audience or without their knowledge). Ethics calls for improving the world, and you are a part of the world – the one you control most. Improving yourself is a service to others.

APPLY THE WINDOWPANE STANDARD. In Aristotle's view, rhetoric reveals how to persuade and how to defeat manipulative persuaders. Thus, top students of rhetoric would be master speakers, trained to anticipate and disarm the rhetorical tactics of their adversaries. According to this tradition, language is only useful to the extent that it does not distort reality, and good writing functions as a "windowpane," helping people peer through the wall of ignorance and view reality. You might think this precludes persuasion. You might think this calls for dry academic language. But what good is a windowpane if nobody cares to look through it? What good is a windowpane to reality if, on the other wall, a stained-glass window distorts reality but draws people to it? The best windowpane reveals as much of reality as possible while drawing as many people to it as possible.

RUN THROUGH THESE INTROSPECTIVE QUESTIONS. Are the means truly unethical or merely distasteful, unpopular, or unwise? Is the end truly good, or does it simply appear good because we desire it? Is it probable that bad means will achieve the good end? Is the same good achievable using more ethical means if we are creative, patient, and skillful? Is the good end clearly and overwhelmingly better than any bad effects of the means used to attain it? Will the use of unethical means to achieve a good end withstand public scrutiny? Could the use of unethical means be justified to those most affected and those most impartial? Can I specify my ethical criteria or standards? What is the grounding of the ethical judgment? Can I justify the reasonableness and relevancy of these standards for this case? Why are these the best criteria? Why do they take priority? How does the communication succeed or fail by these standards? What judgment is justified in this case about the degree of ethicality? Is it a narrowly focused one rather than a broad and generalized one? To whom is ethical responsibility owed – to which individuals, groups, organizations, or professions? In what ways and to what extent? Which take precedence? What is my responsibility to myself and society? How do I feel about myself after this choice? Can I continue to "live with myself?" Would I want my family to know of this choice? Does the choice reflect my ethical character? To what degree is it "out of character?" If called upon in public to justify the ethics of my communication, how adequately could I do so? What generally accepted reasons could I offer? Are there precedents which can guide me? Are there aspects of this case that set it apart from others? How thoroughly have alternatives been explored before settling on this choice? Is it less ethical than some of the workable alternatives? If the goal requires unethical communication, can I abandon the goal (Johannesen et al., 2007)?

VIEW YOURSELF AS A GUIDE. Stories have a hero, a villain who stands in his way, and a guide who helps the hero fulfill his mission. If you speak ineffectively, you are a nonfactor. If you speak deceitfully, you become the villain. But if you convey truth effectively, you become the guide in your audience's story, who leads them, teaches them, inspires them, and helps them overcome adversity and win. Use your words to put people on the best possible path. And if you hide an ugly truth, ask yourself this: "If I found out that *my* guide omitted this, how would I react?"

KNOW THAT THE TRUTH WILL OUT. The truth can either come out in your words, or you can deceive people. You can convince them to live in a fantasy. And that might work. Until. Until truth breaks down the door and storms the building. Until the facade comes crashing down and chaos makes its entry. Slay the dragon in its lair before it comes to your village. Invite truth in through the front door before truth burns the building down. Truth wins in the end, either because a good person spreads, defends, and fights for it, or because untruth reveals itself as such by its consequences, and does so in brutal and painful fashion, hurting innocents and perpetrators alike. Trust and reputation take years to create and seconds to destroy.

MAXIMIZE THE TWO HIERARCHIES OF SUCCESS: honesty *and* effectiveness. You could say "Um, well, uh, I think that um, what we should… should uh… do, is that, well… let me think… er, I think if we are more, you know… fluid, we'll be better at… producing, I mean, progressing, and producing, and just more generally, you know, getting better results, but… I guess my point is, like, that, that if we are more fluid and do things more better, we will get better results than with a bureaucracy and, you know how it is, a silo-based structure, right? I mean… you know what I mean." Or, you could say "Bravery beats bureaucracy, courage beats the status quo, and innovation beats stagnation." Is one of those statements truer? No. Is one of them more effective? Is one of them more likely to get positive action that instantiates the truth into the world? Yes. Language is not reality. It provides signposts to reality. Two different signposts can point at the same truth – they can be equally and maximally true – and yet one can be much more effective. One gets people to follow the road. One doesn't. Maximize honesty. Then, insofar as it doesn't sacrifice honesty, maximize effectiveness. Speak truth. And speak it well.

APPLY THE WISDOM OF THIS QUOTE. Mary Beard, an American historian, author, and activist, captured the essence of ethical rhetoric well: "What politicians do is they never get the rhetoric wrong, and the price they pay is they don't speak the truth as they see it. Now, I will speak truth as I see it, and sometimes I don't get the rhetoric right. I think that's a fair trade-off." It's more than fair. It's necessary.

REMEMBER YOUR RESPONSIBILITY TO SOCIETY. Be a guardian of the truth. Speak out against wrongdoing, and do it well. The solution to evil speech is not less speech, but more (good) speech. Create order with your words, not chaos. Our civilization depends on it. Match the truth, honesty, and vulnerable transparency of your words against the irreducible complexity of the universe. And in this complex universe, remember the omnipresence of nuance, and the dangers of simplistic ideologies. (Inconveniently, simplistic ideologies are persuasive, while nuanced truths are difficult to convey. This is why good people need to be verbally skilled; to pull the extra weight of conveying a realistic worldview). Don't commit your whole mind to an isolated fragment of truth, lacking context, lacking nuance. Be precise in your speech, to ensure you are saying what you mean to say. Memorize the logical fallacies, the cognitive biases, and the rules of logic and correct thinking. (Conveniently, many rhetorical devices are also reasoning devices that focus your inquiry and help you explicate truth). But don't demonize those with good intentions and bad ideas. If they are forthcoming and honest, they are not your enemy. Rather, the two of you are on a shared mission to find the truth, partaking in a shared commitment to reason and dialogue. The malevolent enemy doesn't care about the truth. And in this complex world, remember Voltaire's warning to "cherish those who seek the truth but beware of those who find it," and Aristotle's startling observation that "the least deviation from truth [at the start] is multiplied a thousandfold." Be cautious in determining what to say with conviction. Good speaking is not a substitute for good thinking. The danger zone is being confidently incorrect. What hurts us most is what we know that just isn't so. Remember these tenets and your responsibility, and rhetoric becomes the irreplaceable aid of the good person doing good things in difficult times; the sword of the warrior of the light.

KNOW THAT DECEPTION IS ITS OWN PUNISHMENT. Knowingly uttering a falsehood is a spoken lie of commission. Having something to say but not saying it is a spoken lie of omission. Knowingly behaving inauthentically is an acted-out lie of commission. Knowingly omitting authentic behavior is an acted-out lie of omission. All these deceptions weaken your being. All these deceptions corrupt your own mind, turning your greatest asset into an ever-present companion you can no longer trust. Your conscience operates somewhat autonomously, and it will call you out (unless your repeated neglect desensitizes it). You have a conscious conscience which speaks clearly, and an unconscious conscience, which communicates more subtly. A friend of mine asked: "Why do we feel relieved when we speak truth? Why are we drawn toward it, even if it is not pleasant? Do our brains have something that makes this happen?" Yes, they do: our consciences, our inner lights, our inner north stars. And we feel relieved because living with the knowledge of our own deceit is often an unbearable burden. You live your life before an audience of one: yourself. You cannot escape the observation of your own awareness; you can't hide from yourself. Everywhere you go, there you are. Everything you do, there you are. Some of the greatest heights of wellbeing come from performing well in this one-man theater, and signaling virtue to yourself; being someone you are proud to be (and grateful to observe). Every time you lie, you tell your subconscious mind that your character is too weak to contend with the truth. And this shapes your character accordingly. It becomes true. And then what? Lying carries its own punishment, even if the only person who catches the liar is the liar himself.

Bᴇ ᴀ ᴍᴏɴsᴛᴇʀ (ᴛʜᴇɴ ʟᴇᴀʀɴ ᴛᴏ ᴄᴏɴᴛʀᴏʟ ɪᴛ). There is nothing moral about weakness and harmlessness. The world is difficult. There are threats to confront, oppressors to resist, and tyrants to rebuff. (Peterson, 2018). There are psychopaths, sociopaths, and Machiavellian actors with no love for the common good. There is genuine malevolence. If you are incapable of being an effective deceiver, then you are incapable of being an effective advocate for truth: it is the same weapon, pointed in different directions. If you cannot use it in both directions, can you use it at all? Become a monster, become dangerous, and become capable of convincing people to believe in a lie… and then use this ability to convince them to believe in the truth. The capacity for harm is also the capacity for harming harmful entities; that is to say, defending innocent ones. If you can't hurt anyone, you can't help anyone when they need someone to stand up for them. Words are truly weapons, and the most powerful weapons in the world at that. The ability to use them, for good *or* for bad, is the prerequisite to using them for good. There is an archetype in our cultural narratives: the well-intentioned but harmless protagonist who gets roundly defeated by the villain, until he develops his monstrous edge and integrates it, at which point he becomes the triumphant hero. Along similar lines, I watched a film about an existential threat to humanity, in which the protagonist sought to convey the threat to a skeptical public, but failed miserably because he lacked the rhetorical skill to do so. The result? The world ended. Everyone died. The protagonist was of no use to anyone. And this almost became a true story. A historical study showed that in the Cuban Missile Crisis, the arguments that won out in the United States mastermind group were not the best, but those argued with the most conviction. Those with the best arguments lacked the skill to match. The world (could have) ended. The moral? Speak truth… well.

MASTERING COMMUNICATION, ONE SKILL AT A TIME

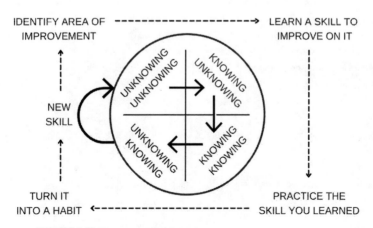

FIGURE I: The proven path to mastery.

public speaking

....

noun
> the world's most common biggest fear

mastery

....

noun
> complete authority or control

CONTENTS

PREPARATION: 101

ASPECTS OF DELIVERY: 277

BEFORE YOU GO…

Rhetoric, Motivated by Love, Guided by Reason, and Aimed at Truth, Is a Powerful Force for the Greatest Good.

POLITICAL DISCLAIMER

Throughout this book, and throughout all my books, I draw examples of communication strategies from the political world. I quote from the speeches of many of America's great leaders, like JFK and MLK, as well as from more recent political figures of both major parties. Political communication is ideal for illustrating the concepts revealed in the books. It is the best source of examples of words that work that I have ever found. I don't use anything out of the political mainstream. And it is by extensively studying the inaugural addresses of United States Presidents and the great speeches of history that I have discovered many of the speaking strategies I share with you.

My using the words of any particular figure to illustrate a principle of communication is not necessarily an endorsement of the figure or their message. Separate the speaker from the strategy. After all, the strategy is the only reason the speaker made an appearance in the book at all. Would you rather have a weak example of a strategy you want to learn from a speaker you love, or a perfect example of the strategy from a speaker you detest?

For a time, I didn't think a disclaimer like this was necessary. I thought people would do this on their own. I thought that if people read an example of a strategy drawn from the words of a political figure they disagreed with, they would appreciate the value of the example as an instructive tool and set aside their negative feelings about the speaker. "Yes, I don't agree with this speaker or the message, but I can clearly see the strategy in this example and I now have a better understanding of how it works and how to execute it." Indeed, I suspect 95% of my readers do just that. You probably will, too. But if you are part of the 5% who aren't up for it, don't say I didn't warn you, and please don't leave a negative review because you think I endorse this person or that person. I don't, as this is strictly a book about communication.

PUBLIC

SPEAKING

MASTERY

HOW TO SPEAK WITH CONFIDENCE, IMPACT, AND INFLUENCE

SPEAK FOR SUCCESS COLLECTION BOOK

V

PUBLIC SPEAKING MASTERY CHAPTER

I

WANT SUPERPOWERS?

Unleash the Power of Your
Words and Leap Forward

LET ME TELL YOU MY STORY (THE SHORT VERSION)

W HY DOES IT MATTER? WHY DO YOU need to communicate? How will it help you? A better question is "how won't it help you?"

You need to communicate to succeed. Weak communication skills will condemn your ideas to a slow and painful death in your mind. An idea born in your mind wants, above all else, to grow; to spread from mind to mind, until a critical mass of persuaded people makes it happen in reality. How can your brilliant idea move from mind to mind if not by communication? And what better way to guarantee it spreads than effective communication?

Effective communication – in other words, communication that uses the strategies I will teach you in this book – is what sets otherwise similar people apart: middle-managers and CEOs, mediocre salesmen and top performers, the 119 people who interviewed, and the one who got the job.

Those who speak well do well. Those who influence with grace lead with strength. Those who persuade with subtle strategy sell with stunning ease. Those who communicate like experts are respected like experts.

And let me ask you this: What would you rather be seen as? What do you want the people making decisions about your pay, your future, and your work to think of you? That you are capable of leading, or not? That you can change the minds of others, or not? That you are an expert, or not? That you are competent at the one skill that counts, or not? That you can communicate exceptionally and thus succeed exceptionally, or not?

The key to the minds of those you need to influence to get what you want is often the right word, and if not the right word, the right set of words, combined in the right way, spoken in the right way, and delivered at the right time.

It's so simple and easy. It's within your reach. If you're reading these words right now, and go on to read this book cover to cover, the power of communication will be yours. The secret of success – or rather, one of the particularly important secrets of success – will be unlocked.

And what, specifically, is this secret to success? Let us assume that success is turning reality from what it is to what you want it to be. How would you do that, if not by selecting a favorite idea, and communicating it effectively to one, then ten, then one-hundred people? How would you do that if not by replicating in the minds of others the immense belief in the idea that exists in yours?

The people who get ahead, and live the lives they want to live, are the people who can take an idea they love, and manifest it in the real world. And the people who can do that are the people who can communicate. And the people who can communicate are the people who use the secrets in this book. Stick with me. You'll be glad you did. Don't give up the pursuit of success. The moment you give up the pursuit of perfect communication, you inherently give up the pursuit of success as well. Success demands communication. Succeeding in manifesting an idea demands that others are aware of the idea, impassioned by it, and excited to help you bring it into being.

So, how did I create this book you hold in your hands? How did I discover the secrets of communication that you'll find buried in it? How did I find out the proven secrets of communication that changes minds and influences people?

The mission of my life, at least this part of my life, is to arm the world's good and ambitious people with the communication tools they need to turn their good ambitions into their beautiful realities. There are three principal ways I do that.

SECRETS OF HUMAN PSYCHOLOGY

The human mind works in certain ways, and effective communication plays upon these mechanisms of human psychology. Many of the secrets you will learn in this book are the result of taking the latest groundbreaking psychological study, and applying its lessons to communication. If you want to communicate to humans, you must communicate in a way that plays upon the inherent intricacies of the human mind. I will teach you exactly how to do this in a way nobody else will. Instead of giving you useless and shallow best practices based on some weak intuition, I give you proven and bullet-proof techniques built upon an infallible foundation: the mechanisms of psychology.

UNPACKING THE MECHANISMS OF HUMAN PSYCHOLOGY

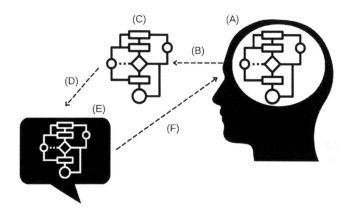

FIGURE 2: The human mind is filled with predictable, algorithmic through processes (A). I learn (B) and simplify these thought processes (C), applying them to communication (D) and developing communication models (E) that appeal to them (F).

METHODS OF PERSONAL EXPERIENCE

I have given hundreds of presentations on hundreds of subjects to thousands of people. I have narrowed down communication fact from fiction; I have broken down effective communication to its guaranteed truths, and ignored the rest. I have ignored what worked once, twice, ten, or even fifty times for me, and only accepted what worked every single time, under every single circumstance, speaking about every single subject, to every single audience. In addition, I' have broken down not only what worked for me, but what worked for my hundreds of students too. I have controlled for every single lurking variable: speaker, audience, subject, and circumstance being the most notable. And from this methodology, I draw not wishy-washy pieces of circumstantial advice, but proven strategies that work.

ANALYZING MY PERSONAL EXPERIENCE

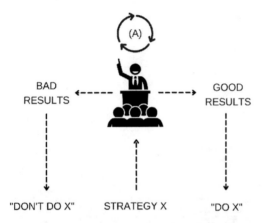

FIGURE 3: I try strategy X. I try it multiple times (A). If I get good results, I incorporate the strategy. If I get bad results, I tell you to avoid the strategy or mistake.

THE STRATEGY OF REVERSE-ENGINEERING

I'm pretty great at this stuff. But I have a coach that knows everything about communication that there is to know. I have a coach who makes my experience look like dirt; like nothing; like useless garbage. I have a coach who makes the experience of the top 100 communication coaches in the United States combined look like dirt; like nothing; like useless garbage. I have a coach who has the aggregate experience of every single major piece of communication ever created at the ready.

Who is this coach? I just said it: every single major piece of communication ever created. So, why don't you go to this coach instead? Because it is incredibly difficult and arduous to work with him; he demands dedication and effort, and only after spending a significant amount of time with him will he give you a small golden nugget of communication wisdom. It would be far more efficient for one person to work with this coach and then pass on his wisdom to a general audience, than for everyone to get it on their own. I'm that person.

THE WORLD'S MOST IMPACTFUL SPEAKING COACH

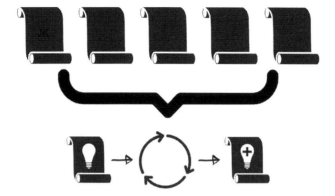

FIGURE 4: I analyze the legendary messages of legendary leaders and extrapolate communication algorithms from them: proven, step-by-step processes that turn a "starting message" into a superior version of itself.

MASTERY VISUALIZED

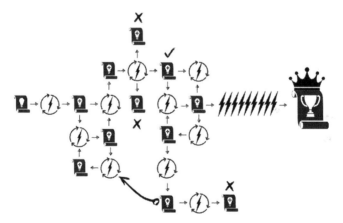

FIGURE 5: Communication mastery is the result of chaining these algorithms together.

...............................Chapter Summary...............................

- This book is based on many years of accumulated public speaking experience, including teaching the skill.
- I was not a naturally effective speaker: I had to make the shift from bad to good, and then from good to great.

- Mastering public speaking will allow you to gain power, persuade others, and develop confidence.
- This book is deeply comprehensive, covering practically everything there is to know about public speaking.
- Virtually all major principles and strategies of effective public speaking are contained in this book.
- Use these principles to make a better world for yourself, help others, and advocate for the truth and the good.

KEY INSIGHT:

We Stand atop a Mountain of Moral Truth Conveyed with Rhetorical Excellence.

We Can Mine the Rhetorical Riches of the Words that Shaped Our World and Culture.

Email Peter D. Andrei, the author of the Speak for Success collection and the President of Speak Truth Well LLC directly.

pandreibusiness@gmail.com

Claim These Free Resources that Will Help You Unleash the Power of Your Words and Speak with Confidence. Visit www.speakforsuccesshub.com/toolkit for Access.

18 Free PDF Resources

12 Iron Rules for Captivating Story, 21 Speeches that Changed the World, 341-Point Influence Checklist, 143 Persuasive Cognitive Biases, 17 Ways to Think On Your Feet, 18 Lies About Speaking Well, 137 Deadly Logical Fallacies, 12 Iron Rules For Captivating Slides, 371 Words that Persuade, 63 Truths of Speaking Well, 27 Laws of Empathy, 21 Secrets of Legendary Speeches, 19 Scripts that Persuade, 12 Iron Rules For Captivating Speech, 33 Laws of Charisma, 11 Influence Formulas, 219-Point Speech-Writing Checklist, 21 Eloquence Formulas

Claim These Free Resources that Will Help You Unleash the Power of Your Words and Speak with Confidence. Visit www.speakforsuccesshub.com/toolkit for Access.

30 Free Video Lessons

We'll send you one free video lesson every day for 30 days, written and recorded by Peter D. Andrei. Days 1-10 cover authenticity, the prerequisite to confidence and persuasive power. Days 11-20 cover building self-belief and defeating communication anxiety. Days 21-30 cover how to speak with impact and influence, ensuring your words change minds instead of falling flat. Authenticity, self-belief, and impact – this course helps you master three components of confidence, turning even the most high-stakes presentations from obstacles into opportunities.

Claim These Free Resources that Will Help You Unleash the Power of Your Words and Speak with Confidence. Visit www.speakforsuccesshub.com/toolkit for Access.

2 Free Workbooks

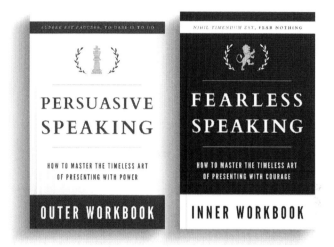

We'll send you two free workbooks, including long-lost excerpts by Dale Carnegie, the mega-bestselling author of *How to Win Friends and Influence People* (5,000,000 copies sold). *Fearless Speaking* guides you in the proven principles of mastering your inner game as a speaker. *Persuasive Speaking* guides you in the time-tested tactics of mastering your outer game by maximizing the power of your words. All of these resources complement the Speak for Success collection.

SPEAK FOR SUCCESS COLLECTION BOOK

V

PUBLIC SPEAKING MASTERY CHAPTER

II

THE BACKGROUND:
Mastering the Basics of
Effective Public Speaking

ESTABLISHING THE FOUNDATION

L IKE EVERYTHING ELSE IN LIFE, PUBLIC SPEAKING will be a journey. It will require dedication, and the journey will bring with it high points and lows; successes and failures; joys and struggles. By embarking on this journey, you are living up to be your best self and pursuing a truly meaningful endeavor which will empower you to change the world. Let this thought give you perspective during the good times that will come on this journey, and determination during the difficult ones. By traveling this journey, you are working to improve yourself. This is a journey which many regret not taking earlier in life, but just as it's never too early, it's never too late. This journey is a keystone to success. Public speaking is an incredibly valuable, empowering skill. Are you ready? Let's begin.

MOST PUBLIC SPEAKING BOOKS

I don't intend to specifically call out any other public speaking books or authors. The vast majority of public speaking books are written by brilliant authors with love and care. But there's just one problem, in my opinion. Maybe in your opinion, it's not even a problem at all. In fact, maybe you think it's actually a good thing.

Here's the problem with the traditional approach in public speaking books, as I see it. They usually suffer from one of these problems (or have one of these benefits, depending on how you view it): Long speech transcripts to teach a lesson that would have been teachable by just a small segment of the speech.

Very abstract lessons and truisms like "feel the room," "know your voice," or "be present," without any direction on how to do so. Lengthy anecdotes from other speakers with little relevance to your individual circumstances. Too much theory, and not enough specific techniques. Too many specific techniques, and not enough theory. Windy, unclear structure. Narrative based writing. Focused on writing a speech, but not delivering it, or the other way around. Either too short, with missing information, or a public speaking textbook that is very expensive. Simply an incomplete picture that leaves out powerful methods.

Again, maybe you think these are good things. Indeed, long speech transcripts might help to illuminate other public speaking lessons aside from the one intended. Abstract lessons might give you an intuitive feel for public speaking. Narrative based writing might entertain you.

Nonetheless, when I set out to write *Public Speaking Mastery*, I wanted to create a book that was truly different, and not only different, but better. And while I have nothing but the utmost respect for the majority of public speaking resources, I disagree with the traditional approach. Instead, I believe public speaking is a skill that can be learned, nurtured, and mastered because it is a skill that can be decomposed into simpler and simpler skills. The natural follow up to this is that public speaking is not as abstract as some other resources make it out to be.

Even the most magical speeches, I believe, can be broken down into a set of powerful techniques and practices being used masterfully. If you can learn and master the skills that fall under the broad umbrella of "public speaking," then you have mastered public speaking. Congratulations.

Instead of a book that tells you to "feel the room, like this one speaker I once coached who learned how to feel the room and suddenly experienced massive improvement," I want to give you a book that says "read your audience by noticing these specific signs your audience gives you, knowing what the signs mean, and reacting to them in these specific ways." Maybe that's not what you're looking for. If it's not, then I apologize. If it is, then you're reading the right book.

INTRODUCTION TO THIS BOOK

This book is a straightforward, in-depth, and all-encompassing guide to mastering public speaking. It provides a broad range of information concisely and in an easy to read way. This guide provides actionable public speaking knowledge, which you will be able to apply instantly. You can read a section from this book five minutes before a speech, and then use it. And you'll be using rock-solid advice proven to work.

MY THREE-PRONGED APPROACH TO COMMUNICATION

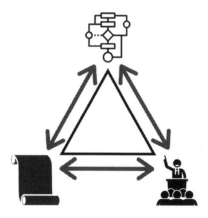

FIGURE 5: I combine my personal experience, the reverse-engineering of psychology, and the reverse-engineering of legendary messages to discover and compile patterns of communication that work. The evidentiary basis for my advice is – and I say this humbly – drastically stronger than that of most authors on this subject, who typically rely on one of these three ingredients.

If you gain nothing from this guide except one or two tips or tricks, such as gesturing with palms outward or using the four-corner crowd eye-contact trick, then I will still consider it a success because seemingly insignificant aspects of a speech can make or break it.

The guide is broken down into six sections: Background, Preparation, Content, Use of Voice, Use of Body, and Aspects of Delivery. These sections are organized to present the information in an intuitive order. The same applies to the subsections within each of the six sections. The subsections are written as short, punchy, but highly informative segments on a topic that relates to the main topic of that section.

The Background section provides you with the baseline information regarding public speaking (mixed into this section you will find some mindset advice which applies to everything, not just public speaking). The Preparation section provides you with tips and tricks regarding how to prepare your speech. The Content section describes what you should put in your speech. The Use of Voice section explains how to harness the power of your voice in very specific ways. The Use of Body section shows you how to accompany your voice with powerful bodily gestures. Lastly, the Aspects of Delivery section informs you on techniques to perfect the actual delivery of your speech. The information is split into these sections because they ultimately reflect the journey of a public speaker.

First, a public speaker adopts the proper mindset and decides what kind of speech they want to give and where, information covered in the Background section. Next, they familiarize themselves with the principles of preparing a speech, which are covered in the Preparation section. Then, they apply those principles to content that is compelling, as shown in the Content section. The speaker proceeds to deliver their speech and, in the process, confronts the question of how to use their voice and body to the greatest effect, which is answered in the Use of Voice and Use of Body sections. Lastly, during their delivery, the speaker makes several conscious decisions and applies several skills such as interacting with the audience. These skills are described in the Aspects of Delivery section.

Through reading countless self-improvement books, it's become clear to me that many of them explain a concept inefficiently and exhaustingly. This guide does not bog itself down with excessively long anecdotes and gets straight to the point.

I hope you enjoy it, and that it truly helps you master the rewarding skill of public speaking. Use this guide, and use it well, to supercharge your journey of becoming a brilliant public speaker and making your voice heard.

WHY PUBLIC SPEAKING IS IMPORTANT

Public speaking is one of the most valuable skills to possess in all realms of life. It is applicable to all vocations, and is not a skill that is, as some people believe, limited to only the worlds of business and politics. Public speaking is a skill that will revolutionize your daily life, unlock countless doors for you, and open new paths that would have otherwise been closed. It allows you to breathe new life into your ideas and spread them from isolation in your mind to a wider audience. Once an idea is presented to an audience, it now belongs to the minds of people who can present it to others, thereby spreading the idea yet further and truly giving it a life of its own.

All good ideas are energized by good presentation, and the ability to inspire appreciation for an idea in others is what makes some ideas rise above the rest and truly have an impact on the world. Mahatma Gandhi's belief in nonviolent resistance would not have altered history were he not able to replicate his belief into the minds of millions of followers. Winston Churchill's faith in the ability of Great Britain to stand alone against the impending Nazi tyranny, and stay strong despite overwhelming odds, would not have altered the course of World War II were he not able to inspire the same faith in the people of his nation. Franklin Delano Roosevelt's economic policies that promised to pull the United States out of the Great Depression would not have done so were he not able to impart his ideas to the people of the United States, and reassure them that everything will be okay with the power of his voice.

The course of human history has been molded by determined individuals who harnessed their most powerful gift: their voices. The voices of impassioned men and women are responsible for creating the world that we live in today. Their ideas alone would not have created change, but there is nothing that can stand in the way of ideas that are given a voice. So, harness yours.

COMMUNICATION EMPOWERS YOUR SUCCESS

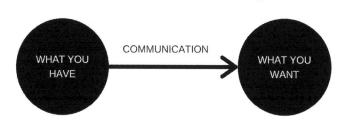

FIGURE 6: Communication is a critical component of success; of turning what you have into what you want.

WHAT WILL PUBLIC SPEAKING DO FOR YOU

Public speaking will empower your life through an unprecedented wellspring of benefits. Some of the benefits unlocked through public speaking are the ability to convince a third party that your school of thought is better than another, or even to convert someone from an opposing school of thought to yours.

Public speaking will help you make great strides in your career, and is often the skill that sets otherwise similar people apart. The ability to inspire, inform, entertain, or persuade through public speaking is what sets apart a CEO and a mid-level office manager. The ability to channel passion to an audience through speech alone is what helps some politicians rise above others and make a difference in this world. All effective leaders have used public speaking to accomplish their goals and push their followers forward. The power of public speaking will impact your success, happiness, and earnings.

THE POWERFUL 80/20 PRINCIPLE VISUALIZED

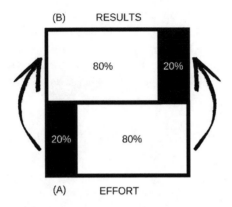

FIGURE 7: The 80/20 principle states that in many situations, 20% of the efforts (A) produce 80% of results (B), or more broadly that 20% of the causes observe 80% of the observed effects.

The vast majority of people fear speaking publicly. Doing what most people are afraid of doing is an attribute that will untether your potential for success. You will be the figure that others rally around. You will be the one to advocate for a group, and in doing so, will become the de facto leader. You will willingly take up the challenge of a presentation because your confidence will be unleashed by your public speaking ability, and you will view the presentation not as an obstacle but as an opportunity. Employers seek employees with a talent for public speaking. Managers favor subordinates who have demonstrated their ability to speak publicly. The world looks fondly upon leaders who can inspire people with the power of their words.

The confidence that comes from the ability to speak publicly infuses itself into all other aspects of your life. Public speaking is essential: it is a skill that will take you ever closer to achieving your ambitions.

THE POSITIVE IMPACTS ON YOUR CAREER

Public speaking will help you find a job. From a pool of otherwise similar applicants, employers will frequently choose the one who lists "public speaking" as a special skill (and backs it up with evidence), or has some resume item that suggests public speaking competency. This conclusion is supported by extensive data.

In 2018, the National Association of Colleges and Employers (NACE) produced an annual study through its Center for Career Development and Talent Acquisition. The purpose of this study? To give the college graduates of 2018 data and analytics on the current job market so that they can take informed first steps to starting their careers. Part of this report is a segment describing what attributes are most attractive to employers, based on polling. This segment of the report found that 67.5% of respondents sought verbal communication skills in the resumes of their applicants. 67.5% might not seem like much, but let's compare that percentage to how sought after some other skills we tend to overemphasize really are.

13 skills are reported to be sought less than communication skills. Only 29.1% of employers sought creativity. *Creativity*. Does that not go to show how much of an advantage competent public speaking is? So important that it is sought after *over twice as much as creativity*? Some other skills which are sought after less than verbal communication are strategic planning skills (39.3%), organizational ability (48.7%), computer skills (48.7%), and technical skills (59.8%).

The two other skills which 67.5% of respondents seek in applicants are analytical/quantitative skills and initiative. Effective communication skills are just as important as *math*, and the ability to get things moving.

We've gone through the numbers, now let's break down what they really mean. These numbers suggest that the ability to give a clear, compelling, and confident speech or presentation is a skill valued more than the ability to think of new solutions for problems (creativity), to plan the opening of a new store location (strategic planning / organizational skills), to create a well-formatted and functional website (computer skills), and to integrate IT systems (technical skills).

If the fact that 67.5% of employers seek strong verbal communication skills isn't enough, and if the fact this skill is sought after more than several other skills which many assume are more important isn't enough, than hear this: two of the few skills ranked above verbal communication skills are the ability to work in a team (82.9%), and leadership (72.6%). What do these two skills have in common? They are directly tied to public speaking. To work well with others and especially to lead others *demand* the ability to communicate; to inform, persuade, or inspire. Without it, one can neither work well in a group nor function as the leader of one.

While the NACE report is indeed one of the most recent and comprehensive reports indicating that public speaking will help you find employment, let's move beyond it.

In 2014, an article titled "New Survey: 70% Say Presentation Skills Are Critical for Career Success" was published on Forbes. Its finding? 70% of employed Americans who gave presentations at work affirmed that doing so was crucial for their career advancement.

In 2017, an article titled "15 Fear of Public Speaking Statistics" found that public speaking is the number one phobia, and that it has a *10% impairment on wages*. That could mean thousands of dollars a year. That could mean a vacation to Paris, or Costa Rica.

In 2018, an article titled "5 Shocking Public Speaking Statistics" found that public speaking anxiety *prevents chances of promotion to management by 15%*. The upper management position that someone has been seeking for years, yet is always just out of reach? One thing keeping them from it could be poor communication skills.

The number of articles suggesting the same thing are endless. Public speaking will help you excel in the workplace. If you aren't convinced yet, go look at the hundreds of other studies telling us the same, exact, thing.

The question that remains to be answered, then, is not *if* public speaking is important in the workplace, but *why*? Why is public speaking valued more than 13 other skills? Because without presentation skills, those 13 other skills become much less useful.

Let's look at creativity yet again. Creativity is certainly valuable in the workplace. The ability to think of new solutions to old problems, dream up new products, or develop new business methods cannot be understated; and yet, this skill is worth very little without the ability to *convey those new solutions, products, or methods to others.*

Let's take a look at strategic planning and organizational skills. Being able to organize complex plans that will methodically lead to a desired outcome is crucial. One crucial aspect of plans in the current business climate is their dependency on people. Every plan, whether large or small in scope, is executed by people. Can a plan, then, be executed smoothly if the people tasked with executing it don't understand it? No, of course not. Therein lies, once again, the importance of verbal communication skills. Without them, the ability of organized planning becomes less useful.

Are you beginning to see why public speaking, presentation skills, strong verbal communication, or whatever you want to call it is so highly emphasized in the workplace? Because so many other skills rely upon it to fulfill their fullest potential. Every other skill on the list is supercharged by strong communication skills. Every single profession benefits from them.

I want to do an exercise with you. Think of an idea you have. It can be anything. Visualize it. Try to make it something related to your career.

I guarantee that whatever idea you thought of, public speaking will help turn it from an idea into reality.

WHAT IT FEELS LIKE TO START

To deliberately immerse yourself in public speaking and to pursue it as a skill can be a nerve-wracking experience. People who perform with extreme confidence in other realms of life will likely see that confidence waver when it comes to speaking publicly. A high school superstar quarterback can perform with complete confidence on the football field and in every other aspect of life, yet when it comes to giving a speech to his team, his confidence miraculously disappears into thin air. A valedictorian may perform brilliantly in the classroom, yet when asked to give her speech at graduation, she will fear it despite confidently acing any academic test thrown at her.

What is seen time and time again, however, is that the confidence developed from mastering the art of public speaking will spill over into other areas of life. The football quarterback may break down when tasked with a speech, but an avid public speaker will feel confident on the football field (even if that's not a good idea).

In *The Power of Habit*, author Charles Duhigg discusses the idea of a "keystone habit." A keystone habit is a very central positive habit in someone's life that not only produces its own benefits, but actually helps the person maintain other positive habits. An example cited by Charles Duhigg was exercise.

WHAT IS THE HABIT LOOP?

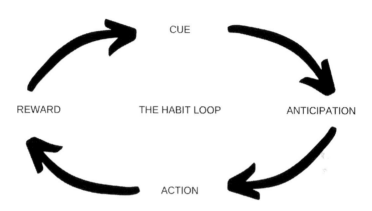

FIGURE 8: This is the habit loop. A cue leads to anticipation of reward that results in action and reward.

Public speaking is similar. Public speaking may not be a keystone habit, but public speaking is a keystone skill. It is a skill that makes someone, overall, more confident and capable. It empowers other skills.

Unfortunately, the abundance of universal confidence which public speaking brings comes at a price: the trial of overcoming the emotions which will confront you when you start.

These emotions include temporary fear and a sense of excitement when the fear is confronted. These emotions include doubt as to whether or not you are experiencing progress, and whether or not it is even a worthy endeavor; a doubt which will hopefully be overpowered by your sense of unwavering determination and a strong desire to learn the skill. These emotions can even include jealousy of those who speak effortlessly; jealousy which dissipates when you remind yourself that they are simply at a different place in the same journey as you and that it is a place you will soon reach if you earnestly persist in your efforts.

Lastly, if you push on with public speaking, this maelstrom of emotions will be replaced by a feeling of fulfillment like none other because whether or not public speaking is your passion, you will be able to apply it to whatever makes you happy. The universality of public speaking is what makes it a journey like none other.

Public speaking has been proven time and time again to be one of the biggest irrational fears known to humankind. Estimates of how many people fear public speaking vary, but some are as high as 75%. If you push through that and reach the light at the end of what is, in reality, a deceptively calm tunnel, only good things will come. To push through this tunnel, you will need to develop the proper mental frame to keep you going throughout all the lows and the highs.

Just keep in mind one thing: the disappointment which *might* come from the lows of public speaking will be greatly outlived by the joys you will *certainly* experience.

WHAT DOES PUBLIC SPEAKING ENTAIL

The art of public speaking is speaking in front of a few people, speaking in front of entire nations, or anywhere in between.

Public speaking can mean convincing a potential client to give you their business in a conference room, or it can mean addressing the entire world through a nationally televised program. The scope of public speaking is endless. There is no norm or average for what the number of people receiving a public speech will be, especially in the digital era when a speech can be viewed online, over and over again, decades after it was actually delivered. A speech delivered to a live audience of just ten people can eventually be viewed by millions through the power of the internet. For example, a man named Sir Ken Robinson gave a Ted Talk to a live audience of a few hundred people. That Ted Talk went on to accumulate over 55 million views with the power of the internet.

Public speaking involves a motive, whether it be to inform, persuade, inspire, entertain, or a combination of these. Public speaking involves preparation. Public speaking involves having a vested interest in an idea and using your body and voice to inspire interest in your audience. Lastly, particularly in less experienced speakers (but also surprisingly often in veteran speakers), public speaking involves overcoming anxiety to effectively deliver a speech.

The magic of public speaking is grounded in a three-way connection between a speaker, an idea, and an audience.

The speaker must connect to the idea to draw upon a reserve of knowledge and passion when speaking. The idea must connect to the audience because if it is not relevant to their lives, they will rapidly lose interest. The speaker must connect to the audience to properly impart the idea by commanding their attention. If they do not connect to their audience, they will be unable to deliver their points effectively, and if they do not connect to their idea, they will lack the dynamism required to connect to their audience. If an idea is not connected to the audience, or more commonly, if the speaker doesn't make the connection obvious, then the audience will lose interest in the speaker and the idea.

THE PUBLIC SPEAKING TRIAD REVEALED

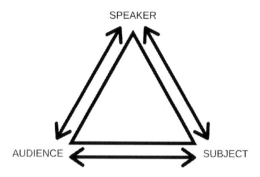

FIGURE 9: The public speaking / communication triad is foundational to effective communication. It is the three-way connection between speaker, audience, and subject.

Understanding, balancing, and perfecting the triad between speaker, idea, and audience is public speaking at its very core. Every other aspect of public speaking relates back to mastering this triad. Whether it's using metaphors in your speech or making eye-contact with your audience, you do it to support the public speaking triad. To quote Alexander Gregg, "there are three things to aim at in public speaking: first, to get into your subject, then to get your subject into yourself, and lastly, to get your subject into the heart of your audience." Mastering public speaking by learning to construct a triad between yourself, *any* idea, and *any* audience is the goal to set before you continue reading this book.

THE MENTAL FRAME

Success in any activity will be a product of the mental frame with which you approach it.

A Forbes article written a psychotherapist and mental strength author states that "thoughts are a catalyst for self-perpetuating cycles." This holds especially true for public speaking.

If you approach public speaking with a positive mindset, you will succeed. If you approach it with a negative mindset, success will come with much more difficulty. It is as simple as that. Luckily for you, your mindset is completely and totally under your control. You can alter it, master it, but if you neglect to seize control of it, fail because of it.

MASTERING THE MENTAL GAME OF CONFIDENCE

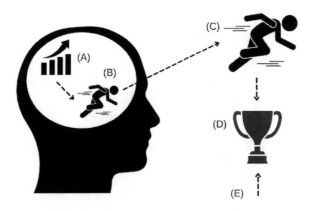

FIGURE 10: The correct mental climate (A) produces the correct potential actions, or thoughts (B), which transmute into reality as correct actions (C) that produce positive reactions, or results (D) from the world (E).

Your mindset is determined by whether you have a favorable ratio of abundance-based thoughts to scarcity-based thoughts. Examples of abundance-based thoughts are "I can do this. There is no speech which I cannot handle. I know that I have prepared well enough, and by placing faith in myself and my preparation, I will have the confidence to ace this speech. If I make a mistake, it is not the end of the world; I will just correct it and continue. If I do poorly altogether, it is still not the end of the world; I will understand the mistakes I made and learn from them in such a way that I will not repeat them next time. Yes, next time. There will always be a next time. I am looking forward to this because it is an opportunity; an opportunity to speak publicly about a topic I love in such a way that will positively alter both my own reality as well as the realities of others. I am not nervous because I fear failure, but excited for the opportunity to experience success. I do not fear failure, nor do I dwell on it as a possibility. I know that failure doesn't really exist. Failure is only final if I accept it as such. I know, beyond the shadow of a single doubt, that this speech will go brilliantly. I have the skills to do this. This is another step on the journey of mastering public speaking and I will succeed and move forward. I'm thankful for everyone and everything that has helped me achieve what I have, and that will help me succeed with this speech. I feel ready, strong, and confident."

On the other hand, scarcity-based thoughts are "Can I do this? I don't think I can handle this speech. Did I prepare well enough? I'm not sure if I have faith in myself and my preparation. I just need to be confident, but why can't I be? What if I make a mistake? What if I make two mistakes? What if I fail? Failure is very real and very scary. If I fail, I'm giving up on public speaking. The universe better not let me fail. Failure isn't a teacher, it's just an awful experience. Will this speech work out? Do I have the necessary public speaking skills? This isn't part of a journey like the author of *Public Speaking*

Mastery said it was, this is just one speech. I wish I had a better mentor. I should have taken classes on this. There are so many things to blame for how badly I will do in this speech. I feel queasy."

As sure as anything can be, the reality imagined in your mind is often the one that actually happens. Your mindset, and the reality your mindset produces, is based on your balance between thoughts of abundance and thoughts of scarcity. A positive mindset is the product of an overwhelming amount of abundance thoughts, while a negative mindset is one polluted by thoughts of scarcity. Thoughts of abundance are affirmative and strong. They dwell on the possibility of success, and thus they reap success as a reward. Thoughts of scarcity are doubtful and weak. They dwell on the possibility of failure instead of success, and thus that possibility becomes reality. Abundance thoughts are called so because they attract abundance in life, while scarcity creates, well, scarcity.

Your thoughts create your reality. Your thoughts can even give you your voice. A negative mindset will produce a quaking, wavering voice; the very voice it dwelled on the fear of having. A positive mindset will produce a voice of strength and powerful resonation; the very voice it convinced itself it had.

It is impossible to have a totally positive mindset, especially at first. It is inevitable to have the occasional thought of scarcity. To maintain a positive mindset, acknowledge the thoughts of scarcity which may occur, and seize control of them before they seize control of you and multiply. Thoughts of scarcity are like a virus, and just like a virus, they can cripple somebody. Thoughts are like battles, and mindsets are wars. The battles between the two types of thoughts will ultimately determine the outcome of the war: your mindset. Whichever side you cultivate will be the victor.

HOW TRYING TOO HARD INHIBITS YOUR PERFORMANCE

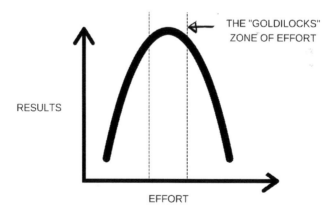

FIGURE 11: If you don't try, you don't succeed – it's as simple and obvious as that. However, if you try too much, you often undermine your own results.

All accomplishments in public speaking, and in life, are first achieved in your mind. If you're interested in learning more about the power of your mind, I highly recommend my all-time favorite book: *Think and Grow Rich*, by Napoleon Hill.

KEY INSIGHT:

The Biggest Factor Deciding the Success or Failure of a Speech Is, Bar None, the Speaker's Mindset.

All Successful Speaking Starts with Successful Thinking, Which Eases Nerves and Strengthens Us.

SEIZING THE OPPORTUNITIES

Opportunities come and go. Whoever seizes an opportunity before it's gone will enjoy the spoils of their own foresight and positive mindset. A positive mindset sees opportunities for success everywhere, while a negative mindset sees opportunities for potential failure everywhere.

There are and forever will be many opportunities to speak publicly. If you see them and then take advantage of them, you will experience exponential progress as opposed to those who deny an offer to give a presentation at work or neglect an offer to make a toast at a social gathering.

Every opportunity is a chance to work on improving your skills and moving towards mastery of public speaking. Every opportunity is a step on the journey; a rung on the ladder to success. While opportunities to speak publicly are infinitely categorizable, they typically fall under one of the following distinctions: speaking at social gatherings, career driven speaking, public speaking-oriented events, and non-public-speaking oriented events.

Speaking at social gatherings includes any sort of celebration, such as a birthday party. In such cases, a toast is an opportunity to speak publicly. Make sure, however, that a toast is actually called for and that what you say is in good taste.

An example of career-driven speaking is giving a presentation to your branch on a new technology coming to the office. In such cases, make sure that you present yourself professionally and actually know the information you are presenting.

Public speaking-oriented events consist of groups like Toastmasters, Ted / TedX talks, or competitions held by organizations like the National Speech and Debate Association. These opportunities are everywhere and are one of the best ways to develop your skills as a speaker. They are public speaking events for public speaking's own sake.

Non-public-speaking oriented events are more formal than typical social gatherings, and consist of events such as graduations.

As always, seek the opportunities out, and you will succeed in mastering the art of public speaking.

DIFFERENT KINDS OF PUBLIC SPEECHES

There are many kinds of public speeches; those delivered to inform, persuade, inspire, or entertain, those delivered formally, those delivered conversationally, those delivered on the spot, and those prepared in time. A public speech can be characterized by its goal (inform, persuade, inspire, entertain), its delivery (conversational, formal), and its preparation (on the spot, prepared in time). There are further sub-characterizations, but at the simplest of levels, this is it.

A speech prepared ahead of time can be intended to inform an audience with a formal delivery. On the opposite end of the spectrum, a speech given on the spot can be intended to entertain an audience with a conversational delivery. All speeches can be characterized by the attributes of purpose, mode of delivery, and type of preparation. There are pros and cons that come with all possible approaches. One of the keys to effective public speaking is choosing wisely. There is no best approach, but there is always an approach better suited for a given situation than others.

SPEAKING TO INFORM

One of the most common forms of a public speech is one with the purpose of informing an audience. Consider a college lecture, for example. In this setting, what should establish the three-way connection between speaker, idea, and audience, is that the audience is there with the purpose of being informed on an idea, and the speaker is there to inform the audience on that idea.

HOW TO AVOID CONFUSING YOUR AUDIENCE

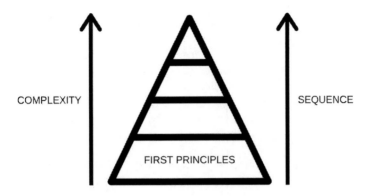

FIGURE 12: Arrange your informative message in a logical progression from less complex and more foundational information to more complex and less foundational information. Move in sequence up the pyramid.

The audience connects with the idea because they have an interest in learning it. The speaker connects with the idea because they understand it thoroughly. Lastly, the audience connects with the speaker because he or she is viewed as a trusted authority on a subject the audience wants to learn about.

The triad of effective public speaking for speeches designed to inform is built upon the honest and unbiased exchange of information from an engaging speaker to an interested audience. For a speech to properly inform, it is important that the speaker makes his authority on the topic known to the audience in a humble but assertive way. By doing this, the speaker builds a necessary level of trust.

The public speaking triad for speeches designed to inform can fall apart in several ways. The connection between audience and idea can be cut by the audience not having a genuine desire to understand the idea or information. This can be fixed by explaining to the audience why the information is important and what they can gain by understanding it.

The connection between speaker and audience can be cut by the speaker being un-engaging in such a way that even if the audience wants to understand the idea, they simply cannot keep their attention on the speaker for too long. This can be fixed by the speaker using the engagement techniques disclosed further in this book.

The connection between speaker and idea can be cut by a lack of understanding of the idea by the speaker. This can be fixed by the speaker familiarizing themselves with the idea to the fullest extent, or not trying to teach something they don't actually know.

By avoiding these pitfalls and employing these remedies if necessary, a speaker with the desire to inform an audience can rest well-assured that they will fulfill that purpose.

Lastly, always keep in mind when speaking to inform that the success of your presentation will be judged not by the knowledge you disseminate, but by the knowledge your audience receives and remembers.

SPEAKING TO PERSUADE

Public speeches with the purpose of persuading an audience to think a certain way, perform a certain daily routine, or buy a certain product are the type of speeches with the most real-world applications. An example of such a speech is a salesperson pitching an idea to potential customers in a conference room.

THE TWO IRREFUTABLE INGREDIENTS OF PERSUASION

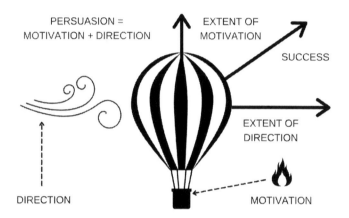

FIGURE 13: Persuasion is motivation plus direction. Think of it like a hot air balloon: the fire produces the motivation; the fire produces the potential for movement. The wind directs it in a particular direction. Proper persuasive success demands both motivation and direction. This is a powerful model that will allow you to conceptualize the key components of effective speaking.

For speeches to persuade, what should establish the three-way connection between speaker, idea, and audience is that the audience is there with a need to be filled or with a potential area of improvement in their lives, and the speaker wants to offer their service or product as a way to fulfill that need.

The audience connects with the idea or product because they have a desire that they believe it could resolve. The speaker connects with the idea or product because they will get money (or another incentive) if they win over the audience. Indeed, money should never be the only motivation. Lastly, the audience connects with the speaker because the speaker is viewed as a source from which the audience can obtain a helpful idea or product.

The triad of effective public speaking for persuasive speeches is built upon the audience having a desire or problem, and the speaker trying to convince the audience that a specific product, service, or idea will be more helpful than others towards helping them.

The public speaking triad for speeches designed to persuade can fall apart in several ways, but can be saved just as readily. The connection between audience and idea can be severed by the audience not having an actual desire for the idea. This can be fixed by the speaker inducing in the audience a desire, or pointing out a problem which the product fixes.

The connection between speaker and audience can be cut if the speaker does not truly believe that their product or idea can help the audience, or doesn't understand the needs of the audience. This can be fixed by the speaker actively seeking to understand the needs of the audience they are trying to persuade.

The connection between speaker and idea can be cut if the speaker does not actually want to sell the idea or product. This disconnect can be fixed by the speaker inspiring in themselves a desire to sell the idea or product, or not trying to persuade the audience of something they are not passionate about in the first place.

By side-stepping these dangers and using these remedies when necessary, a speaker with the desire to persuade an audience will almost always be successful. Joseph Conrad once said, "he who wants to persuade should put his trust not in the right argument, but in the right word. The power of sound has always been greater than the power of sense." In the true spirit of this quote, it is true that people often buy lower quality products which were sold to them more effectively instead of higher quality ones which were not sold to them effectively.

SPEAKING TO INSPIRE

The speeches that go down in history are almost always delivered with the purpose of inspiring an audience. An example of such a speech is a United States president-elect delivering his inaugural address. It is usually hopeful, reflective, and retrospective; painting a picture of the dawn of a new, brighter era in American history. Many of these speeches are delivered with great conviction and vocal inflection at strategic points, as well as beautifully flowing sentence structure and diction. Intensity and passion are also common aspects of these speeches.

Email Peter D. Andrei, the author of the Speak for Success collection and the President of Speak Truth Well LLC directly.

pandreibusiness@gmail.com

VISUALIZING THE CORE PRINCIPLE OF INSPIRATION

SET OF POSSIBLE QUALITIES

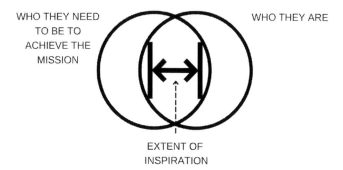

WHO THEY NEED
TO BE TO
ACHIEVE THE
MISSION

WHO THEY ARE

EXTENT OF
INSPIRATION

FIGURE 14: The core of inspiration is presenting the overlap between who they need to be and who they are.

For speeches to inspire, what should establish the three-way connection between speaker, idea, and audience, is similar to what establishes the triad for speeches to persuade. The audience usually has an area of improvement, impending danger, or hope, and the speaker uses his or her words to push the audience towards achieving the best outcome.

The audience connects with the idea because it has massive implications for their lives (such as Winston Churchill speaking to his country about the impending Nazi air raids).

The speaker connects with the idea because they are filled with conviction, determination, and purpose to impart the idea to others.

Lastly, the audience connects with the speaker because the speaker is someone that can lead them, give them direction, and be a catalyst for progress.

The triad of effective public speaking for inspirational speeches is built not only upon a need for change and the speaker inspiring that change in the audience, but also upon the audience actually being receptive to the speaker's ideas.

The public speaking triad for speeches designed to inspire is particularly fragile, because the goal of inspiring drastic change in people who inherently dislike change is more difficult than entertaining, informing, or persuading minor change. The public speaking triad for speeches designed to inspire can fall apart in several ways, and in this case, the consequences can be much more harmful.

The connection between audience and idea can be cut by the audience rejecting a need for change or a possibility for improvement. This can be fixed by the speaker showing the audience why there is a need for change.

The connection between speaker and audience can be cut by the speaker not channeling the passion they feel for the idea in their speech. This can be fixed by the speaker tapping into a reserve of passion and reminding themselves why the speech is of the utmost importance.

The connection between speaker and idea can be cut if the speaker lacks passion and belief in it. This disconnect must be avoided to begin with. A speaker cannot inspire others to pursue change or improvement by adopting an idea if they themselves don't believe in it.

To deliver a truly inspiring speech that will move the audience, these harmful scenarios should be avoided. If the speaker avoids these damaging scenarios, the public speaking triad will be intact, and they will be able to move any audience towards progress.

SPEAKING TO ENTERTAIN

Speeches with the purpose of entertaining an audience are the most lighthearted of them all. Think of a comedy act. The speaker is conversational, light, and humorous. The audience's laughter fills the room, and no bad sentiment is spoken of whatsoever.

For speeches designed to entertain, what should establish the three-way connection between speaker, idea, and audience, is that the audience is there with the purpose of being entertained, and the speaker is there to provide entertainment to the audience.

The audience connects with the ideas, or humor in this case because they are designed to be entertaining.

The speaker connects with the ideas because they want to entertain through them.

Lastly, the audience connects with the speaker because the speaker is a source of entertainment.

The triad of effective public speaking for speeches to entertain is built upon the exchange of engaging and humorous ideas from a speaker with humorous and lighthearted delivery, to an audience receptive to the speaker's unique brand of entertainment. The public speaking triad for speeches designed to entertain can fall apart in several ways.

The connection between audience and idea can be cut by the audience not being receptive to the speaker's brand of humor. This can be fixed by reading the audience and adjusting the brand of humor accordingly.

The connection between speaker and audience can be cut by the speaker failing to deliver the humorous ideas with lighthearted vocal inflection, or timing it poorly. This can be fixed by the speaker mastering conversational, lighthearted delivery.

The connection between speaker and idea can be severed by a lack of preparation and understanding of comedic value. This can be fixed by the speaker familiarizing themselves with what brand of humor is most entertaining to the demographic that makes up their audience.

By maintaining the three-way connection, and preventing the unraveling of the triad, any speaker will be able to entertain any audience.

COMMON TRAITS UNITING ALL SPEECHES

While the four types of public speeches are all distinctly different from one another, they are still united by similar traits. First and foremost, all public speaking triads collapse if the speaker is unengaging, and doesn't make use of the knowledge and techniques shared further in this book. Additionally, they collapse if the idea lacks meaning. No matter how engaging a speaker is, nobody can induce an audience to have genuine interest in a meaningless idea. Lastly, the public speaking triads fall apart if the audience doesn't have any desire to consume the content of the speech, or more commonly, if the speaker neglects to spark a desire in the minds of the audience.

All four types of speeches demand the speaker to have an interest in the idea. All four types of speeches demand the speaker to connect with the audience. All four types of speeches require the idea to have relevance to the lives of the audience members, and for the speaker to point out the relevance if it's not obvious.

By understanding and mastering the relationship between speaker, audience, and idea, you will succeed as a public speaker. It's that simple. Every single special technique you come across ultimately relates to one purpose: building the public speaking triad. The stronger that connection is, the more successful your speech will be.

MULTI-PURPOSED SPEECHES

We've all heard the phrase "kill two birds with one stone." There are many speeches that do just that by fulfilling more than one purpose. In fact, the majority of speeches go beyond just informing, entertaining, inspiring, or persuading.

A speech delivered by a climatologist could simply inform an audience of recent findings in the field, but to maximize real-world impact, the speech would need to do more than just inform. It could first present the information and then go beyond that to inspire listeners to adopt more climate-friendly habits. It could then end by persuading them to buy a book on how to lead more environmentally friendly lives. By accomplishing more than one goal, a speaker can create much more positive change in the world.

The distinction between inspiring and persuading is very important, especially in the context of this example. To inspire an audience is to alter their worldview, give them strength in the face of overwhelming odds, and open their eyes to their own potential for greatness. To persuade an audience is to convince them of something they might justifiably have reservations about, such as exchanging money for a product.

Inspiration is free and demands no immediate action from the audience, but rather a long-term change. Persuasion is convincing an audience of something that a case could be made against. Urging an audience to believe in humanity's ability to stop climate change and personally aid the effort by changing their long-term habits is to inspire. On the other hand, convincing an audience to buy a book on how to cut down their carbon footprint is persuasion because "don't buy it, that money could be spent better elsewhere" is quite a compelling argument. To inspire is to help an audience tap into their unknown reserve of strength, willpower, and determination. To persuade is to convince an audience to make a choice that is not inherently better than another choice. A particularly noteworthy combination of purposes is a comedic political commentary. There are countless political comedians who entertain and persuade an audience through comedic interpretations of recent political events, with their own biases injected into the humor to persuade an audience to adopt a political stance. Any political comedian that makes a joke out of a Senate bill is using entertainment to persuade the audience, in a non-threatening way, to see the bill as a failure. Note that this is persuasion, not inspiration, because a stance against the bill is not inherently superior to a stance for the bill (at least in most cases).

Another trend becoming more and more common is the inspirational speaker who uses entertainment to help drive home their message. Entertainment and inspiration can be blended together when an inspirational speaker describes an embarrassing, saddening, yet funny anecdote from their past to show how far they've come.

There are countless examples of entertainment, inspiration, information, and persuasion all being accomplished synergistically. In some cases, it is better to accomplish just one exceedingly well than to accomplish three or four in a less stellar way. In other cases, doing three or four competently can surpass doing one extremely well.

A SPEAKER'S TOOLBOX

Effective, powerful, and compelling public speaking is built around three tools which you can use to convey a message. These three tools are your voice, body, and words. By mastering these three aspects of communication, any public speech you give will be successful and serve the purpose you sought to achieve.

Use of Voice: The most obvious aspect of effective public speaking is, well, *speaking*. To maximize the impact of your voice when you speak publicly, make sure to project it so that everyone can hear you. Make sure to emphasize words to grant your speech a more vivid message, and to use dramatic pauses. Modulate your talking pace according to the effect you want to have on your audience, and make sure you choose a specific and deliberate tone. Avoid repetitive verbal patterns. Speak with the proper vocal tonality so that the subconscious impact of your words is maximized. Perform vocal exercises before you speak to warm up your voice.

Use of Body: Using your body to help you convey your message and engage your audience is a facet of effective public speaking often overlooked. Stand with a confident posture, and make eye contact with your audience. Use gestures when appropriate in such a way that your message is emphasized, and move across the stage to engage different sides of the audience as your speech progresses. Lastly, use facial expressions that match the sentiment of your words.

Use of Words: While your words are certainly a crucial part of a speech, good words alone will not convince an audience if they are not delivered well. In fact, it's very possible (and common) for a speaker to convince an audience of an idea that they wouldn't agree with if they came across the idea in written form. Why? Because of the way the speaker is speaking. It's not just what you say, it's how you say it. That's one of the fundamental principles of effective public speaking.

Nonetheless, strive to maximize the impact of your words by writing a hook to captivate your audience from the start of your speech, and writing a call to action to give your speech a way to make tangible, real-world impacts. Include the basics of persuasion in your speech, as well as ethos, pathos, and logos. Use the components of compelling sentence structure to develop strong rhetoric in your speech, and be sure to include metaphors and analogies as well. Choose your diction strategically, and your word choice wisely. Use positive and inclusive language, and do not be afraid to use personal anecdotes. Find a salient, intense, and stable subject, invoke the core human desires, and maximize the substance of your words. Use metaphors, similes, and analogies. Maintain simplicity and produce novelty of subject. Master the intricacies of sentence structure.

This section was a short framework of what is to come in this book. Further, you will learn how to use your communication toolbox to its fullest potential by reading extremely sophisticated strategies that will help you fulfill the purpose of your speech.

KEY INSIGHT:

One Language Speaks Louder and Means More Than All the Others. The Language Not of Words, Not of Voice, Not of Gestures, But of Action.

Standing By One's Word, Living According to One's Own Conscience, Is the Most Persuasive Rhetorical Device.

THE COMMUNICATION TOOLBOX REVEALED

FIGURE 15: The public speaking / communication toolbox reveals your tools as a communicator: your words, your body language, and your vocal modulations. You may consider yourself as having a fourth: visual aids, like presentation slides.

HOW THE TRIAD AND THE TOOLBOX CONNECT

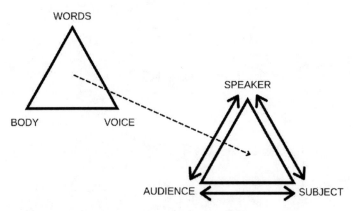

FIGURE 16: You use your communication toolbox to form the public speaking triad. You use your words, body, and voice to connect speaker, audience, and subject.

HOW TO MASTER THE FOUR LEVELS OF COMMUNICATION

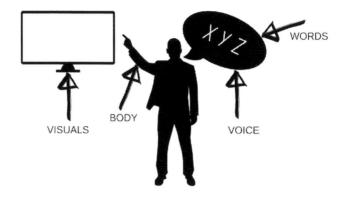

FIGURE 17: You speak with four languages: words, voice, body language, and visuals. This book deals primarily with maximizing the impact of your word language.

BACKGROUND CONCLUSION

In life, it's very important to know exactly what you want from an endeavor. That rule certainly applies to public speaking. It's important to have a clear picture of what you want to achieve with your speech. It's critical that you know whether you want to inform, persuade, inspire, entertain, or do more than one of those. Determine clearly which public speaking triad you want to construct, and have a plan to do so.

True public speaking mastery comes down to one thing. If you take only one idea from the background section of the book to form your base of knowledge for the rest of it, let it be this: to succeed as a public speaker, connect yourself to your audience. Then, connect your audience to the idea. Then, connect yourself to the idea. Then use that connection to accomplish amazing things.

There's a complex toolbox which you recently just glimpsed in the "your three tools" section that will be uncovered for you in greater depth throughout the book. Just remember the fundamental principle of effective public speaking, the three-way connection, as you read further. That's what it all comes down to.

...............................Chapter Summary...............................

- The core of effective public speaking is forming a three-way connection between speaker, subject, and audience.
- You have three languages: your words, your body language, and your vocal language. Consider visual aids as a fourth.
- These three tools comprise the public speaking toolbox; use this toolbox to form the public speaking triad.

- There are four principal kinds of speeches: informational, persuasive, entertaining, and inspirational.
- Many speeches are combinations of these four essential ingredients, using them in a sequence.
- Mastering public speaking will be drastically beneficial for your career and life, helping you seize more opportunities.

KEY INSIGHT:

Simplicity Is Sophistication, Not Only Because the Audience Follows, But Because It Prevents Mistakes the Speaker Would Otherwise Make.

Don't Let the Complex Theories of Public Speaking Overwhelm You When You Are Speaking.

HOW TO MASTER PUBLIC SPEAKING (PART ONE)

1	Background
1.1	Many Public Speaking Books Fail to Teach the Subject Optimally
1.2	This Book Is Designed to Correct Their Mistakes
1.3	Public Speaking is Part of the Foundation of Success
1.4	Public Speaking Will Massively Improve Your Career and Life
1.5	You Will Be More Likely to Get Hired, Promoted, and Paid More
1.6	Starting the Public Speaking Journey Demands Beating Anxiety
1.7	Public Speaking Means to Speak to 10-1,000,000,000 People
1.8	Adopting a Mental Frame of Abundance Will Improve Your Results
1.9	Multiple Opportunities Arise for Practicing the Skill: Seize Them
1.10	Vastly Different Speeches Are Similar at Their Fundamental Level
1.11	The First Type of Speech is Speaking to Inform
1.12	The Second Type of Speech is Speaking to Persuade
1.13	The Third Type of Speech is Speaking to Inspire
1.14	The Fourth Type of Speech is Speaking to Entertain
1.15	All Speeches Share Some Common Fundamentals
1.16	Most Speeches Fulfill More Than One of the Four Purposes
1.17	A Speaker Uses His Words, Body, and Voice to Convey His Message
2	Preparation
3	Content
4	Use of Voice
5	Use of Body

6 Aspects of Delivery

Email Peter D. Andrei, the author of the Speak for Success collection and the President of Speak Truth Well LLC directly.

pandreibusiness@gmail.com

KEY INSIGHT:

Public Speaking Is One of the World's Biggest Fears.

Beating It, Even Just Confronting It for a Moment, Generates a Great Deal of "Spillover" Confidence.

Speaking Publicly Is an Act of Immense Self-Belief. That Self-Belief Sticks Around After the Speech Is Over.

Access your 18 free PDF resources, 30 free video lessons, and 2 free workbooks from this link:
www.speakforsuccesshub.com/toolkit

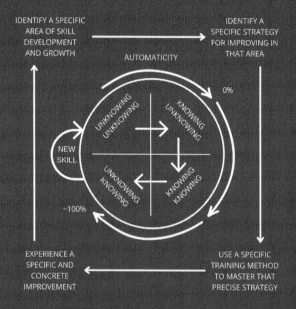

How do anxious speakers turn into articulate masters of the craft? Here's how: With the bulletproof, scientifically-proven, 2,500-year-old (but mostly forgotten) process pictured above.

First, we identify a specific area of improvement. Perhaps your body language weakens your connection with the audience. At this point, you experience "unknowing unknowing." You don't know you don't know the strategy you will soon learn for improving in this area.

Second, we choose a specific strategy for improving in this area. Perhaps we choose "open gestures," a type of gesturing that draws the audience in and holds attention.

At this point, you experience "knowing unknowing." You know you don't know the strategy. Your automaticity, or how automatically you perform the strategy when speaking, is 0%.

Third, we choose a specific drill or training method to help you practice open gestures. Perhaps you give practice speeches and perform the gestures. At this point, you experience "knowing knowing." You know you know the strategy.

And through practice, you formed a weak habit, so your automaticity is somewhere between 0% and 100%.

Fourth, you continue practicing the technique. You shift into "unknowing knowing." You forgot you use this type of gesture, because it became a matter of automatic habit. Your automaticity is 100%.

And just like that, you've experienced a significant and concrete improvement. You've left behind a weakness in communication and gained a strength. Forever. Every time you speak, you use this type of gesture, and you do it without even thinking about it. This alone can make the difference between a successful and unsuccessful speech.

Now repeat. Master a new skill. Create a new habit. Improve in a new area. How else could we improve your body language? What about the structure of your communication? Your persuasive strategy? Your debate skill? Your vocal modulation? With this process, people gain measurable and significant improvements in as little as one hour. Imagine if you stuck with it over time. This is the path to mastery. This is the path to unleashing the power of your words.

Access your 18 free PDF resources, 30 free video lessons, and 2 free workbooks from this link: www.speakforsuccesshub.com/toolkit

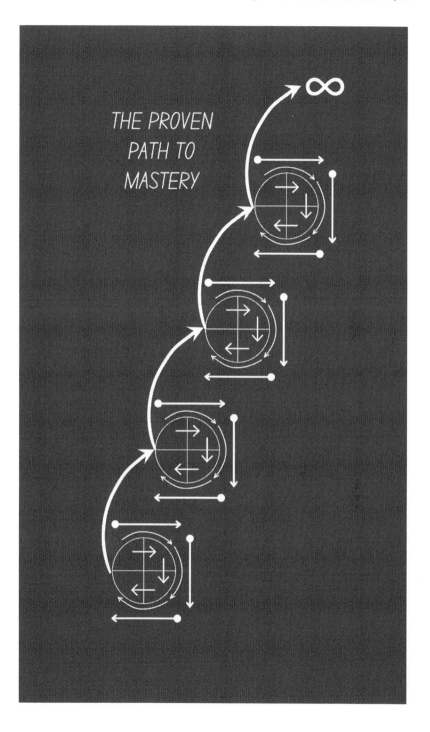

THE PROVEN
PATH TO
MASTERY

SPEAK FOR SUCCESS COLLECTION BOOK

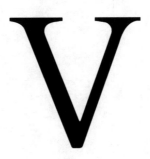

PUBLIC SPEAKING MASTERY CHAPTER

III

PREPARATION:

How to Guarantee a Perfect Presentation

ENSURING SUCCESS

T O SUCCEED IN ANY ENDEAVOR, YOU MUST prepare for it. There is no substitute for preparation when it comes to a football game, or a piano performance. The same applies to public speaking. The preparation involved with public speaking includes mastering your mind, and conquering yourself. It also includes dedicated repetition or studious analysis of a set of themes and ideas.

CONFIDENCE

This is, beyond the shadow of a single doubt, the most important section of this book. And this, beyond the shadow of a single doubt, is the most important word: *confidence*.

Confidence is what will push you towards success as a speaker, or hold you back from it. You have to truly believe in your ability to be an amazing speaker. Believe in it, and the hard work will become much easier because you will see the desired outcome as *genuinely attainable*. See yourself as an unstoppable speaker, and you will become one. Keep this thought in the back of your mind – that you are a good public speaker – every time you speak publicly. Find your own variation of that thought. Some people prefer "I'm an unstoppable public speaker," while others prefer the humbler "I'm a solid public speaker who can give a good presentation to these wonderful people gathered here today."

Don't be afraid to get out of your comfort zone. Your ability to be an effective public speaker is split not only into *what* you say, but *how* you say it. Be confident in yourself to maximize the power of the "how you say it." The first stepping stone to completely uninhibited speech is confidence in oneself. Master confidence and all else in public speaking will come much more easily.

Understandably, it's not quite as easy as saying "I'm going to be confident now." The secret in developing public speaking confidence lies in facing anxiety, time and time again, until it disappears and you've conquered it once and for all. Being at that point is incredibly tranquil and it is here where the confidence gained from public speaking finally spills into other areas of life. Audiences can hear confidence. They can see it, and they can notice when it's missing.

Developing public speaking confidence doesn't come easy, but once it does, everything else will fall into place.

UNPACKING THE ANXIETY

Some people are more anxious to speak publicly than others. Why? How can these people overcome the anxiety? Well, first we have to understand why it happens in the first place. We have to figure out what makes public speaking so scary to some people.

The first reason public speaking is so fearsome to many people is because of a set of traits evolution has developed in us. They were helpful in the past, but they no longer serve a purpose in the modern age. The emotion of anxiety is a response to environmental stimuli: in the past, a large animal attacking us would cause our nervous systems to go into "defense" mode. In this case, our nervous systems respond in a beneficial way.

Now, to our rational minds, getting attacked by a tiger and getting up to give a speech in front of one hundred people are radically different. Rationally, the latter shouldn't scare us at all. To our nervous system, however, those situations appear far more similar than they really are. Our nervous system can't distinguish between the threat of a predator and what it perceives as the threat of hundreds of eyes looking at us when we're vulnerable on a stage. Unfortunately, this means that our nervous system sometimes reacts the same way to a saber-tooth tiger as it does to an audience. This fight or flight response produces the symptoms of what we know as anxiety. Thanks a lot, evolution.

In some cases, the fight or flight response can serve to confuse us even more. We become anxious not about the physical act of giving a public speech itself, but about the anxiety we're feeling. We become anxious about our being anxious.

Public speaking anxiety exists on a broad spectrum: some people simply shake a little on stage, while others completely panic. There are many solutions out there for all ranges of public speaking anxiety. These solutions include hypnosis, virtual-reality therapy, rational-emotive therapy, simulated reconditioning, and many other exceedingly complex approaches.

In my experience, the solution which is most reliable, most effective, and simplest is retraining the nervous system by exposing it to public speaking time and time again until it can override its previous impulses and react in a less harmful way. This process takes time, effort, and grit, but it pays off. It can be done in a very controlled, safe way. For example, instead of starting to expose themselves to massive crowds hoping that they won't be anxious from the start, an aspiring public speaker can start small: four close family members. Then eight. Then twelve strangers. By starting small and working one's way up, this process of retraining the nervous system becomes much gentler.

Public speaking anxiety can also occur in specific circumstances. Someone might be a perfectly confident speaker in most situations, but become very anxious when they are being evaluated, when they are giving a speech to people of "higher status" then themselves, and when there are higher stakes than usual. As with any activity, external and additional pressures can apply.

The solution to public speaking anxiety is this: practice, learn, and get as much experience as possible. Study public speaking with commitment, diligence, and determination; soon enough, anxiety will be a thing of the past.

COMPARTMENTALIZING THE ANXIETY

Everyone gets anxious before speaking publicly, at least until they become more experienced. Even the best speakers sometimes get anxious right before a big speech. There are only two types of speakers in the world: those who are nervous, and those who lie by saying they are never nervous. Very rarely nervous? Sure, that's certainly possible. But *never?* That can't happen.

Believe it or not: confidence and anxiety can, and often do, coexist. Anxiety can be present, and confidence can acknowledge it and counterbalance it. You can feel anxiety, and your confidence can remind you that it's caused by your nervous system, and that you have no control over it. You can worry that you won't do well, and your confidence can remind you that you're ready to ace the speech.

When you're feeling anxious prior to a speech, keep in mind that it is a very natural reaction. Don't shy away from an opportunity to speak publicly due to anxiety. As soon as you start, it'll all melt away. Time and time again, speakers describe how anxious they were before a speech but how it all went away when they began speaking. What was it replaced by? It was replaced by elation, joy, and a feeling of fulfillment and success.

Never try to suppress your anxiety. Acknowledge the way you're feeling, and acknowledge that you're still going to do great. Remember that almost every person who ever gave a public speech felt some measure of anxiety at one point or another. If you're anxious, place faith in your preparation and your ability. Fake it until you make it. No matter how anxious you are, start your speech as confidently as you possibly can and by the end of it, the abundance of anxiety will be replaced by a wellspring of confidence.

Think of it not as anxiety to speak in front of an audience, but excitement to do an amazing job. And lastly, after all is said and done, no matter how "awful" you think a speech may have gone, it was infinitely better than the one not given, the audience likely didn't notice the mistakes you noticed, and you are now a more experienced speaker.

KEY INSIGHT:

Yes, Your Audience *Might* Be Judging You. But Do You Care About Their Judgment More Than Your Own? You Are Bravely Confronting a Fear. What Does Your Judgment Say About That? Good. Forget Theirs

---

PRE-SPEECH RELAXATION TECHNIQUES

There will be times when no matter what, you'll find that you can't shake speaking anxiety and you can't put yourself in a confident state of mind. In this case, there is a technique you can perform to ease your anxiety.

First, focus on your breathing. Sit still with good but relaxed posture in a comfortable chair, with the palms of your hands placed on your legs, and take deep breaths. Take the breaths all the way into your stomach. This is called diaphragmatic breathing. Imagine that the anxiety is all physically located in your stomach, and you have to breathe deeply enough to exhale it out. Make sure you breathe through your nose. You might be skeptical of this technique, but there are countless studies that hold the benefits of diaphragmatic breathing in high acclaim.

While you're in the process of performing diaphragmatic breathing, close your eyes and meditate by attempting to push all thoughts out of your mind. If they come, simply observe them and accept them. Do not engage in a train of thought. Once you've reached mental clarity through meditation, begin to actively visualize positive scenarios. Picture yourself receiving thundering applause after your speech. You can even try to remember a particularly comforting memory and recreate it in your mind as best as you can. As with diaphragmatic breathing, many reputable studies conclude that meditation can ease anxiety.

Listening to either mellow background music that is specifically designed to relax the mind or to upbeat music with triumphant lyrics while you perform this relaxation process can be beneficial as well. Never stop picturing a positive outcome as you perform this technique.

After performing this technique, exercise of any form will further alter your brain chemistry in a positive way. Exercising while repeating positive, non-exercise related affirmations to oneself is a secret weapon for inducing a calm state of mind. It's important when listening to music to ease anxiety that you don't listen to what seems the most relaxing, but to your favorite genre. Listening to your favorite genre of music, or your favorite songs, has several positive impacts on your mental state.

While these strategies almost always work if done properly, in the case of an impromptu speech, you may not have time to do them. Luckily, in this case, not only will you not have time to perform these relaxation techniques, you'll also not have time to get anxious and wrapped up in your head.

Email Peter D. Andrei, the author of the Speak for Success collection and the President of Speak Truth Well LLC directly.

pandreibusiness@gmail.com

HOW THESE SHIFTS GIVE YOU ENERGY IN TOUGH MOMENTS

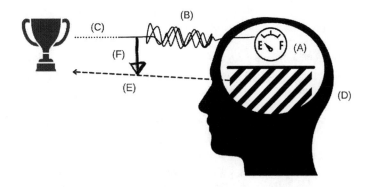

FIGURE 18: In stressful, high-stakes situations, or when you are tired or anxious, your conscious mind lacks the energy (A) to meet the moment effectively, producing incorrect actions (B) that fall short of achieving your goal (C). However, your subconscious mind is capable of meeting this moment (D), producing correct actions that hit the mark (E). Thus, these shifts give you the energy in difficult moments to perform well instead of poorly (F).

If you're skeptical about these techniques, try them with an open mind before your next speech. If they don't work for you, try to find a different routine. If they do work for you, which they likely will, then use them any time you feel anxious, not just before a public speech.

IMPROMPTU AND EXTEMPORANEOUS SPEECHES

Imagine this: you are a branch manager for a technology company, and your superior asks that you give a speech on an out-of-the-blue branch merger that caught you by surprise. This is a speech that you could not have possibly prepared for. If anything, you can consider reading this book or the past speeches you've done as the preparation for this one. You might have only five to ten minutes to prepare a speech. Doing so is certainly a daunting endeavor.

If this happens, just write down the main ideas on a piece of paper, memorize them, and remain confident. The successful delivery of an impromptu speech relies mostly on the confidence of the speaker, and their ability to remain calm and collected. A speaker lacking confidence who has been asked to give an impromptu speech will spend the little time they have to prepare in the grips of panic as opposed to actually preparing. Giving an impromptu speech is a difficult affair, and to do so effectively you must have faith in your ability.

Imagine this: you are a branch manager once again, but this time your superior has elected to give the speech herself. She speaks for a few minutes, and then in front of everyone turns to you and asks, "would you like to say any words?" Of course, you could just say no, but that wouldn't further your career, and that would be passing up on a good opportunity. In this scenario, you have less than 5 seconds to prepare.

What do you do? Start saying what's on your mind, and be genuine. The first sentence is the hardest part. Delivering the first sentence of your impromptu speech confidently will make the rest of the speech easy. Whatever you say first, whether it is "this is a big step forward for the branch," or "nobody will lose their jobs," the words will begin to freely flow out of you, as your following statements will build off of the first one. Giving an impromptu speech is essentially just saying what's on your mind, in a slightly more eloquent and ordered way than you normally would.

THE LITTLE-KNOWN STRATEGY FOR IMPROMPTU ELOQUENCE

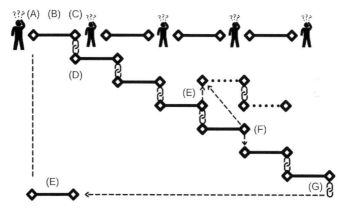

FIGURE 19: When you must speak extemporaneously, you may experience some difficulty fluently finding your content; your sentences (A). When you find your first sentence after some effortful thinking (B), you have two choices. You can either proceed in this manner (C), effortfully thinking of your content and appearing unsure, nervous, and inhibited as you need to brainstorm every sentence all-over again, or you can apply the sentence-chaining principle (D). Your first sentence was the most important piece of content you needed to get across. The sentence-chaining principle then uses this as a launching pad into the second sentence, chaining the start of the second sentence to the end of the first one. Perhaps three sentences later, you receive another two sentences to incorporate (E), but you have a more important sentence to deliver. After you deliver it, you may find that you don't have an easy, natural chain from your previous sentence. So, you recall and use the deferred two sentences (F). When you conclude, you chain the final sentence (G) back to the first (E).

A helpful tool for impromptu speeches is the use of dramatic pauses (more on these later). These give you time to carefully consider your next words while building suspense.

Remember to not get down on yourself if you make an error as this will affect the rest of your speech. Simply stay focused, accept any mistakes you make, and continue delivering your speech in a confident manner. Chances are people will simply overlook the small mistakes in favor of the overall tone, delivery, and message of your speech.

Nobody expects a perfect impromptu speech: the audience will understand the circumstances and accept mistakes or stumbles as they come, without judging you for it. They will be filled with admiration for you for putting yourself out there to communicate information in a candid way. You giving an impromptu speech to inform, persuade, inspire, or entertain an audience is something anyone should be able to appreciate.

SPEECHES PREPARED IN TIME

The majority of speeches are prepared in time. This, however, does not always mean that they are memorized. Many speeches are merely centered around a core set of ideas. This allows for a human-to-human transmission of the ideas. A speech centered around a core set of ideas might occur differently every time it is given. The words chosen might not be the same, but the concepts will be.

The difference between a speech prepared in time that is loosely centered around a set of ideas and an impromptu speech is that with the former, you can and should spend time familiarizing yourself with what you will say. Speeches prepared in time that are not written word for word allow for an honest exchange of information between speaker and audience simply because the speaker can't artificially rearrange words and phrases to suit his or her liking. Words come out the way they were thought, which is usually the best way. When beginner speakers write speeches, they typically first write down their thoughts, and then deliberately refine them. This is certainly beneficial, but the language usually isn't as natural as it was when the speech was first written.

A manuscript makes for indirect communication. The speaker goes to the manuscript for words, the manuscript returns words to the speaker, and then the speaker gives these words to the audience. A speech centered around a core set of ideas is direct communication because words go straight from the mind of the speaker to the audience. Thus, the speaker centering a speech around a set of ideas as opposed to memorizing it word for word can still exchange the ideas effectively, if not more effectively, because the first way to describe an idea that comes to the speaker's mind is usually the most straightforward and natural. It will be a direct connection from speaker to audience as opposed to a connection from manuscript to speaker to audience.

Having a completely memorized speech that you strictly adhere to can be an inhibition, and while it may make you feel more confident and prepared, it is not always a worthy sacrifice. Speakers often feel the urge to ditch the manuscript as soon as they start speaking. It should be there as a failsafe, in case you need it, but not as a crutch. Memorization is certainly recommended, especially for speeches with higher stakes such as a president addressing the nation, or a keynote speaker addressing an auditorium of thousands of listeners. Complete and thorough memorization is excellent, and allows for a truly polished speech. Achieving the necessary level of complete and total memorization, however, demands committed practice.

Complete memorization is excellent if possible, and if not, centering a speech around a set of ideas and spending time memorizing only a few key portions of it is even better. When a manuscript is completely, thoroughly memorized, it becomes a part of you. Therefore, a truly memorized manuscript is direct communication. It's very difficult, however, to memorize and practice a manuscript to the point that it becomes a part of you. The worst case is attempting to memorize a speech, not doing so fully, and then relying on a hazy memory of the manuscript when you speak. This is a 3-step pattern of communication. Step 1 is the speaker searching for words to say to the audience from either the manuscript, or a hazy memory of it. Step 2 is the speaker getting words from the manuscript, or a hazy memory of it. Because the process of searching a manuscript (or a hazy memory of one) for words becomes cumbersome and frequent, it ends up detracting from step 3, which is the speaker delivering the words to the audience.

The pattern of communication when speaking with a well memorized manuscript is also 3-step communication. However, in this case, the manuscript represents either a physical manuscript or the speaker's memory of a manuscript which he or she didn't bring on stage. The manuscript is well memorized, and thus the process of searching the manuscript for words (or the memory of the manuscript for words) is reduced in frequency and difficulty. Therefore step 3, the communication between speaker and audience, remains unhindered.

Now let's talk about the 3 steps in the pattern of communication for speaking fluidly around a core set of ideas. Step 1 is the process of searching for words, Step 2 is the process of receiving, or finding words. In this case, both of these steps occur within the speaker's mind. When you speak freely about a subject, you are searching your cache of knowledge for words, a place from which you can readily draw. When you memorize a speech, you are sifting for words through your memory of a manuscript, which is only effective if that memory is crystal clear. It can be very difficult to maintain an engaging presence and also use an unmemorized manuscript. Sure, it might be comfortable because you have the words right in front of you, but this often diminishes your ability to be an engaging presence in the room. What's worse is that time and time again, speakers who use manuscripts speak less eloquently than if they simply spoke in a natural, direct way. Why? Because they misread a word, their eyes jump to the wrong line, they can't understand their own handwriting, etc. These are just some of the barriers that can occur between step 1 (looking to the manuscript for words) and step 2 (finding them), which ultimately hinder step 3 (speaking to the audience).

THREE-STEP COMMUNICATION IS FAKE COMMUNICATION

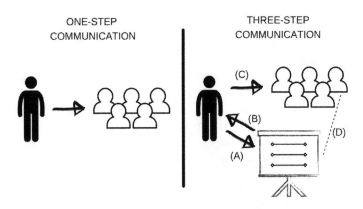

FIGURE 20: One step communication is when the speaker directly pours the message into the hearts and minds of the audience; when the speaker connects his heart and mind to their hearts and minds, and communicates by way of this connection. Three-step communication is when the speaker looks to a manuscript, memory, visual aid, or external apparatus for the message (A), finds it there (B), and then relays it to the audience (C). In this case, the audience can circumvent the speaker and still get the message by going directly to the external aid (D). While calling this "fake" communication is a bit of an exaggeration, it is true that in this situation, the speaker is superfluous in some measure.

If you can memorize your speech fully and completely, do so. If you can't, center it around a set of ideas and familiarize yourself with those ideas.

MEMORIZATION TRICKS AND SPEECH PRACTICE

When Anton Chekhov, a Russian playwright and short-story writer said "knowledge is of no value unless you put it into practice," it was a broad statement that can be adapted to public speaking: trying to convey knowledge is of no value unless you practice doing so. If you choose to memorize and practice your speech, there are several tricks that make doing so easier.

The first is relying on muscle memory, and handwriting your speech over and over again. Say the words out loud as you write them, the way you plan to when you actually deliver your speech. Many career public speakers have drawers filled with handwritten copies of speeches they wrote simply to memorize them. This is an effective way to memorize a speech because muscle memory is stronger than regular memory, and because the act of simultaneously writing and saying the words activates more of your brain towards memorizing the speech and roots the words in a more solid form of memory. Eventually, you will be able to handwrite it from memory alone, and then to deliver it from memory alone.

When you're attempting to write the speech from memory alone, pay attention to segments in the speech where you forget what to write, or write the wrong thing. These are the moments in your speech when you would have made a mistake during actual delivery. It usually has something to do with the way it's written, so rewrite these problematic segments in a more natural way. You'll find that once you rewrite them in a more natural way, it's less likely that you stumble over them.

The second method is practicing it verbally. Split your speech into five segments and memorize the first one by delivering it over and over again, until you no longer need the manuscript. Do the same with the second segment, and try seamlessly delivering the first two segments one after the other. Repeat this until you've memorized the entire speech. Break down your speech into as many segments as you want. In fact, if you think this might help you, you can even perform this technique sentence by sentence.

The third strategy is to draw pictures that you associate with each portion of the speech, and then memorize the order of pictures. Studies have shown that the brain can remember pictures better than it does words. You can use this strategy in tandem with the other two.

Another important element of memorization and practice is not only the words, but the vocal inflections, gestures, volume shifts, pacing, and tonalities that will be used at certain points in the speech. Not only should you memorize the words, but practice delivering them with the techniques shared in the Use of Voice and Use of Body sections. It is also very valuable to have a trusted friend or even a more experienced public speaker listen to your speech and critique it. You can even place a smartphone or camera on a table and perform your speech in front of it. This will allow you to analyze exactly what you may need improvement on.

The best way to guarantee a good performance and ease anxiety is to prepare. Prepare weeks, even months in advance. Prepare with dedication, and your speech will go well. You get out what you put in. Garbage in, garbage out. Gold in, gold out.

GENERAL PUBLIC SPEAKING PRACTICE TECHNIQUES

You can practice public speaking the same way you can work out your muscles. There are many techniques, strategies, and methods which you can use to improve as a public speaker. I'm not referring to just practicing one speech until it's ready to be delivered, I'm talking about actually improving, in a very broad and general way, as a public speaker over time. Not all of these techniques require other people around. Some could benefit by being done with other people, and some couldn't. By doing each of these once a day in the morning or before going to bed, over time, you will experience a massive improvement in your abilities.

The first technique, my personal favorite, is to find a random topic by looking at news headlines, asking someone, or by choosing one yourself. After finding a topic, spend two to five minutes considering what you will say (perhaps writing main ideas on a notecard). Then, give a five-minute speech in the mirror, filmed with your own phone, or in front of others. This is perhaps one of the most practical types of public speaking. Being able to give a confident, intelligent, and well-structured speech on a topic with only five minutes is an indispensable skill. Try going just off of your knowledge without spending the preparation time researching further. It might be challenging at first, but you'll realize you know more than you think you know. This first technique is designed to improve your impromptu speaking skills, and can be adapted to informational, inspirational, persuasive, and entertaining speeches. Think of processes that you need to discuss in your field of work, and try this practice technique with them. If you are a chemist, for example, try explaining a chemical process relevant to your work. Maybe one day you'll need to, and you'll already have practiced it.

This game is especially useful when you gradually limit your preparation and research time, because it teaches you how to form connections between things you already know and the topic you are speaking about.

A fun variation of this is the "um" game. Speak for as long as you can without introducing a conversation filler (uh, umm, like, you know, etc). Time yourself, and try to increase the time until you can go endlessly without saying any conversation fillers.

The second technique is designed for speeches prepared in time, and is effective if you have a speech which you need to give over and over again. A salesman, for example, might be going on a sales circuit in a different state. He will likely be giving the same pitch over and over again, so he should practice it three times a night, every night for one to three weeks before he departs. Motivational speakers, who are paid to give the same speech or very similar versions over and over again, use this technique only until their first few speaking contracts have been fulfilled. Then, their speech becomes second nature. As always, practice while filming yourself so that you can critique yourself afterwards.

None of these techniques need other people, but it's always better to do them with others around. If you have a friend or two who want to learn public speaking (or have upcoming presentations), you can meet once a week and practice these skills together. They can ask questions, give you detailed feedback, and you can hold each other accountable.

Public speaking is not as abstract as it seems, and is a skill that can be practiced, polished, and improved. Just like any other skill, it requires dedicated practice of a set of core principles. This book supplies the core principles for you: the next step is to practice them.

VISUAL AIDS AND READING A SPEECH

Posture, eye-contact, gestures, movement, and charisma. What do these all have in common? Reading your speech to an audience from a piece of paper kills them all. Reading from a paper degrades your stage-presence, engagement, and confidence. If you feel that having the manuscript with you is necessary, bring the paper, briefly glance down at it, and deliver it sentence by sentence. Read the next sentence quickly, then look up and deliver it while facing the audience.

The best alternative, especially when you're basing your speech around a set of core concepts, is just writing down the main points you want to deliver. Speaking naturally always beats reading from a piece of paper. If you're bringing a set of notecards, ensure that you get them ready five minutes before you go up to speak so that you have them all in the right order. Additionally, find a way to attach them together so that if you drop them, they don't all go flying everywhere. One of the most successful approaches, however, is just one three by five-inch note card with brief notes and a few of the most important word for word phrases in your speech. This is a good compromise between having the entire speech in front of you, and having no visual aids whatsoever.

This notecard is not obvious, does not intrude on the speaker's ability to be an engaging presence, and still gives the benefits of having some sort of visual aid by lending the sense of direction and security that comes with having a physical resource while you speak.

While some might feel that it is not enough, it is just the right amount. It is enough to give you direction, but not so much that it impacts your fluidity.

SPEAKING ATTIRE

Even Shakespeare knew that "apparel oft proclaims the man." The clothes you wear when speaking should match the venue you are speaking at. If you are giving a conversational speech to a group of high-schoolers, then you don't need a suit and tie. If you are speaking in a professional setting, a suit and tie is recommended.

The advice that clothes are important when it comes to public speaking is wrongfully framed by many as vain, trivial, and useless, when in reality it is just the opposite.

People tend to connect with those who they can identify with. That is why you should dress only slightly fancier than your audience, in such a way that they can still identify with you but at the same time respect you. If you are speaking to a group of high-schoolers, jeans are okay but instead of a regular t-shirt, a polo shirt is more respectable but still relatable. If you are speaking to an office of employees wearing white collared shirts, ties, and khakis, wear something similar but throw on a blazer to be slightly better dressed than your audience. This may seem vain and insignificant, but psychologically speaking, it is very important. Do not be so much more well-dressed that you sacrifice audience relatability, but do not wear the exact same thing because doing so sacrifices your respectability.

Your audience being able to identify with you is crucial and worth the effort of choosing the right clothes for the occasion. A politician appealing to a constituency of struggling, hard-working blue-collar citizens would be foolish to approach the podium in an expensive suit and tie. Instead, he would be wise to take off the blazer, loosen the tie, and roll up the sleeves. This subconsciously indicates to the audience that the politician is not afraid to get his hands dirty, and is willing to forego his appearance in favor of comfort and functionality. This is something that the constituency can identify with. Suddenly the way the politician decided to dress added another layer to the connection between speaker and audience. Even the act of dramatically loosening a tie and rolling up sleeves mid-speech says something about the speaker.

Be creative with it, but remember to not let your clothes distract your audience from your speech. The clothes should never speak louder than the speaker.

PRESENTATION TOOLS

There are a variety of presentation tools available such as PowerPoint, Google Slides, and many more. Ever since these softwares hit the market, public speakers have used them in ways that are both effective and detrimental to their speeches. Bad use of PowerPoint is to project word for word what you will say and simply read off the slides. This is one of the single biggest mistakes a speaker can make. The phrase "death by PowerPoint" was coined because of this, yet some people still make this mistake over and over again. You are not there to read. Hopefully, everybody in your audience knows how to do so themselves. Instead, you are there to passionately convey your ideas to the audience.

Effective use of PowerPoint is projecting a few key phrases, statistics, data, graphs, and visuals. Using PowerPoint as an aid, not a guide, and certainly not as a manuscript, is the best method. You should not rely on the PowerPoint. It should be there for the audience, not for you. An example of a bad PowerPoint slide is this:

WHAT YOUR SLIDES SHOULD NOT LOOK LIKE

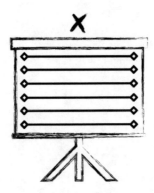

FIGURE 21: Your slides should not be big blocks of text. In the "hook" section of this book, we reveal the underlying psychological dynamics of attention that explain why big paragraphs do not work well in slides.

Such a PowerPoint slide is harmful because it takes attention away from the speaker by confusing the audience as to whether they should read the slides or listen to the speaker. Additionally, it is harmful because it is designed to be read by the speaker instead of the audience, and because big blocks of text on slides have been shown to be uninteresting and also visually daunting to an audience. They might not commit to reading the entire slide, and thus they can tune out. On the other hand, if they do commit to reading the slides, you risk clicking to the next slide before they finish and this will frustrate them. It is also quite possible that they decide to ignore the slides, and in this case, the speaker robbed themselves of the benefits of having slides in the first place. A better alternative to this slide is this:

A BETTER ALTERNATIVE

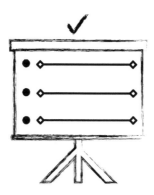

FIGURE 22: This is a superior alternative, shortening the sentences and making them bullet-points.

This slide improves on the previous slide because it conveys the same information more concisely, but ultimately faces many of the same issues in a less extreme way. An even better alternative is the example on the next page.

KEY INSIGHT:

We Are Wired to Feel Deep Compassion Toward People, Not Abstractions.

THE BEST EXAMPLE

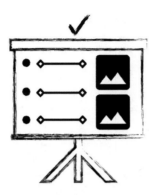

FIGURE 23: This is even better, breaking down the sentences further and including images.

It's better to have an audience actually remember three main ideas from a slide rather than to have them try and fail to remember a massive block of text. The rule of three is a well-known speech-writing, speaking, and prose writing technique. It allows you to explain concepts with more depth, completion, and thoroughness. It is also inherently satisfying to hear and read. Why say "Climate change is a problem caused by human activity" when you can say "Climate change is a problem caused by car emissions, industrial emissions, and plastic waste in our oceans." The rule of three originates from the Latin phrase *"omne trium perfectum,"* which means everything that comes in threes is perfect, or, every set of three is complete. Sets of three ideas allow for simplicity. Aim for three main ideas on each slide.

This slide is the best alternative because it greatly simplifies the information while retaining the essence of it, and because it synergizes visuals and text to improve information retention. It also, of course, takes advantage of the following principle: reading, seeing, and hearing information all at the same time maximizes the chance that it will be retained. Additionally, this slide lacks the overwhelming amounts of text that was clearly abundant in the first two. The audience can quickly read each brief, punchy statement, analyze the pictures, and then return to the voice of the speaker as opposed to having their attention divided.

This slide still provides guidance and helps the speaker maintain the direction of his or her speech, but it doesn't feed them the words which kills their naturality, charisma, and spontaneity.

This slide could be improved yet further by splitting it up into three slides.

BREAKING IT UP: PART ONE

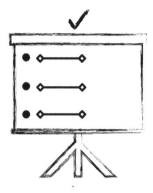

FIGURE 24: Breaking up the slides into three is even better. First, the sentences.

BREAKING IT UP: PART TWO

FIGURE 25: Then, the first image. Now, it gets complete and undivided attention.

KEY INSIGHT:

Complex Slides Slide Off the Mind. Simple Slides Slide Into It.

BREAKING IT UP: PART THREE

FIGURE 26: Lastly, the final image. Once again, it doesn't compete with anything for attention.

DON'T INTRODUCE UNNECESSARY DISTRACTIONS

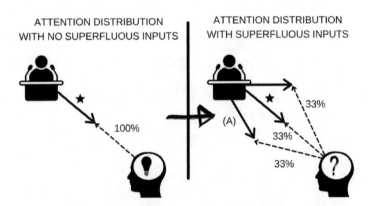

FIGURE 27: When you introduce one input – the most important input you are presenting – it receives 100% of the attention you have obtained. Unnecessary inputs (A) dilute the attention, distracting away from the important input, spreading it out among the unimportant ones.

The speaker could speak about the concepts on the first slide, and then stop on the image of the cars for 10 or so seconds and say "here we see something that our society can't seem to function without... mass transportation into cities and commercial centers. We can't seem to get rid of it, so we have to find a way to make it more carbon efficient." Then, the speaker could click to the slide of the smokestacks and once again hover for 10 or so seconds, saying "here we see the smokestacks of factories which may have produced the iPhone in your pocket, the car you drove here, and even the clothes you are wearing right now." It is important that upon clicking to a new picture, the speaker remains silent for a few second to allow the audience to take it in.

Lastly, after you've shown a slide long enough for your audience members to have taken it all in, blank the screen in order to put focus back on you. You can even make some sort of "background" depending on the size of your projector screen. If the screen is large, and low to the ground, you can make it be light blue, for example, which accentuates your silhouette. You can make it the skyline of the city you are speaking in. The possibilities are endless, just make sure it doesn't distract from you. To "blank" a slide after you're done showing it, use software specific commands, or simply add an empty slide in between every content slide.

Presentation softwares can be wonderfully advantageous, or seriously harmful. It all depends on how they are used.

PREPARATION CONCLUSION

Success comes to those who prepare themselves to create it and receive it. Public speaking, like any other worthy endeavor, takes preparation. If you ever feel that you lack control of the situation when you're actually giving a public speech, take solace in this: in most cases, your ability to prepare for a speech is 100% under your control. Use this principle in every possible way. Make a clear plan as to how you will prepare, and then execute it. Do whatever it takes to get ready for the speech. The amount of control you can exert over yourself and your audience when you're actually giving your speech, as well as how calm you feel, are both directly proportional to how diligently you prepare.

As you gain experience, you'll need to prepare less and less. Experienced public speakers reach a point where they can briefly glance over a five-page summary of a topic and then give a ten-minute speech on it directly after. This is a very useful manifestation of public speaking mastery. However, until you are there, take the time to prepare. A long time ago, a calculus teacher of mine used to say "there's no such thing as luck, only preparation" before handing out our tests. It's really that simple. Prepare yourself, and you'll succeed as a public speaker.

Use the principles learned in this section to guide your preparation, and combine them with a diligent and motivated approach. Success will be yours.

..............................Chapter Summary................................

- Proper preparation produces perfect performance. The better you prepare, the higher your chances of success.
- Public speaking anxiety is one of the most common fears in the United States of America.
- One powerful method for reducing public speaking anxiety is the strategy of progressive exposure therapy.

- Speak to the smallest possible audience in the least fearsome circumstances imaginable. Then, progress forward in steps.
- You can practice public speaking the same way you practice any other skill: diligently on a daily basis.
- Garbage in, garbage out: The worse your preparation, the worse your performance.

KEY INSIGHT:

How Many Times Do You Need to Practice Your Speech to Memorize It? 10?

Aim To Do It 100 Times.

How Many Hours Do You Need to Review Your Research to Capture Your Main Points? One?

Aim To Do It For 10.

Your Preparation Is Entirely in Your Control. Preparation Can't Be Overdone, Only Underdone.

HOW TO MASTER PUBLIC SPEAKING (PART TWO)

1	Background
1.1	Many Public Speaking Books Fail to Teach the Subject Optimally
1.2	This Book Is Designed to Correct Their Mistakes
1.3	Public Speaking is Part of the Foundation of Success
1.4	Public Speaking Will Massively Improve Your Career and Life
1.5	You Will Be More Likely to Get Hired, Promoted, and Paid More
1.6	Starting the Public Speaking Journey Demands Beating Anxiety
1.7	Public Speaking Means to Speak to 10-1,000,000,000 People
1.8	Adopting a Mental Frame of Abundance Will Improve Your Results
1.9	Multiple Opportunities Arise for Practicing the Skill: Seize Them
1.10	Vastly Different Speeches Are Similar at Their Fundamental Level
1.11	The First Type of Speech is Speaking to Inform
1.12	The Second Type of Speech is Speaking to Persuade
1.13	The Third Type of Speech is Speaking to Inspire
1.14	The Fourth Type of Speech is Speaking to Entertain
1.15	All Speeches Share Some Common Fundamentals
1.16	Most Speeches Fulfill More Than One of the Four Purposes
1.17	A Speaker Uses His Words, Body, and Voice to Convey His Message
2	Preparation
2.1	The First Determinant of Speaking Success is Confidence
2.2	Public Speaking Anxiety is Normal, Natural, and Beatable
2.3	There Are Multiple Powerful Strategies For Defeating the Anxiety

2.4	Apply Pre-Speech Relaxation Techniques to Ease the Nerves
2.5	Impromptu and Extemporaneous Speeches Call for Different Styles
2.6	Speeches Prepared Ahead of Time Offer You Time to Practice
2.7	Apply Memorization Tricks and Practice Techniques
2.8	Practice the Skill of Public Speaking Generally, Not Just For a Speech
2.9	Remember the Common Visual-Aid Mistakes
2.10	Choose Your Attire Strategically, As It Communicates Too
2.11	Apply the Principles of Effectively Using Presentation Tools
3	Content
4	Use of Voice
5	Use of Body
6	Aspects of Delivery

KEY INSIGHT:

Put In the Preparation Work Your Future Self Will Thank You For While Reflecting On a Successful Presentation.

Claim These Free Resources that Will Help You Unleash the Power of Your Words and Speak with Confidence. Visit www.speakforsuccesshub.com/toolkit for Access.

18 Free PDF Resources

12 Iron Rules for Captivating Story, 21 Speeches that Changed the World, 341-Point Influence Checklist, 143 Persuasive Cognitive Biases, 17 Ways to Think On Your Feet, 18 Lies About Speaking Well, 137 Deadly Logical Fallacies, 12 Iron Rules For Captivating Slides, 371 Words that Persuade, 63 Truths of Speaking Well, 27 Laws of Empathy, 21 Secrets of Legendary Speeches, 19 Scripts that Persuade, 12 Iron Rules For Captivating Speech, 33 Laws of Charisma, 11 Influence Formulas, 219-Point Speech-Writing Checklist, 21 Eloquence Formulas

Claim These Free Resources that Will Help You Unleash the Power of Your Words and Speak with Confidence. Visit www.speakforsuccesshub.com/toolkit for Access.

30 Free Video Lessons

We'll send you one free video lesson every day for 30 days, written and recorded by Peter D. Andrei. Days 1-10 cover authenticity, the prerequisite to confidence and persuasive power. Days 11-20 cover building self-belief and defeating communication anxiety. Days 21-30 cover how to speak with impact and influence, ensuring your words change minds instead of falling flat. Authenticity, self-belief, and impact – this course helps you master three components of confidence, turning even the most high-stakes presentations from obstacles into opportunities.

Claim These Free Resources that Will Help You Unleash the Power of Your Words and Speak with Confidence. Visit **www.speakforsuccesshub.com/toolkit** for Access.

2 Free Workbooks

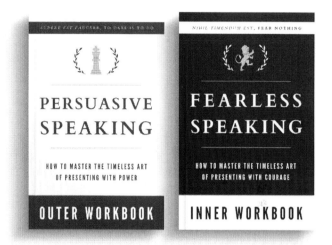

We'll send you two free workbooks, including long-lost excerpts by Dale Carnegie, the mega-bestselling author of *How to Win Friends and Influence People* (5,000,000 copies sold). *Fearless Speaking* guides you in the proven principles of mastering your inner game as a speaker. *Persuasive Speaking* guides you in the time-tested tactics of mastering your outer game by maximizing the power of your words. All of these resources complement the Speak for Success collection.

SPEAK FOR SUCCESS COLLECTION BOOK

PUBLIC SPEAKING MASTERY CHAPTER

IV

CONTENT:

What to Say to Impact, Influence, and Inspire

CRAFTING A MASTERPIECE

A "PAPER TIGER" IS A PHRASE COINED TO DESCRIBE something that is superficially significant, but folds up when a true challenge arises. A speech can be a "paper tiger." No matter how much you practice delivering your speech, use engaging body movements, and achieve masterful command of your voice, if the content at the core of it is lacking, it will fold up upon scrutiny. It's especially important when moving into the Use of Body and Use of Voice sections that you remember this: the content of your speech is just as important as how well it is delivered. Without excellent content, excellent delivery alone will not make an excellent speech. Likewise, without excellent delivery, excellent content alone won't make an excellent speech either. In this section, you will learn many techniques that will help you make the most of your words.

SPEECH STRUCTURE

No matter how beautiful a house might be, if it lacks in structure what it has in beauty, it will collapse. Similarly, no matter how beautifully a speech is worded and delivered, if it lacks structure and content, the beauty of it will be wasted.

Every time you speak publicly, especially when informing or persuading an audience, try to center your speech around three main points that support one message. Always keep in mind that if you can't write your message in a sentence, you can't say it in an hour. If your thesis is that climate change is harmful, choose the three strongest supporting arguments and drive them home. Do not try to be subtle or clever; be deliberate and obvious.

Do not come up with 17 different arguments for why you're right. You usually do not have enough time to deliver more than three supporting arguments in a convincing and thorough way. You can't properly drive home 17 different supporting arguments in a reasonable timeframe. Additionally, if you use 17 obscure and non-essential arguments, it dilutes and takes attention away from your most convincing arguments.

If you present more arguments, one of them is more likely to be faulty than if you only presented your most convincing three. The skeptical members of your audience will disregard your strong arguments and focus on the weak ones. Stick to a smaller, more reasonable number when trying to decide how many supporting pieces of evidence you should use to back up your message.

Your speech should follow a linear train of thought. Avoid tangents. Be straightforward and don't over complexify your point by saying unnecessary things. Your audience will (usually) only remember three things from your speech a year later. This is an unfortunate truth that applies to all speeches by all speakers.

This is a simple, common, and straightforward structure for a fifteen-minute speech: personal introduction (1 minute), hook (1 minute), speech introduction (2 minutes), subpoint A (3 minutes), subpoint B (3 minutes), subpoint C (3 minutes), closing (2 minutes) wrap it all up, call to action (1 minute).

This is only an example, not a rule. Ultimately, you should structure your speech based on what you feel will be most tailored to the subject matter, the audience, and your own personal preferences as a speaker. Some speeches have no structure at all, and in some cases, the type of spontaneity that occurs in these situations can actually make the speech better. Other speeches are less structured and seem to follow a winding train of thought.

Lastly, your speech should have an underlying theme that acts as a common thread woven throughout it. Choose your theme wisely. It should really strike through to the very core of the issue at hand. For example, our climatologist could build a speech around the theme of short-term comfort versus long term prosperity, and how we sacrifice one for the other when neglecting to solve climate change. We'll discuss theme in greater detail later.

THE PAST, PRESENT, MEANS STRUCTURE VISUALIZED

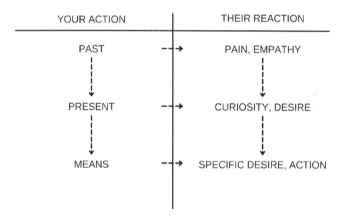

FIGURE 29: The past, present, means structure arouses immense curiosity, instigating the pressing, urgent question of "how did you make the change?"

KEY INSIGHT:

"The Past Was Difficult. Here's Why. The Now Is Amazing. Here's Why. I Changed Things. Here's How."

THE PATH-CONTRAST STRUCTURE VISUALIZED

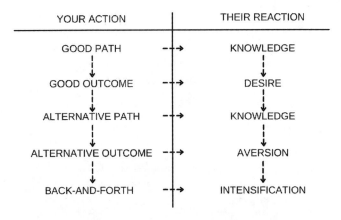

FIGURE 28: The path-contrast structure uses both contrast persuasion and aspirational persuasion. It persuades people to move both away from an alternative to your position and toward your position.

THE PROBLEM-SOLUTION FORMULA VISUALIZED

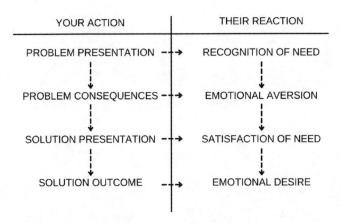

FIGURE 30: The ubiquitous problem-solution structure is foundational. Almost all structures incorporate problems and solution to some extent.

THE PROBLEM, AGITATE, SOLUTION, AGITATE STRUCTURE

STRUCTURE	"PASA" Structure			
BEHAVIORAL DUALITY	Escape		Approach	
SEMANTIC DUALITY	Problem		Solution	
EMOTIONAL DUALITY	Pain		Pleasure	
TEMPORAL DUALITY	Now		Later	
EXISTENTIAL DUALITY	Here		There	
DESIRE DUALITY	Aversion		Desire	
MODAL DUALITY	Chaos		Order	
STATE DUALITY	Actual		Potential	
KAIROS DUALITY	Conflict		Resolution	
THE SEQUENCE	**Problem**	**Agitate**	**Solution**	**Agitate**

THE SHORT-FORM THREE-POINT PUNCH VISUALIZED

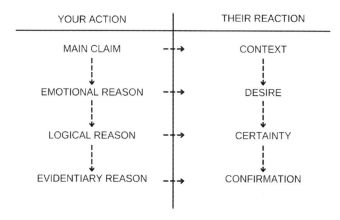

FIGURE 31: This structure is simple and straightforward, and it appeals to the three essential elements of persuasive communication.

KEY INSIGHT:

Emotion, Logic, and Evidence Are Not Disparate Domains. Logic and Evidence Can Impact Us Emotionally.

THE LONG-FORM THREE-POINT PUNCH VISUALIZED

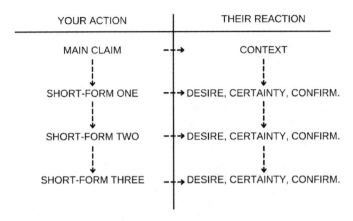

FIGURE 32: This structure extends the short-form three-point punch, achieving more desire, certainty, and confirmation.

THE GAIN, LOGIC, FEAR TRIFECTA VISUALIZED

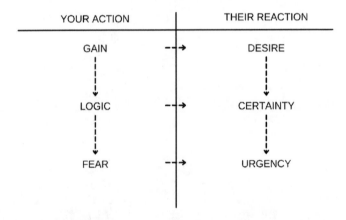

FIGURE 33: This structure is particularly effective at motivating enthusiastic action because it doesn't only answer the question "why should I do this?" but the more important question "why should I do this now?"

OPENINGS

First impressions form very, very quickly. In a matter of seconds. It's easy to form a first impression, and hard to overcome it later on. Just like there are ways to make a strong first impression when you're speaking to a single person: strong handshake, eye contact, clear speaking, there are ways to make and maintain a good first impression when you are giving a public speech.

WHY SOME INSTANTLY LOSE WHILE OTHERS INSTANTLY WIN

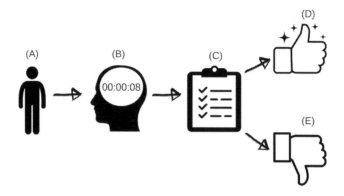

FIGURE 34: When a new speaker (A) appears to the audience, in about eight seconds (B) they run through a mental checklist (C) to decide if they approve (D) or disapprove (E); trust or distrust; like or dislike.

THE HALO EFFECT VISUALIZED

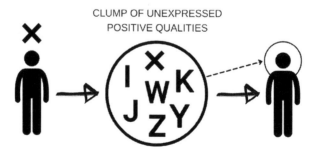

FIGURE 35: When people perceive positive quality "X" in you, the halo effect causes them to also judge you as possessing a clump of unexpressed positive qualities.

VISUALIZING THE SNAP CATEGORIZATION PRINCIPLE

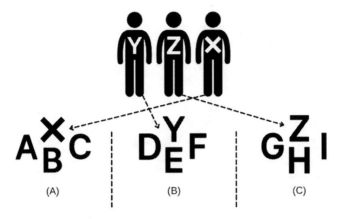

FIGURE 36: The audience perceives three people. The first person portrays quality Y. The audience has a mental category that includes items with the quality Y (B). Items in this category also have qualities D, E, and F. The audience lumps the first person into this category, transmuting the qualities D, E, and F to them. The second portrays quality Z, and he gets lumped into a category that transmutes the qualities G, H, and I to him (C) – qualities he never portrayed. Person X portrays quality X. You know the story: Now, he is not only a person who portrayed X, but a member of a mental category that includes the un-portrayed qualities A, B, and C (A), which the audience now transmutes onto him. This is a form of influence by mere association.

To make giving off a strong first impression easier, always make a deliberate effort to understand your venue. Will you have a microphone? A stage? What size is the expected audience? Also, you should show up early so that you can set up your PowerPoint and deal with any technical issues before the audience arrives. It's not terrible if you have technical difficulties in front of them, but might throw *you* off. The audience will usually be sympathetic, but it might ruin *your* flow. It's always better to fix any potential problems by showing up early.

Openings fall under the same distinctions as speeches: conversational or formal; to inform, inspire, persuade, or entertain; prepared in time, or impromptu.

Conversational, impromptu openings can be a back and forth with your audience members: "where are you guys from?", "that's a very nice watch," "I'm not enjoying this rain," etc. Formal openings prepared in time are usually more orchestrated: "How many people know when climate change will be in full effect?"

You can have a speech that is prepared in time, but an impromptu opening. You can also have a speech that is impromptu, but an opening prepared in time. Your opening should, after opening pleasantries, be a window and gateway into the rest of your speech.

Spend extra time practicing your opening. First impressions are crucial and form quickly.

TRANSITIONS

When making a speech, you give contextual and introductory information as well as core information. This means that you aren't just going through the information blindly, but that you are actually giving information about the information. You are introducing it and providing context. This is accomplished through transitions, which are a necessary part of any speech. They tell your audience something about what you are going to say before you say it. In doing so, they prime your audience's minds to receive whatever it is that you're going to say next.

HOW TO SPEAK WITH PRISTINE ELOQUENCE

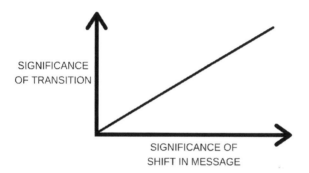

FIGURE 37: As the significance of the shift in your message rises, so too should the significance of your transition. This is the principle of the transition map.

Transitions smooth out the information transferring process: a speech without them sounds very choppy and staccato.

Email Peter D. Andrei, the author of the Speak for Success collection and the President of Speak Truth Well LLC directly.

pandreibusiness@gmail.com

TRANSITIONS SERVE AN INVALUABLE FUNCTION

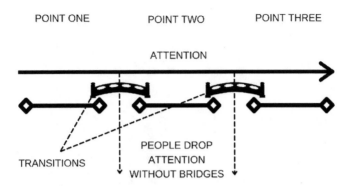

FIGURE 38: Moving from point one to two to three and bridging the points with transitions carries attention across. The vertical dotted arrows reveal the path of attention without the transitions: slipping away from your points through the cracks between points – cracks that the transitions fill. Build bridges to close the gaps between points, so attention doesn't leak out through the. This is the essence of transitioning. The greater the gap, the bigger the bridge. We will revisit this with the "transition map" principle revealed at the end of this section.

ANSWER THIS CRITICAL QUESTION TO CAPTURE ATTENTION

FIGURE 39: What links what I just said to what I am about to say? What bridges what I just said to what I am about to say? Answer this question to find your transition.

There are many kinds of transitions, firstly those of difference. These are used to indicate that you're moving into an idea that is different from the one you just presented, and they prime your audience accordingly. They sound like this: "however," "on the contrary," "conversely..." There are also transitions of similarity, which sound like this: "similarly," "just like this," "a similar trend appears if we examine..." There are also transitions to dive deeper into an idea: "if we look even more closely," "furthermore," "additionally..." Listing several steps in a process is also a useful transition: "first," "second," "third..." There are transitions for going back to something mentioned previously: "as I said," "if you recall my earlier point," "if you think back to when I said..." as well as transitions for concluding your speech: "now, to wrap up," "let me close by saying," "in conclusion..." Similarly, there are transitions for beginning your speech after you finish your introduction: "so, to start," "let's begin," "time to get into it..." Cause and effect transitions sound like: "consequently," "therefore," and "because of this..." Transitions to examples are: "for example," "as is shown by," or "this is made evident by..." Transitions to quotations sound like: "as ___ said in 2013," "in 2013, the university of ___ found that," and "to quote ___." Transitions to summaries sound like: "now, to summarize the big ideas," "here are the main takeaways," "to give you the big picture."

When you make a statement about something, and then say "on the contrary," it signals to your audience that they should be prepared to pay attention to the differences between what you are going to say and what you previously said. This is why transitions are so useful. They tell your audience where you are going to go next, and how it relates to what you have previously said. They put every statement you make in context.

Try to make your transitions smooth, natural, and simple. Never overlook transitions: without them, your audience will end up feeling lost.

Tell your audience where you are taking them next with transitions, the guiding signposts along the road.

HOOK

Just as a fisherman casting in the surf can't catch a fish without a metal hook, you can't catch an audience's attention without a verbal one. Your verbal hook is a sentence at the beginning of your speech meant to engage the audience.

KEY INSIGHT:

What Would Someone Have to Hear in the First 15 Seconds to Not Be Able to Resist Listening to The Next 15 Minutes?

REVEALING THE INFORMATION-FORAGING DYNAMIC

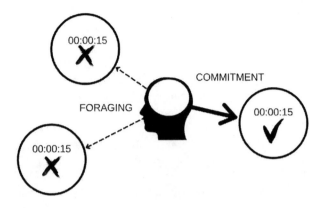

FIGURE 40: This visualizes the information foraging dynamic. They will test one patch of information for 15 seconds to determine its "information scent." Based on this, they will commit or reject it. Then, they will move on to patch after patch, until they find one that passes the 15-second information scent test. Then, they will commit.

IT ONLY GETS HARDER FROM THE START

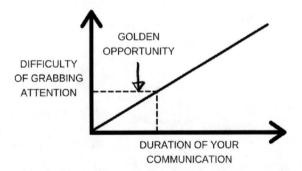

FIGURE 41: It only gets more difficult to grab attention as the speech progresses. As the duration of your communication extends, the difficulty of grabbing attention rises. The start of your speech acts as a moment of golden opportunity, when it is easiest to grab attention.

REVEALING THE GOLDEN OPPORTUNITY AND DEAD ZONE

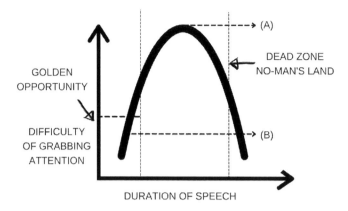

FIGURE 42: The previous figure left out some nuance. It is more accurate to say that the difficulty of grabbing attention acts as a bell curve. At the start, it is the easiest to grab attention. Likewise, at the end, it is roughly as easy as it was at the start. In the middle, the difficulty tends rises. Take advantage of the golden opportunity at the beginning. Make sure you have attained attention by the time you get into the dead zone. Grabbing attention in the middle is both significantly harder and less valuable, as you only keep it for half of the speech (A). If you grab it at the golden opportunity – which is easier – and if you don't lose it, you keep it throughout the entire speech (B). At the start, they are fresh slates. Toward the end, they perceive the conclusion of the speech and tune in again.

REVEALING THEIR TOLERANCE FOR COMPLEX INFORMATION

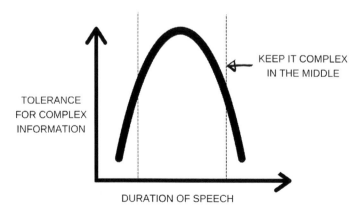

FIGURE 43: The audience has the lowest tolerance for complexity at the beginning and at the end. Keep it simple at the beginning at

the end. Focus on the dynamics of attention. Present complexity in the middle.

KEY INSIGHT:

Domain One: Complex, Evidence-Driven Talk of Policies, Plans, and Hard Mental Models.

Domain Two: Simple Talk of Eternal Moral Truths. Master Both, Forget Neither.

Hooks are most often used in speeches designed to persuade or to inspire, and often take the form of a rhetorical question or a particularly powerful statistic. An effective way to augment your hook is to follow it with a two to six second pause. Dramatic pauses and moments of silence are attention grabbers on their own, but more so when combined with a hook.

A hook can be anything you want it to be. It just has to get people's attention and thus, the more eccentric and unusual, the better. There are several strategies that will help you write an effective hook.

First and foremost, the hook must be of real impact and echo the sentiment of your speech, such as "why is it that climate change is caused the most by the nations which will be affected the least?" for our climatologist. More jarring, perhaps, would be "there are little boys and girls in developing nations who will be even hungrier than they are now because the world leaders who pledged to help them neglected climate change as a credible threat despite all evidence pointing to the contrary." It depends on the approach and personal style of the climatologist, of course. But no matter what a speaker's personal style is, their hook must be impactful.

Secondly, the hook must be a phrase that points out the relevance of the topic to everyone in the audience, such as "every single person in this room - yes, every single one - will experience some hardships due to global warming." Cast as wide a net as possible to catch the attention of your entire audience. An effective way to make your hook relevant to everyone is to paint a picture. Use words like "imagine," or "what if" to transition into a narrative that hooks your audience.

Thirdly, the hook should establish urgency or immediacy, which can be accomplished by stating that "the problem grows worse and worse as I speak. To stop climate change, we need to start ten years ago." It's not enough to make people think they should care about your subject. You have to show them that they need to care *now*.

By combining these three aspects of hook writing, the audience's attention will be yours from the very start of your speech.

CALL TO ACTION

No matter how brilliant a speech made to persuade or inspire is, it needs a call to action to be truly useful. A call to action is something towards the end of your speech designed to rouse your audience to aid your cause in a specific way. An example of a powerful call to action is "if you were in any way moved by what I've had to say today, and if you want to help me in my effort to stop climate change, please start carpooling in order to reduce carbon emissions."

A call to action needs to be direct to be effective. It must have a tangible impact. After persuading the audience to agree with your purpose, give them exact steps on how to help and contribute to the effort. The implication that they would actually be helping themselves by helping you is very powerful as well. Implying that through helping you, they would be creating a better future for themselves and their families is a powerful motivator.

Keep your call to action reasonable. If a climatologist told their audience to trade their cars in for electric cars, the vast majority of people wouldn't. Would you trade in your care for an electric car because a speaker told you to? No, probably not. If a climatologist made the call to action more reasonable, like recycling and carpooling, it's more likely that the audience would actually do it. The effectiveness of a call to action is, in many cases, determined by how well you persuaded, inspired, and moved your audience leading up to it.

KEY INSIGHT:

Persuasion Rarely Produces Wholesale Converts. It Often Works Subtly, Slowly, Converting Through Little, Gentle Nudges Over Time.

THE FRAMEWORK OF POWERFUL SPEAKING

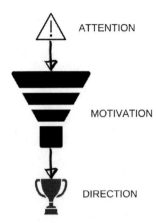

ATTENTION

MOTIVATION

DIRECTION

FIGURE 44: Powerful speaking is capturing attention, putting it into a persuasive funnel that achieves motivation, and channeling this motivation in a specific direction.

Never forget a call to action. It is important because it answers the following question for your audience: "Okay, I agree with you, and I want to help. How can I help? What do you want me to do?" If you neglect to answer that question, then your speech may be engaging, beautiful, and masterful, but little real-world change will come of it.

RHETORICAL STRATEGIES

Pathos, ethos, and logos. These are the big three rhetorical strategies that persuade an audience. Pathos is playing upon the emotions of your listeners. Ethos is referencing authorities on the topic of your speech to lend yourself authority. Logos is the use of hard logic to prove your point. While one of these may be better suited to a topic than the others, an argument is most persuasive when it employs all three.

Pathos: Pathos is the art of playing upon an audience's emotions. This is seen in PETA commercials, which induce sympathy for abused animals in viewers. But pathos goes beyond that. Emotion is a broad spectrum of feelings and sentiments. Anger, happiness, sadness, love, desire, and jealousy are all emotions that you can tap into with pathos. Luckily for you, emotion is a very powerful motivator: the majority of decisions are made on emotional impulses. You can tap into an audience's happiness just as readily as you can tap into an audience's anger. Determine which emotion will make people follow your call to action, and then focus on inducing it in the audience.

Many revolutionaries throughout history played on the anger of their audience, which was usually made up of poor and angry people living through difficult times, and used that anger to direct the audience towards the goal of toppling old regimes in favor of new ones that promised change. A wedding ring salesman taps into an audience's emotion of the love they feel for their soon to be fiances to induce them into spending an extra two to three thousand dollars on a piece of metal with a rock. A car manufacturer builds beautiful automobiles to create a desire in those who see them drive by. Emotion is powerful. Pathos will help you harness emotion, and use it to your advantage.

Ethos: Ethos is using expert testimony to support your idea. It most often takes the form of quoting statements made by experts in a field. A pharmaceutical salesman might say something along the lines of "two in every three doctors agree on the effectiveness of this medicine," or according to Dr. Martin, this medicine is a surefire and safe way to get rid of a headache." Both of these statements have the same effect: they bring in an outside source to convince the audience that a claim made by the speaker is valid. Ethos can also take the form of personal ethos. In this case, a speaker uses conviction and has the necessary credentials that outside testimony becomes unnecessary because their word stands on its own. For example, were Dr. Martin himself giving a speech on that medicine, his word would carry enough ethos that he wouldn't have to quote another doctor.

Logos: Logos is the use of pure logic that, combined with ethos and pathos, will form a rhetorically powerful speech. Logos is making the audience understand why your ideas are true by showing them the logical steps connecting your evidence to your claim. While humans do indeed make decisions primarily based on emotion, they also prefer rationalizing those decisions, and use of logos in a speech provides a way to do so. Ethos is the pure facts, while Logos is the set of logical connections, or warrants, that connect the facts to the conclusion.

ARISTOTLE'S PERSUASIVE FRAMEWORK

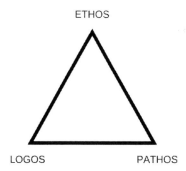

FIGURE 45: Thousands of years ago, Aristotle conveyed a timeless persuasive framework. He argued that all effective persuasion and impactful rhetoric was the result of successfully appealing to pathos (emotion), logos (logic), and ethos (evidence). Ethos has also been understood as a characteristic of the speaker:

his credibility, character, and the extent to which he has the audience's interests at heart. This definition is valuable as well.

BASICS OF PERSUASION

There are six basics of persuasion. While this is not necessarily a direct aspect of public speaking, injecting these into your speech, leading up to it, or even after it when interacting with audience members, will make you very persuasive. These are all scientifically backed and have been proven to work time and time again. Know them, and use them. You'll see how effective they are for yourself.

Reciprocity: People tend to feel the need to repay any kind behavior they receive. If a friend buys you lunch, there's an obligation to buy them lunch in the future to return the favor. If you give another speaker a standing ovation, they are likely to reciprocate this behavior back to you later on. If you want to persuade the audience to buy a product from you, giving them a discount on it will make them more likely to buy it because you are essentially giving up money you would have earned for them to give up money in return.

Interestingly enough, how you give the discount is just as important as the discount itself. If you say "there's a 10% discount on my product," that may only attract a few buyers from the audience. However, if you say "now I normally only offer a 5% discount on my product at the end of these speeches, but because you were such a great audience, I'll give a 10% discount. Make sure you don't tell anyone!", the results will be much more profitable. You are giving the same discount in both cases, but in one situation you are doing it in a much more personal way. Additionally, by including the "don't tell anyone!" you are entering into a lighthearted, friendly conspiracy with the audience.

To appear more genuine, you can even announce the 5% discount, leave the microphone, but then turn back and say "actually, I think such a great audience deserves a 10% discount." By exchanging this kindness with the audience, they are much more likely to buy the product because they will be supporting someone they like. People will never admit the reason they bought it is because they like you; they will form a logical rationalization to use as an explanation of their purchase. If you recall, most decisions are made on emotion, not logic, and yet most decisions are consciously rationalized by logic after they are made on an emotional impulse.

Scarcity: People want things that other people don't have. That is why people buy expensive jewels. They serve no real function, but are desirable because of their rarity. An example of scarcity in action is when a consumer product in the market decreases in availability, and the prices go up. The product itself is the same, but because there is less of it available on the market, people are willing to pay more for it.

The underlying subconscious assumption behind this behavioral phenomenon is that a rare resource will run out faster, and that more people are competing for the same resource.

You can use the principle of persuasive scarcity in a speech by portraying your idea or product as one your audience should adopt soon, because if they do not, they will soon regret losing the opportunity as it will be sold out or too late. Loss aversion is a very powerful motivator: people typically don't play to win, just not to lose. Losing out on the opportunity to buy or do something, even if one hasn't already, triggers loss aversion as well.

Many online stores use scarcity to spur purchases, which is a highly effective strategy. They do so by putting a timed discount, or a decreasing stock number. Just as scarcity can work on an online store, it can work in your speech. Don't create fake scarcity: if fake scarcity is detected by your audience, which it likely will be, then they will feel manipulated or lied to. If there is even a small amount of scarcity, then expose it. Don't make it up, just express it if it already exists.

Authority: Ethos and the persuasive principle of authority are both very similar. They are using what people of authority on a subject have said about it to help validate your point. The principle of personal authority is when you try to generate the appearance of being an authority on a subject, and thereby ethos is automatically generated whenever you say something. You can create this appearance by explaining complex aspects of an idea, problem, or product to your audience. Additionally, you can briefly mention the amount of research that supports what you are saying, or briefly allude to your credentials. Anything that makes you appear as an expert on a subject generates personal ethos. Personal ethos is a very powerful tool for persuading an audience. Harnessing this principle of persuasion can go a long way; you are making use of the reason why patients defer to the judgements of doctors, and athletes listen to their coaches.

An interesting example of the principle of authority is the Milgram experiment, which showed that people would willingly shock what they believed to be a real person in another room at higher and higher voltages. Even lethal voltages. They did so because an authority figure told them to. Nobody was actually shocked; the test participant was just made to believe that someone was being shocked. Why did they do this? Why did they willingly shock another human being, despite having clear reservations about it? Because an authority figure told them to.

Determining what people are willing to do just because an authority figure told them to was the purpose of the famous Milgram experiment, and it was found that authority is an incredibly powerful quality. Just make sure you use it for good.

Consistency: People want to be consistent with themselves. The principle of persuasive consistency suggests that it is easier to get someone to agree to something substantial if you've gotten them to agree to something smaller in the past.

If you approach someone and ask them directly for a donation to a nonprofit, they will likely say no, but if you approach someone and first ask them to verbally endorse a nonprofit, and then ask for a donation later on, they are much more likely to say yes to making the donation if they previously agreed to a verbal endorsement.

People like to be consistent with themselves. If you've gotten someone to agree to something small, they are more likely to agree to something bigger later on. If you try to get someone to agree to something big immediately, they are far more likely to turn you down than if you ease them into it by first getting them to make smaller commitments. Doing so is essentially forming a "ladder" in which each rung of the ladder represents a slightly larger commitment than the last. Whether the commitment is to purchase something or to agree with someone, the principle of consistency applies. If your audience agrees first to a small claim you make, and then to a slightly more controversial claim, and then to your most contentious point, you are more likely to get them to agree to your most contentious point than if you started with it.

You can flip the principle of consistency around, and combine it with the principle of reciprocity. To do this, you can ask someone for something which they will obviously deny. After they've denied it, ask them for something comparatively small (which is the only thing you truly wanted from them all along) and they will be more likely to agree to it because they feel bad for having turned you down the first time. An example of this: *You:* "Hey, can you help me write this speech?" *Other person:* "Sorry, I can't commit to that at this time." *You:* (appear crestfallen to play on their emotions) "I'm sorry to hear that. Could you help me practice it once I finish?" (which is the only thing you actually wanted all along).

Likability: Aesop had a fable in which the wind and the sun competed to get a traveler's coat off. The wind took its turn first, and battered the traveler with violent gust after violent gust to blow off his coat. The traveler only pulled his coat tighter. When it was the sun's turn, it shined its gentle rays of warmth on the traveler. This time, the traveler took the coat off on his own. Here's the fable:

The North Wind and the Sun had a quarrel about which of them was the stronger. While they were disputing with much heat and bluster, a Traveler passed along the road wrapped in a cloak.

"Let us agree," said the Sun, "that he is the stronger who can strip that Traveler of his cloak."

"Very well," growled the North Wind, and at once sent a cold, howling blast against the Traveler.

With the first gust of wind the ends of the cloak whipped about the Traveler's body. But he immediately wrapped it closely around him, and the harder the Wind blew, the tighter he held it to him. The North Wind tore angrily at the cloak, but all his efforts were in vain. Then the Sun began to shine. At first his beams were gentle, and in the pleasant warmth after the bitter cold of the North Wind, the Traveler unfastened his cloak and let it hang loosely from his shoulders. The Sun's rays grew warmer and warmer. The man took off his cap and mopped his brow. At last he became so heated that he pulled off his cloak, and, to escape the blazing sunshine, threw himself down in the welcome shade of a tree by the roadside.

There is a lot to learn from this fable. In some cases, it is better to be gentle when persuading. Some people grow defensive when faced with aggressive persuasion tactics, and instead of getting anything out of them, they tighten their metaphorical coats. The sun gently shined its warmth on the traveler, and the traveler took off the coat on his own.

In many cases, subtle and gentle persuasion beats obvious persuasion. The coat represents an inherent aversion to be persuaded that many carry like a shield. Indeed, persuasion resistance is a well-documented psychological phenomenon. Many assume that if you try to persuade them of something, it must be beneficial for you at their expense. Do not try to rip the shield from people for that will surely fail. On the other hand, get them to willingly give up their shield just as the traveler took off his coat.

The principle of likeability embodies the moral of Aesop's fable. People prefer to help those who they like. People tend to like those who are similar to them, have complimented them, or who are working towards similar goals as them. Employ these to get people to like you before trying to persuade them to your cause.

It is well known that in business, if you want to convince someone to make a big purchase or commitment, you don't want to get right to business. Take them to a business dinner, ask about their day, exchange pleasantries, see how their family is doing, and ignore the business for the first half hour or so. During this time set aside the business and focus on establishing similarity, complimenting them, and looking for common goals. Only after establishing a bond of friendship with the prospective buyer is it time to bring up business.

At this point, because they view you as a friend, they will subconsciously not want to turn you down in fear that they might lose the connection. Humans are inherently social creatures, and we are genetically predisposed to value a large social network. Many businessmen say that it is better to "get right into it," but it has been proven time and time again that the approach of fostering likeability for a few minutes and then getting into the business is much more effective and results in more profitable agreements for both parties.

Use the principle of likability often in your speech. It can often make the difference between people following your call to action or ignoring it. You can use the principle of likability in your speech by establishing common goals with your audience, expressing similarity, and complimenting them. Specifically how to do this will be answered in the Audience Interaction section.

A last word on the principle of likability and soft persuasion is this: you cannot force anyone to listen to your speech. They may be sitting there, but it is up to you to make them listen. Just because you have an audience, doesn't mean your audience is really listening. How do you make them listen? By making them *choose* to listen. They cannot be forced. This evokes the same truth as the fable of the wind and the sun. Be so valuable as a speaker, with such important ideas and engaging presence, that they almost have to choose to listen. Much of the rest of this book helps you achieve that.

Consensus: The herd mindset is an interesting phenomenon. A study conducted by researchers at Leeds University concluded that 10 confident people who pretended to know what they were doing in an unfamiliar situation were able to influence 190 people to follow them. The principle of consensus plays off of the tendency people have to follow the crowd, or a few particularly confident people from the crowd. This principle applies especially in times of uncertainty. You can use this principle to your advantage by asking a group of friends who you know will be attending your speech to give a standing ovation after you finish. Upon seeing five or six people stand, others will begin to follow their lead. This is simply how human beings are wired.

REVEALING THE SIX MOST SCIENCE-BACKED STRATEGIES

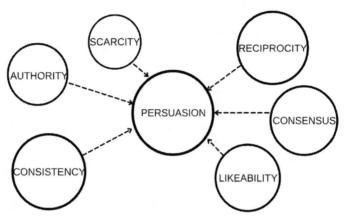

FIGURE 46: These are six of the most well-supported and extensively science-backed persuasive methods.

KEY INSIGHT:

Our Millenia-Old Cognitive Wiring Can Misfire.

These Misfires Can Make Us Believe the Wrong Things for the Wrong Reasons. They Can Also Make Us Believe the Right Things for the Wrong Reasons.

KAIROS

This is the dictionary entrance for Kairos: "Kairos (καιρός) is an Ancient Greek word meaning the right, critical, or opportune moment. The ancient Greeks had two words for time: chronos (χρόνος) and kairos. The former refers to chronological or sequential time, while the latter signifies a proper or opportune time for action. While chronos is quantitative, kairos has a qualitative, permanent nature. *Kairos* also means *weather* in Modern Greek. The plural, καιροί (*kairoi* (Ancient and Modern Greek)) means *the times*."

The concept of Kairos is, perhaps, much more fundamental than even ethos, pathos, and logos. It simply means biding your time. It means waiting to attempt persuading people until a time comes when persuasion is most likely to work.

In business, for example, if you have a radical new way of doing things that challenges the status quo of company operations, then Kairos is your friend. Unless you are sure of your ability to persuade the organization to adopt the change you want to see, then simply bide your time. Wait, and while you wait, keep developing your idea as well as a plan for implementing it. Keep it at the ready, but keep it concealed.

Eventually, there will be a time of crisis. Investors will get cold feet, manufacturing will fail, a public relations scandal will occur, etc. As Kairos suggests, the time of crisis will be the time to attempt to persuade the company into changing its operations. That is because during this time of crisis, people are especially persuadable and willing to try new things. The status quo is not working, and thus they will be much more malleable and open to your ideas.

Wait for the opportune time, and use your persuasion when it will be most effective. If you can combine ethos, pathos, logos, reciprocity, authority, scarcity, likeability, consensus, and consistency with kairos, then you maximize your persuasive power. Don't give a speech trying to persuade a company to change the way of doing things when the status quo is working and people are happy. Wait for the status quo to fail, and once it does, your persuasive power will be maximized. A huge part of using Kairos to your advantage is being in tune with the motions of collective opinion. Any group tends to experience opinion-convergence: over time, given no drastic changes, many common opinions will develop within the group. Be sensitive to these collective opinions, especially when they might be in flux. That will help you find the right time, and as you may have heard, timing is everything.

KEY INSIGHT:

Take Your Stand Before the Crisis, even if Nobody Believes You. When It Comes, They'll Remember. Then Take Your Stand Again.

NO PROBLEM? BIG PROBLEM

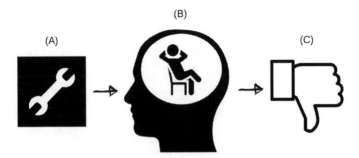

FIGURE 47: If you try to sell a solution (A) when the world is telling someone to relax (B), they will reject the solution (B). Why? Because they don't perceive a compelling problem that justifies the solution; that the solution solves.

AVOIDING THE MOST BASIC PERSUASIVE MISTAKE

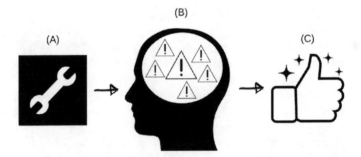

FIGURE 48: If you try to sell someone a solution (A) when the problem is looming large in their consciousness (B), they are much more likely to accept the solution (C). Crucially, you can impact the extent to which a problem shouts to be solved with your words.

THE CORE HUMAN DRIVES

Humans are motivated by a set of core desires. The vast majority of actions humans take are, upon closer inspection, manifestations of one or more of the core desires. A core desire was not filled, so a behavioral change or action was performed in order to satisfy it.

How do these core desires relate to public speaking? Each of the different types of public speeches can satisfy one or more of these drives, and within public speeches each of these drives can be used to achieve the purpose of the speech and increase persuasive power. This is truer for speeches designed to inspire, persuade, or inform than it is for those designed to entertain. The core human drives are as follow:

Getting: People have a natural drive to get "things." We have a natural tendency, which at one point likely conferred an evolutionary advantage, to collect material possessions as well as immaterial accolades. Here's an example of this desire being used in a speech: "Some of these changes we can make to our daily lives to help stop climate change also end up helping our wallets. They save the planet, but they also save us money. Think about how much gas money carpooling saves, in addition to reducing carbon emissions. Over time, it's enough for a fancy new watch, or even a vacation."

Bonding: People have a natural drive to bond with other people and form relationships both deep and shallow. Here's an example of this desire being used in a speech: "By committing to making small, convenient changes in your daily routines that will help spare our planet, you're entering a large but close community of people who understand what you're doing and why you're doing it. And when you carpool, you can form long lasting bonds with the people you drive places with after all that time spent together in the car."

Learning: People have a natural drive to learn as much information as possible to broaden their horizons and become better equipped to live their lives. Here's an example of this desire being used in a speech: "I promise that by the end of this presentation, you will know all about one of the biggest threats we face today as well as the solutions you can use to help stop it. Ultimately, this will make you a much more informed, self-reliant, and capable global citizen as humanity begins to work towards stopping climate change."

Defending: People have a natural drive to defend what is theirs, and even to defend what they wrongfully perceive as theirs. This doesn't necessarily apply only to physical possessions, but also immaterial possessions such as status, accolades, or pride. Here's an example of this desire being used in a speech: "By making climate friendly choices, you are not only saving the planet, but you are defending your beautiful home from climate-change caused natural disasters such as wildfires, hurricanes, and floods."

Feeling: People have a natural drive to feel a wide range of different emotions, even negative emotions if they are being felt in a compartmentalized way. Nobody wants to feel real sadness, yet many people will gladly feel simulated, compartmentalized sadness created by watching a sad movie. However, there's no compartmentalization necessary with positive emotions. Here's an example of this desire being used in a speech: "When I started being more climate-friendly in my daily life, I thought it was going to be very hard. It was made much easier by how good it made me feel to know that I was saving our planet."

Now, before I present the sixth and final core human desire, let me present one of the fundamental frameworks of modern psychology: Maslow's Hierarchy of Needs.

This framework is arranged as a pyramid with five segments. The first is physiological needs, the second is safety needs, the third is belongingness and love needs, the fourth is esteem needs, and the fifth and final is self-actualization needs.

One cannot go further up the triangle without first satisfying the base: one cannot progress to fulfilling the next need if they have not fulfilled the previous one.

Physiological needs are food, warmth, water, and anything needed to sustain human life. Safety needs are, well, the need for safety and security in one's life. Belongingness and love needs are those relating to human relationships: friendship, a romantic relationship, and a role in a social group. Esteem needs are those relating to one's status in society: wealth, trophies, and titles.

THE FIRST LEVEL OF MASLOW'S HIERARCHY

BASIC NEEDS

SAFETY NEEDS:
SECURITY, SAFETY

PHYSIOLOGICAL NEEDS:
FOOD, WATER, WARMTH, REST

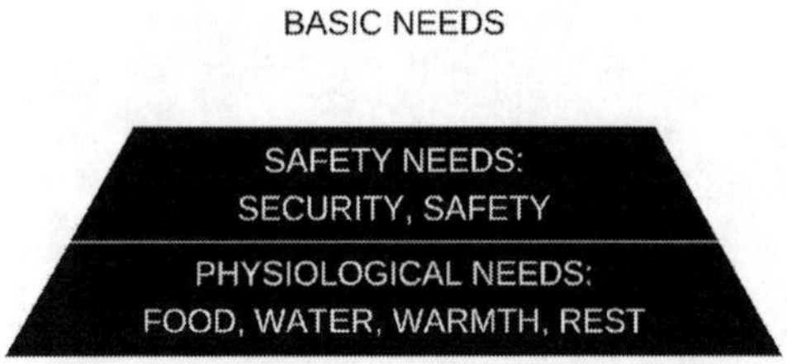

FIGURE 49: This is the first level of Maslow's Hierarchy.

KEY INSIGHT:

Most Corporate Audiences Are Not on The First Level of Maslow's Hierarchy of Needs.

THE SECOND LEVEL OF MASLOW'S HIERARCHY

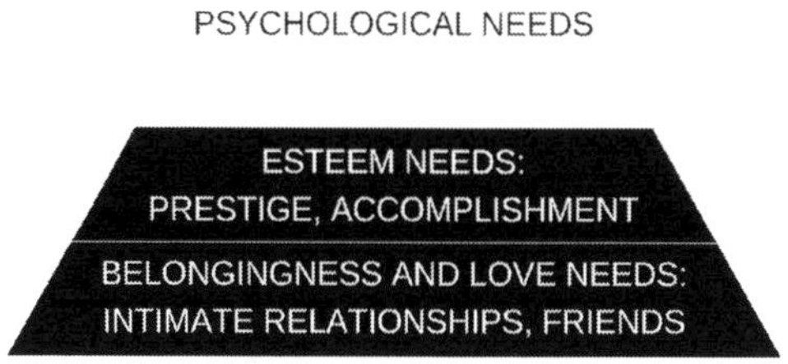

PSYCHOLOGICAL NEEDS

ESTEEM NEEDS:
PRESTIGE, ACCOMPLISHMENT
BELONGINGNESS AND LOVE NEEDS:
INTIMATE RELATIONSHIPS, FRIENDS

FIGURE 50: This is the second level of the hierarchy.

If we re-examine the core human drives, they typically relate to one of the core human needs. The drive to get relates to esteem needs, but also possibly to safety needs and physiological needs. The drive to bond relates to the need of belongingness and love. The drive to learn relates both to the esteem needs and the self-actualization need. The drive to defend can relate to the first four needs. Lastly, the drive to feel relates to the esteem needs and the safety needs.

The need for self-actualization is the need to live up to one's fullest potential: to figure out a purpose in life and make it happen. The first two needs are physical needs, the next two are psychological needs, and the final one is the "self-fulfillment" need. This need for self-fulfillment arises if and only if the previous four needs are satisfied. When it does arise, it creates the sixth and final core human drive:

Self-Actualization: Humans have a desire, upon satisfying all physiological and psychological needs, to actualize their fullest potential and seek their highest selves through self-improvement. Here's an example of this desire being used in a speech: "Now, all else aside, making an effort to become more climate friendly doesn't just help the planet: it helps you be your best self and live a more disciplined life."

Email Peter D. Andrei, the author of the Speak for Success collection and the President of Speak Truth Well LLC directly.

pandreibusiness@gmail.com

THE THIRD LEVEL OF MASLOW'S HIERARCHY

FIGURE 51: This is the entire hierarchy. People progress from the bottom to the top. In order to be motivated by a particular need, people must meet all the lower needs.

TARGET THE RIGHT LEVEL

FIGURE 52: Target the level your audience is on – not above or below. In most professional situations in most developed countries, that means targeting the self-actualization need (and in some cases, the esteem needs).

If you want to influence the decisions people make, motivate a certain action, or convince an audience of a point of view, it's only logical that you should understand how people make decisions, why they take certain actions, and what forces govern their opinion-making. Understanding these six core needs and desires can be very useful when crafting speech that will resonate with your audience. Attach an action you want your audience to take to one or more of the six core drives, and they will be impulsed to do it.

By invoking the needs and core drives of your audience members, you can strengthen the public speaking triad for any of the four kinds of speeches in a very clever, skillful way.

USE OF STATISTICS

If you have a point to make, do not try to be subtle or clever with it. Say it clearly and say it loudly. Be blatant and obvious. Statistics are a way to do this, and are regarded as part of the rhetorical strategy ethos. While statistics themselves are indeed ethos, they rely on logos to connect them to your main claim.

When using statistics, avoid non sequiturs, logical fallacies in which a piece of supporting evidence like a statistic fails to actually support your main argument. This often appears to be the case when it isn't, especially in cases when a piece of evidence supports a claim in an indirect way. This can be avoided by clearly explaining the logical links (also known as warrants) between your evidence and the point you are trying to prove. For some statistics, the logical path connecting to your main point is straightforward, while for others, it needs to be deliberately explained.

Once you use a statistic, follow up and explain its significance. If you are a climatologist advocating for underdeveloped nations, this is an example of what you could say: "It has been scientifically proven that by the year 2025, underdeveloped nations will experience a 30% reduction in GDP due to climate change, while developed nations like the United States will only experience a 15% reduction in GDP due to climate change." Do not stop here, elaborate on the significance: "This shows that the nations actually causing climate change are not going to be hit as hard as the un-industrialized nations which do not contribute to climate change and that are the most vulnerable."

Many speakers who are nervous about giving a speech often fall back on using statistics, but forget to clearly explain the significance of them. Always make sure that you clearly connect a statistic to your claim, otherwise its impact might be diluted.

KEY INSIGHT:

Statistics Are Simple. They Carry an Air of Authority. They Convey Credibility. Use Them.

NUMBERS VERSUS EMOTION: WHICH SHOULD YOU USE?

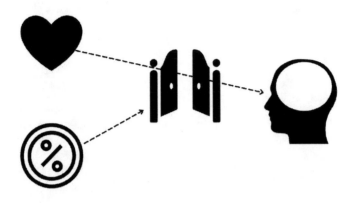

FIGURE 53: Numbers and logical evidence open the gate. Emotional influence goes through it. It is a two-pronged approach.

MONROE'S MOTIVATED SEQUENCE

Monroe's motivated sequence is named after the man who first described it, Alan H. Monroe, who developed it in the mid-1930s at Purdue University. Monroe's motivated sequence is a proven structure for persuasive speeches. It goes like this: attention, need, satisfaction, visualization, action.

In the attention step, your goal is to get your audience listening to you. This is the job of the hook. You can use a personal anecdote, a dramatic quote, a statistic, or anything that gets your audience's attention.

In the need step, your goal is to establish a clear problem, and a clear problem that is directly relevant to your audience. It shouldn't be some abstract, distant problem that affects other people. Make it clear to your audience that the problem directly relates to them and their needs. You have to clearly state the problem, describe the problem, describe the impacts of the problem, and then clearly connect the problem to your audience.

In the satisfaction step, your goal is to show your audience a clear solution to the problem outlined in the need step. This is the solution you want them to adopt. Only now is it time to actually express to your audience what you are trying to persuade them to do. Clearly describe what you are trying to get your audience to adopt. Then, connect that to the need by showing how it solves the problem. Prove how the solution solves the problem with evidence, such as statistics, past experiences, and logos.

In the visualization step, your goal is to help your audience visualize what will happen if they adopt your solution, or what will happen if they don't. You can also show them what will happen if they don't, followed by what will happen if they do, or vice versa. This is called the contrast method.

In the action step, your goal is to motivate your audience towards a specific action. What's the first thing they need to do? This is your call to action.

MONROE'S MOTIVATED SEQUENCE REVISITED

FIGURE 54: This is the proven, five-step process of Monroe's Motivated Sequence.

HOW TO GRAB ATTENTION

FIGURE 55: Reveal a shocking statistic, appeal to curiosity, tease little-known information, and create two-way communication.

HOW TO CREATE A NEED

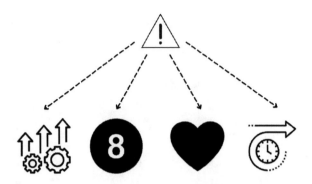

FIGURE 56: Appeal to the self-actualization impulse, the life-force eight desires, emotion, and present a future-based cause.

HOW TO OFFER SATISFACTION

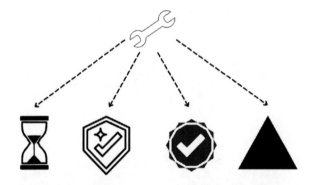

FIGURE 57: Postpone the pitch, apply safety-indicating words, present personal safety-indicators, and use ethos, pathos, and logos.

HOW TO INSPIRE VISUALIZATION

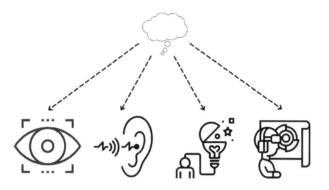

FIGURE 58: Use powerful visual adjectives, the VAKOG senses, the "imagine" phrase, and empower positive counterfactual simulations.

HOW TO GET ACTION

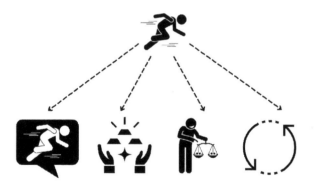

FIGURE 59: Use strong action verbs, offer a tangible takeaway, present a reasonable call to action, and graft your desired action on the audience's preexisting habit loops.

INFORMATIONAL MOTIVATED SEQUENCE

While Monroe's motivated sequence is designed for persuasive speeches, it can be adopted for informational speeches as well. In this case, the motivated sequence takes up significantly less time. For a persuasive speech, Monroe's motivated sequence is the entire speech. For an informational speech, however, the motivated sequence is shorter and is used to motivate the following action: listening to you.

Here's how a 15-minute persuasive speech could be structured with Monroe's motivated sequence: attention (3 minutes), need (3 minutes), satisfaction (3 minutes), visualization (3 minutes), action (3 minutes).

Here's how an informational speech of roughly the same length can be structured with the informational motivated sequence: attention (1-minute maximum), need (1-minute maximum), satisfaction (1-minute maximum), visualization (1-minute maximum), information (10 minutes minimum), action (1-minute maximum, if applicable).

During the attention step of the informational motivated sequence, once again, you should get your audience's attention. In this case, do so in a way that gradually moves them into the information.

In the need step, you should clearly show your audience an area of knowledge that they don't know much about. Tell them why they should listen, and show them what needs your information fulfills. Clearly establish why your information is worth their time. Connect it to their wants and desires. Connect it to their lives. Think of a problem that arises out of not knowing the information you are about to give them, and describe it. Describe the impacts of not knowing what you are about to say.

In the satisfaction step, clearly explain why the information you are going to give them solves the problem or fulfills a need that they have. Present your information as the solution to one of their most difficult, frustrating problems.

In the visualization step, show your audience what life will be like once they understand your information. Perhaps you are speaking to businesspeople who don't understand a crucial business process. Show them how wonderful it will feel to know that business process inside and out.

The information step is, of course, the most crucial. In a persuasive speech, you are trying to convince your audience to take up a certain solution, perform an action, or purchase something. Thus, the entirety of the speech should suit that purpose. With the informational motivated sequence, however, your main purpose is still to inform. The informational motivated sequence is essentially condensing Monroe's motivated sequence and putting it in front of an informational speech. The main focus is still informing. Note that the in the informational motivated sequence, the timeframe is ten minutes minimum for the information, and a maximum of four minutes for the first four steps of the motivated sequence. On the contrary, in Monroe's motivated sequence for persuasive speeches, each step of the sequence gets three minutes.

Lastly, in the action step, tell your audience what to do with your information. Once again, with the example of explaining a crucial business process to unknowing businesspeople, tell them the first point in their organizations where they can begin applying your information. Or if you prefer, tell them how to continue learning more about the subject. Show them how to use what you just told them.

THE INFORMATIONAL MOTIVATED SEQUENCE VISUALIZED

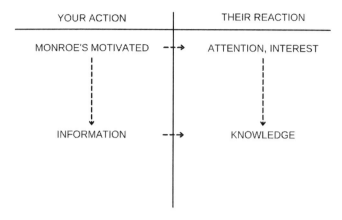

FIGURE 60: Squish Monroe's Motivated Sequence to get attention and build interest before an informational speech – use it as an opener – and then continue with the speech to convey the knowledge you wish to impart.

KEY INSIGHT:

There Should Never Be a Purely Informative Speech. Even Informative Speeches Should Sell.

They Should Sell the Information. Why Is It Important? Helpful? Necessary? Why Shouldn't People Miss Out On Learning It?

AGREE, PROMISE, PREVIEW METHOD

Among the many ways you can begin your speech is the Agree, Promise, Preview method. This method is very effective at starting your speech off on the right foot. In the Agree phase, you simply agree with your audience on something. What, specifically, do you agree with them on? It depends on the speech, but in most cases, it is a problem to be solved, or an area of difficulty that your speech is assisting. So, in most cases, what you are agreeing with your audience on is that a problem they are facing is difficult or frustrating.

EXPLICIT AND IMPLICIT; SPOKEN AND UNSPOKEN

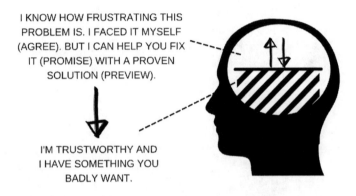

I KNOW HOW FRUSTRATING THIS PROBLEM IS. I FACED IT MYSELF (AGREE). BUT I CAN HELP YOU FIX IT (PROMISE) WITH A PROVEN SOLUTION (PREVIEW).

I'M TRUSTWORTHY AND I HAVE SOMETHING YOU BADLY WANT.

FIGURE 61: All words carry subtext, implication, and a subtle script of meaning layered a level under the literal language. For example, the script above drives directly to the conscious minds of the audience in its literal form, but also has a subtext of "unspoken speech" that hits at the subconscious mind. What cannot be said in "spoken speech" can often be (and often is) layered a level under at the level of "unspoken speech."

Next, in the Promise phase, after you agreed with your audience on a sentiment that they likely all relate to, you need to promise a solution. Promise to them what it will be like when your speech helps solve their problem. Promise to them that you have the solutions that they are looking for.

Lastly, in the Preview section, you should give a brief overview of your speech. This preview should particularly highlight the questions your speech answers. Give them a preview of your content not by simply listing out your content, but by telling them what questions your content answers.

The Agree phase makes the audience members think "Okay, this person really understands my problem." Again, we see that people trust someone who understands a problem to solve it. The Promise phase makes the audience members think "I better listen to this speech so I can have my problems solved." The Preview section makes the audience members think "Those are the specific ways this speech will solve my problems." There's nothing better you can provide to your audience than solutions to a problem.

Here's an example of the Agree, Promise, Preview method in action by a political candidate:

"Believe me: I understand just how frustrating and difficult our tax system can be in this state. Every time tax season rolls around, I'm constantly furious at our politicians for trying to extract even more money from us and trying to hide it. I know that the system is extremely complicated, and I know that we shouldn't have to hire a personal accountant just to pay our taxes. [Agree] But I have good news for you. I promise that there is a way for us to reclaim our tax system and get rid of all the red tape. I promise you that there is a solution we can reach for together. [Promise] Today I'm going to be talking about how we can take advantage of hidden tax deductions to pay less, and about how you can join me in the fight to simplify our tax system with a flat tax. [Preview]"

The Agree section showed the audience that the political candidate understands their difficulties. This is a crucial component of building audience trust, and audience trust is a crucial component of a successful speech. The Promise section made the candidate the source of a solution, which is personally advantageous. The Preview section primed the audience to receive the information coming later in the speech and to maintain their interest as the speech progressed.

The Agree, Promise, Preview method is one of many ways to start a speech. It is very effective at building good rapport with your audience and setting the stage for a successful speech. Keep in mind, it should be fairly brief. It should only be between five to ten sentences.

With the Agree, Promise, Preview method, you will achieve three things. Your audience will believe that you understand them. Your audience will believe that you have a valuable solution for them. Your audience will be carefully listening to your speech because they were primed by the preview phase.

CONCESSIONS

It takes a brave and honest person to admit that an opponent is correct about something. To concede that an opposing idea to yours is indeed partially correct is an action most speakers would never imagine themselves doing. Why would you ever want to admit that an opponent might actually be correct about something? Particularly if you are speaking to inform or persuade, a crucial feeling your audience has to have towards you is trust.

In the case of an informational speech, your audience must trust that you know what you are talking about and that you are impartial. In the case of a persuasive speech, your audience must trust that you aren't holding anything back from them in order to make another sale. To make a small acknowledgement of an opposing viewpoint is to build trust in you. Why? Because it shows that you are impartial and that you are not holding anything back. Trust is one of the most important elements of a successful speaker to audience connection.

For a successful concession, make sure to keep it brief. You don't want to spend too much time talking about an opposing viewpoint. That's not the aim of a concession. What you say about the opposing viewpoint isn't important as long as it's an acknowledgement of partial validity.

THE RELATIONSHIP BETWEEN RESPECT AND OBJECTIVITY

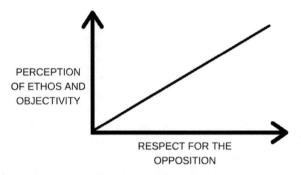

FIGURE 62: As your perceived respect for the opposition rises, so does the audience's perception that you are objective.

THE RELATIONSHIP BETWEEN OBJECTIVITY AND TRUST

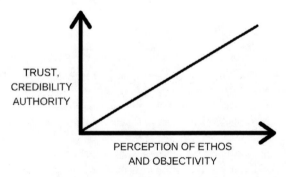

FIGURE 63: As your perceived objectivity rises, so does the audience's trust in you.

THE RELATIONSHIP BETWEEN RESPECT AND TRUST

HOW COMPLIMENTING YOUR ENEMIES HELPS YOU

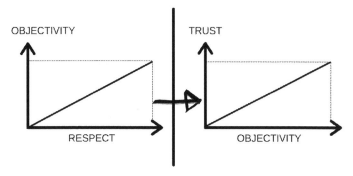

FIGURE 64: Presenting respect for the opposition makes you appear objective; appearing objective earns you trust.

For a successful concession, try to use a format like this one: "Supporters of [product, person, or idea] often say [the opposing benefit]. I actually agree with them, but I would argue that [your product, person, or idea] accomplishes [the opposing benefit] even more, for [reasons and evidence]. And unlike [product, person or idea], [your product, person, or idea] has [additional benefit(s)]." As you can see, this format allows you to acknowledge an opposing viewpoint which builds trust, and then use that to transition to talking about your viewpoint. You are not agreeing with your opponents that their idea is better. You are agreeing with your opponents that a certain benefit is important, and then showing the audience that your idea actually has more of that benefit.

LOGICAL FALLACIES

Logical fallacies can ruin your speech. People can be skeptical, and often deliberately seek out logical fallacies in speeches. If they find one, they will mentally shut you out. The more revolutionary the sentiment of your speech is, the more deliberately some people will analyze it for logical fallacies. If you challenge their status quo, they will attempt to find a way to prove that your thoughts are inferior to theirs to preserve their intellectual status quos. Do not give them a way to do this by avoiding logical fallacies. These below are some of the most common and will give you a general idea about logical fallacies, and how to avoid them. There are hundreds of logical fallacies. Keep in mind that if you are speaking against someone, you can point these out in their argument.

Ad Hominem: Targeting the person who is delivering an argument instead of the argument: "You don't really care about climate change, you just want to sell us your book on how to reduce our carbon emissions!" An argument can be true even if the person delivering it is hypocritical, immoral, or unpopular.

The Bandwagon: Stating that an idea is good simply because many people adopt it: "If driving a car is so bad for our climate then why does every single American do it? Clearly it isn't as bad as you say." An argument can be true even if the vast majority of people contradict it, or wrong even if the vast majority of people agree with it.

The Strawman: Basing a rebuttal off of a misinterpretation of your opposition's point: "You're saying that climate change is caused by us breathing, so if we want to stop climate change that means we have to stop breathing," when nobody asserted that climate change was caused by people breathing. Anybody can effectively challenge an argument if they misunderstood someone's argument and are actually challenging a different one.

The Appeal to Authority: Making an argument and stating that it is true because some testimony supports it: "Climate change cannot be a real thing because the United States president says it is a hoax." Even if authority figures say something is correct, that doesn't mean it is.

One or the Other: A situation that arises when it is misleadingly expressed that a choice between two equally extreme and opposite decisions is required, when in reality a middle ground exists: "We can either sacrifice everything to stop climate change, or we can live luxuriously but all die due to climate change one day," when in reality, a middle ground of making some minor changes in lifestyle will slow down climate change sufficiently. Most arguments tend to be focused around two opposing extremes, when in reality the truth of the matter is somewhere in the middle.

The Hasty Generalization: Making an argument based off of a generalization of insufficient data, or without considering every variable: "One study with two data points showed that the climate is actually cooling, therefore global warming does not exist." There are studies out there that support anything. Literally anything. One study should not impulse someone to an immediate, rapid conclusion.

The Slothful Induction: The opposite of the hasty generalization, not accepting a conclusion which is sufficiently supported by data: "Despite the 75 studies shown to me which supposedly prove climate change, I am not convinced." Although we can't be sure, if there is a lot of evidence suggesting something, one should not refuse to draw the logical conclusion.

The Correlation Causation Fallacy: Stating that A caused B because A and B occurred in correlation: "Climate change started at the same time as organized sports leagues, and thus organized sports leagues caused climate change." It seems intuitive to us that if something happens, and immediately after something else happens, that the first caused the second. This is an extremely common fallacy. Still, it's a fallacy nonetheless.

Anecdotal Evidence: Building an argument based on one insufficient example and stating that the anecdotal example describes the broad trend: "I went to a beach in Florida, where the water level actually went down! Clearly climate change isn't occurring around the world."

The Middle Ground: Asserting that the middle ground between two opposing points of view is the correct choice: "Some experts say that climate change is caused by cars, while some experts say that climate change is caused by trees; therefore, climate change must be caused both by cars and trees as that is the middle ground," when climate change is obviously not caused by trees. The middle ground between two opposing viewpoints is not always correct, especially if one of the opposing viewpoints is extremely wrong.

The Burden of Proof Fallacy: Misplacing the burden of proof: "If you can't disprove my point, then it's true." This is misplacing the burden of proof because it is not other people's job to disprove your point, but it is your job to prove your point. This often takes the form of making a claim that there is little evidence disproving an argument. Sure, but what's the evidence *proving* it?

The Appeal to Ignorance: Assuming something is true because there is no evidence proving its opposite: "Climate change must be real because there is no evidence proving that it isn't." While it is true that there is little evidence disproving climate change, stating that this is the reason climate change is real is a logical fallacy.

The Slippery Slope: Stating that if a certain step occurs, then it will lead to a cascading effect with an ultimately horrible outcome: "If we stop using diesel cars to reduce our carbon emissions, then people who worked in the auto industry will be out of work, which will lead to civil unrest, and civil unrest will obviously lead to increased crime which will lead the government to impose martial law and ultimately to take away all of our civil rights." While this is an exaggerated example, a slippery slope fallacy is still a fallacy if A actually can realistically lead to B, and B can realistically lead to C, etc.

The Circular Argument: An argument in the following form: "He was a good public speaker because he was good at speaking in front of a crowd."

The Red Herring: A logical fallacy, which in this case is also a useful (but deceptive) debate technique. It is deliberately introducing an irrelevant argument to confuse opponents. For example, for someone denying climate change: "Climate change is an issue of economic disparity. We need to discuss economic disparity and how the measures proposed to stop climate change will harm those in lower socioeconomic classes."

The Sunk-Cost Fallacy: A natural, psychological tendency where one continues on a path simply because they have already spent time on it, even if it is not necessarily optimal from a certain point forward. In argument form: "Why re-adjust society to stop climate change when we've already spent so much time living a certain lifestyle?"

The Equivocal Fallacy: A logical fallacy which occurs when someone uses a word ambiguously, and interchanges between two meanings at different parts of the argument. This is relatively uncommon in its literal form, but has been adapted to refer to arguments made with confusing, unclear, and obscuring language.

The Appeal to Pity: Trying to use emotional appeals in a logical argument. This is essentially the use of pathos in an unsubstantiated way: "We have poverty on Earth, and yet you go on raving about climate change? Look at the picture of this struggling third world family. Look at this little boy. Clearly climate change isn't a real problem."

The Spotlight: When someone assumes that the general media portrayal or pop culture presence of a group of people stands for the whole population of that group: "All Republicans deny climate change because the Republican president does!" Obviously, this isn't true. In a broader sense, it can mean assuming that the general portrayal of anything is true.

The Appeal to Tradition: An assumption that an argument is true because it matches tradition: "Climate change is not a real thing! Nobody has ever thought of it as a threat before."

There are many, many more fallacies. These are just the most common ones. If you know these and the others well, and you are speaking in a competitive setting, try exposing them in your opponent's argument. Additionally, try avoiding them in your own. Even in a non-competitive setting, when it is only you speaking, avoid logical fallacies.

From when you begin thinking about the argumentation in your speech, and throughout the process of actually writing it, carefully avoid leaps of logic.

SENTENCE STRUCTURE

This is going to be a longer section than usual. It will put the public address devices of Plato, Socrates, and Aristotle at your fingertips. It will also show you how the great speakers of our world have used these devices in their famous speeches, and how these devices can be used in different scenarios through hypothetical examples.

Examine the following excerpt from Winston Churchill's most famous speech. The purpose of this speech was to inspire fortitude in the people of Great Britain, and to convince them that they can fight off the impending threat of Nazi Germany. Pay attention to which phrases appear to be emphasized by the sentence structure: "We shall go on to the end, we shall fight in France, we shall fight on the seas and oceans, we shall fight with growing confidence and growing strength in the air, we shall defend our Island, whatever the cost may be, we shall fight on the beaches, we shall fight on the landing grounds, we shall fight in the fields and in the streets, we shall fight in the hills; we shall never surrender."

The phrase most emphasized is "we shall never surrender." Consider why: "We shall go on to the end, <u>we shall fight</u> in France, <u>we shall fight</u> on the seas and oceans, <u>we shall fight</u> with growing confidence and growing strength in the air, <u>we shall</u> *defend our Island*, whatever the cost may be, <u>we shall fight</u> on the beaches, <u>we shall fight</u> on the landing grounds, <u>we shall fight</u> in the fields and in the streets, <u>we shall fight</u> in the hills; <u>we shall</u> *never surrender.*"

Email Peter D. Andrei, the author of the Speak for Success collection and the President of Speak Truth Well LLC directly.

pandreibusiness@gmail.com

HOW TO AVOID ACCIDENTALLY BORING YOUR AUDIENCE

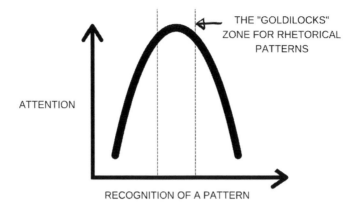

FIGURE 65: As your audience begins to perceive your pattern (or as your pattern begins to announce itself to their perception), attention rises. The pattern continues to captivate attention until it reaches the point of habituation. At this point – which can come quickly – the pattern becomes rote, routine, boring, and droning. As they see the pattern continuing, their attention dips. Bring your patterns to the goldilocks zone, but no further. Unfortunately, there is no hard and fast rule for determining the point of habituation. It depends on the nature of the pattern in question.

WHY PATTERN-INTERRUPTS HOOK AUDIENCE ATTENTION

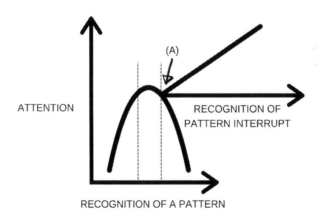

FIGURE 66: Up to the point of habituation, patterns grab attention. After the point of habituation, patterns lose attention. After the point of habituation, pattern-interrupts grab attention. The ideal sequence is this: produce rhetorical patterns until the point of

habituation. Then, apply a pattern-interrupt. This guarantees attention rises (or at least doesn't fall) throughout.

The structure of the sentences preceding "defend our island," and "we shall never surrender" involved repetition of the phrase "we shall fight." The first phrase to break away from this pattern is indirectly emphasized by the previous sentence structure in a very punchy and powerful way. This happens because the repetitive phrases create an expectation that the next phrase will repeat the same phrase again, and when it doesn't, the breakaway phrase is emphasized. When people in the audience expect another "we shall fight," and instead get something else, that new phrase is emphasized. Starting each sentence or portion of a sentence with a repeated word or phrase is a technique called anaphora. Consider this excerpt from a generic speech given by a fictitious politician: "We are being hurt by fiscal irresponsibility. We are being hurt by raised taxes to make up for that fiscal irresponsibility. We are being hurt by failing infrastructure. We are being hurt by a degrading education system. We are being hurt by jobs being outsourced elsewhere. *I will be the one to change these things*, because just like you, I have suffered by them."

The emphasis, once again, is placed indirectly and non-verbally, simply by the sentence structure of the speech, on the breakaway phrase. In this case, that is "I will be the one to change these things, because just like you, I have suffered by them." It is no coincidence that the breakaway phrase is typically more important than those preceding it. The opposite of anaphora is epistrophe. For example, when Lyndon B. Johnson said: "There is no Negro problem. There is no Southern problem. There is no Northern problem. There is only an American problem."

The combination of anaphora and epistrophe is called symploce. For example, a fictitious politician could say: "We are at our best when against hatred we stand together. We are at our best when we refuse petty political rivalries and instead we stand together. We are at our best when through hard times we stand together."

Now consider this sentence from JFK's "moon speech," which was delivered at Rice University, and when he revealed his goal to send a man to the moon: "We choose to go to the moon in this decade and do the other things, not because they are easy, but because they are hard."

This is a classic example of contrasting phrases, otherwise known as antithesis. The "not because they are easy" sets the mental stage for what many in the audience assumed will come next: "*but because they are hard.*" Another example of this is: "I am not up here talking to you all about climate change because the problem is out of our control, but because it still is in our control."

HOW THE CONTRAST EFFECT SHAPES PERCEPTION

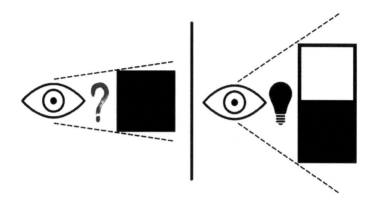

FIGURE 67: Human perception functions through contrasts. We judge items by drawing comparisons between the item in questions and other available items: contextual items, items in memory, or items provided by the speaker. Provide contrasting items which improve the estimation of the item in question. Make your idea appear better both by raising its appeal directly and contrasting it with weaker ideas.

By telling the audience first what something is *not*, they will think of what it *is* before you actually say it. Thus, when you say it, you are fulfilling something they already mentally assumed; a conclusion they already reached. Doing so is very satisfying for the audience. In addition to this, contrasting phrases also place emphasis on the second phrase in the sequence.

Keep in mind that speeches are spoken, not written. A sentence structure, diction, or word choice that may be smooth and sleek on the page might sound garbled when spoken, and the opposite applies as well. Always keep this in mind when choosing sentence structure, diction, or word choice. Next, let's examine this excerpt from one of Ronald Reagan's speeches: "The men of Normandy had faith that what they were doing was right, faith that they fought for all humanity, faith that a just God would grant them mercy on this beachhead or on the next. It was the deep knowledge — and pray God we have not lost it — that there is a profound moral difference between the use of force for liberation and the use of force for conquest. You were here to liberate, not to conquer, and so you and those others did not doubt your cause. And you were right not to doubt."

This example shows us the importance of varying sentence structure. Pay attention to the punchy, short sentences that have been underlined, and consider how they sound when mixed with the long, flowing sentences that have been italicized.

"*The men of Normandy had faith that what they were doing was right, faith that they fought for all humanity, faith that a just God would grant them mercy on this beachhead or on the next.* / *It was the deep knowledge — and pray God we have not lost it — that there is a profound moral difference between the use of force for liberation and the use of force for conquest.* / <u>You were here to liberate, not to conquer, and so you and</u> <u>those others did not doubt your cause.</u> / <u>And you were right not to doubt.</u>"

But let's break that excerpt down a little further: let's break it down into syllable count.

"The men of Normandy had faith that what they were doing was right, faith that they fought for all humanity, faith that a just God would grant them mercy on this beachhead or on the next [Sentence 1: 43 syllables]. It was the deep knowledge – and pray God we have not lost it – that there is a profound moral difference between the use of force for liberation and the use of force for conquest [Sentence 2: 44 syllables]. You were here to liberate, not to conquer, and so you and those others did not doubt your cause. [Sentence 3: 23] / And you were right not to doubt [Sentence 4: 7 syllables]."

We have a sentence with 43 syllables, one with 44, one with 23, and one with 7. There's clear variance between sentences 1, 3, and 4, and 2, 3, and 4, but not much between sentences 1 and 2. This will change if we dive a little deeper. We have to remind ourselves that when spoken, each individual phrase acts almost as its own sentence. Not in a grammatical sense (grammar doesn't change when speaking, of course), but in an auditory way. A portion of a sentence separated by commas on paper is separated by pauses when spoken and these pauses allow it to have its auditory properties independent from the rest of the sentence. Let's break down the excerpt yet further: "The men of Normandy had faith that what they were doing was right [Section 1: 15 syllables], faith that they fought for all humanity [Section 2: 10 syllables], faith that a just God would grant them mercy on this beachhead or on the next [Section 3: 18 syllables] [Sentence 1: 43 syllables]. It was the deep knowledge [Section 1: 6 syllables] – and pray God we have not lost it [Section 2: 8 syllables] – that there is a profound moral difference between the use of force for liberation and the use of force for conquest [Section 3: 30 syllables] [Sentence 2: 44 syllables]. You were here to liberate [Section 1: 7 syllables], not to conquer [Section 2: 4 syllables], and so you and those others did not doubt your cause [Section 3: 12 syllables]. [Sentence 3: 23] / And you were right not to doubt [Sentence 4: 7 syllables]."

It is clear upon breaking down the sentences to this level that Reagan managed to create varying sentence structures despite using two back-to-back sentences of similar length. The first sentence had a section with 15 syllables followed by one with 10 and then one with 18, while the second had a section with 6 syllables followed by one with 8 and then one with 30. It is not expected that any of these techniques happened naturally or on the spot, nor is it expected that Reagan himself actually broke it down to this level (it was probably one of his speech writers). Regardless, combining sentences of varying length and structure makes for a much more pleasing listening experience. Imagine if Reagan had said: "The men of Normandy had faith. Faith that what they were doing was right. Faith that they fought for all humanity. Faith that a just God would grant them mercy. Both on this beachhead or on the next. It was a deep knowledge. Pray God we have not lost it. A deep knowledge that there is a difference. A profound moral difference. A difference between the use of force for liberation and the use of force for conquest. You were here to liberate. You were not here to conquer. You and those others did not doubt your cause. And you were right not to doubt."

HOW TO AVOID INSTANTLY LOSING AUDIENCE ATTENTION

A PATTERN THAT
LOSES ATTENTION

AN ENGAGING
LISTENING EXPERIENCE

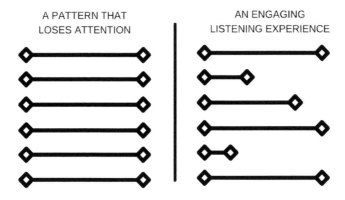

FIGURE 68: Varied sentence lengths produce intrigue and interest, creating an engaging and varied listening experience. Speaking sentences of the same length in sequence for an extended portion of your speech grows tremendously monotonous and loses attention. There is one caveat: it can be beneficial to periodically speak sentences of the same length when the meaning justifies it or when it achieves some rhetorical effect. However, in the absence of these conditions, stay away from same-length sentences. They bore people.

This type of repetitive sentence structure drones on and on. It is robotic and unnatural, and should be avoided. Now, in another excerpt from the same speech, we can examine rhetorical questions as components of sentence structure: "Forty summers have passed since the battle that you fought here. You were young the day you took these cliffs; some of you were hardly more than boys, with the deepest joys of life before you. Yet you risked everything here. Why? Why did you do it? What impelled you to put aside the instinct for self-preservation and risk your lives to take these cliffs? What inspired all the men of the armies that met here? We look at you, and somehow we know the answer. It was faith, and belief; it was loyalty and love."

Before discussing the power of rhetorical questions, let us first re-examine that excerpt without them: "Forty summers have passed since the battle that you fought here. You were young the day you took these cliffs; some of you were hardly more than boys, with the deepest joys of life before you. Yet you risked everything here. You were impelled to put aside the instinct for self-preservation and risk your lives to take these cliffs. You were inspired as men of the armies that met here. We look at you, and somehow we know why. It was faith, and belief; it was loyalty and love."

It is much less interesting, and in a way, much less *interactive*. Speeches should be mentally interactive, and rhetorical questions accomplish that. Using them induces the audience to be more engaged and attentive because they are answering the questions in their minds as you phrase them.

HOW THE SUBCONSIOUS MIND INTERACTS WITH QUESTIONS

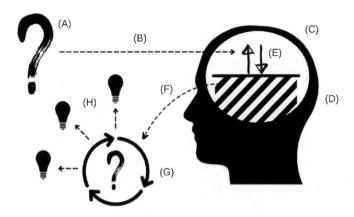

FIGURE 69: When someone hears a question (A), they receive it (B) consciously (C) and subconsciously (D). The conscious and subconscious minds shape each other: your conscious thought habits imprint upon the subconscious mind, and your subconscious mind tosses up conscious thoughts (E) that correspond to what you have imprinted upon it. Your subconscious mind (F) turns the question over, (G) churning its big cognitive factory and producing not one conscious thought (which the may or may not be acted upon) but multiple over time (H).

A way to use rhetorical questions that builds suspense and interest is to ask or describe a question that is very central to your topic, and then to say "I will answer this critical question later on." Bring up the question early in your speech, and answer it towards the end. Doing this builds interest because your audience is now listening ever more closely for the answer. Make sure the question doesn't have a clear answer already; make the question be one that only you have the answer to.

Another technique which falls under the umbrella of sentence structure is rearranging sentences to place key words in places of emphasis, such as the first or last word of the sentence. Consider the following excerpt of a speech: "We need to stop climate change before human progress comes to a grinding halt. The longer we wait, the more danger climate change creates. We are sacrificing short term comfort for our long-term prosperity in a foolish way. It's not hopeless, however, because we can overcome it together if we are smart enough to do so."

The key evocative phrases, which truly give the sentences their meanings, have been underlined: "We need to stop climate change before human progress comes to a grinding halt. The longer we wait, the more danger climate change creates. We are sacrificing our long-term prosperity for short term comfort in a foolish way. However, it's not hopeless, because we can overcome it together if we are smart enough to do so."

Now, the excerpt has been rearranged so that the key phrases are placed either as the first or last word in the sentences. This was done without altering the meaning or nuances of the original excerpt in any way: "Climate change needs to be stopped before it brings human progress to a grinding halt. Danger grows exponentially worse the longer we wait to solve climate change. Long term prosperity is being foolishly sacrificed for short term comfort. We can overcome it together if we are smart enough to address it; it is not hopeless."

The second version is punchier, more vivid, and delivers the message with more clarity. It's not that the first version is unclear or lacks potency; the second version simply uses the two most important places in the sentence, the first and last words, much more strategically and with greater impact.

KEY INSIGHT:

Rhetorical Questions Awaken the Mind. They Grab Attention. They Draw People In.

Don't They? When You Hear One, Doesn't It Grab Your Attention? Doesn't It Make You Think? Doesn't Your Mind Interact with It?

HOW TO USE THE POSITIONS OF INHERENT EMPHASIS

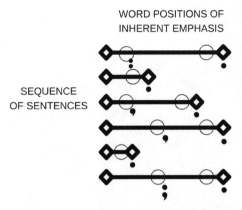

WORD POSITIONS OF
INHERENT EMPHASIS

SEQUENCE
OF SENTENCES

FIGURE 70: The word positions of inherent emphasis in the sequence of sentences are circled. Note that the first word is also a position of inherent emphasis.

"DIFFERENT THAN THE REST" CONTEXTUAL EMPHASIS

FIGURE 71: The different item stands out.

"BEST FOR LAST" CONTEXTUAL EMPHASIS

FIGURE 72: The last item stands out.

HOW TO COMBINE TWO MODES OF CONTEXTUAL EMPHASIS

FIGURE 73: JFK combined the two modes of contextual emphasis by placing the item he wanted to emphasize last and clothing it differently than the items around it.

There are many other techniques for powerful sentence structure. Alliteration creates a pleasing, flowing structure by placing words starting with the same letters or syllables in consecutive (or almost consecutive) places. Consider Barack Obama's speech when he said: "They are part of the finest fighting force that the world has ever known. They have served tour after tour of duty in distant, different, and difficult places."

Anadiplosis paints a sequential cause and effect narrative by starting subsequent phrases with the last word of the preceding phrase. Consider the following example from another fictitious politician: "Outsourcing creates unemployment; unemployment forces more people to rely on welfare; welfare leads to greater taxes for those still employed."

Asyndeton alters pace, heightens intensity, increases clarity, and emphasizes portions of a speech by getting rid of all conjunctions. Consider one of General Douglas MacArthur's speeches: "Duty, Honor, Country: Those three hallowed words reverently dictate what you ought to be, what you can be, what you will be. They are your rallying points: to build courage when courage seems to fail; to regain faith when there seems to be little cause for faith; to create hope when hope becomes forlorn."

It sounds very powerful and intense. The same speech with conjunctions is not quite as emphatic: "Duty, Honor, and Country: Those three hallowed words reverently dictate what you ought to be, what you can be, and what you will be. They are your rallying points: to build courage when courage seems to fail; to regain faith when there seems to be little cause for faith; and to create hope when hope becomes forlorn."

Polysyndeton, on the other hand, is the addition of conjunctions which need not be there. This emphasizes the volume of items in a list. For example, a climatologist might say: "Climate change will destroy our lifestyles, and people's homes, and food supply, and stability, and even the air we breathe."

The repetitive and unnecessary conjunctions (except for the last one, which is necessary) place emphasis on just how many things will be destroyed by climate change. Without the conjunctions, the list sounds shorter, and is therefore registered as a less significant list even though the number of items and the length of each item are the same.

Aposiopesis is frustrating for the audience, in a good way, and in a way that grabs their attention. Aposiopesis is beginning to say a very powerful, impactful statement, and then cutting it off. This is like a hook that can be used anywhere in your speech to regain audience attention. For example: "Because of climate change, each and every one of you will, in your lives, experience- *[pause]* It's very serious, and the impacts can be drastic."

Be wary of overusing it. It can become genuinely frustrating if overused, but in moderation, this technique can be productively frustrating. The audience members are likely thinking "wait, what am I going to experience in my life because of climate change? I'm going to listen closely for the answer." The longer the buildup of the compelling statement, the more attention grabbing it is when it becomes cut off. People want to know. They'll begin listening to every word to possibly find the answer. They will be intrigued, and they will want to satisfy their curiosities by listening closely for the answer.

Catachresis is an extreme metaphor, when something is being equated to another thing that breaks the conventional word choice one would expect in that sentence. For example: "Climate change is a planetary fever that just keeps getting worse and worse unless we do something about it."

Catachresis is very jarring and evocative. It's very vivid, and almost anyone can relate to having a fever. Indeed, this is a metaphor, but it's catachresis because it's a very unusual metaphor, and uses particularly jarring words that are normally not matched together.

Sententia is the summation of a preceding segment with a memorable statement. For example, here's how we could add sententia to a previous example: "We are being hurt by fiscal irresponsibility. We are being hurt by raised taxes to make up for that fiscal irresponsibility. We are being hurt by failing infrastructure. We are being hurt by a degrading education system. We are being hurt by jobs being outsourced elsewhere. I will be the one to change these things, because just like you, I have suffered by them. I know the problems that hurt you, because they hurt me too: a vote for me is a vote for you."

The effectiveness of sententia is that it roots a message, or part of a message, in the minds of the audience in an additional way. Audience members might not always remember the exact words a speaker says, but they will instead remember the general message and overall tone. With sententia, however, they will have a memorable phrase stuck in their minds which summarizes the message. Therefore, instead of having just a memory of the message, they will have both a memory of the words that conveyed that message and the message itself.

Sometimes when we are reading, it seems as though we need to read the same sentence over and over again. For some reason, the words just aren't being rooted in our minds. The same phenomenon can happen in a speech: words can pass through the minds of your audience without being rooted there. Apposition is a rhetorical device which can fight this by putting two words close to each other which clarify one another. For example, a climatologist could say: "And the rising sea levels there, in Boston, will flood many streets, building lobbies, and parks."

It would be even better to avoid saying "there" in the first place, and instead say "in Boston." Replacing pronouns like them, they, or there, with whatever the pronouns are referring to, helps to make your words concrete and takes them out of abstraction. Of course, don't overdo it: if you very recently assigned a word to a pronoun, then you don't need to repeatedly say the word instead of the pronoun. Only do it when you think the assignment needs to be refreshed.

Climax is a technique in which you repeat phrases that are arranged in order of increasing intensity. For example, when Bill Clinton said: "What I think we have to do is invest in American jobs, American education, control American healthcare costs, and bring the American people together again."

As you can see, the most intense and passionate statement, that of bringing the American people together again, was left for last. Each of the preceding statements was more intense than the one before it. We have an upcoming analysis of the speech in which Bill Clinton said this quote.

Enumeratio is dividing up a word into many descriptive parts, and listing them out. For example, a climatologist could say: "My work is studying climate change: the natural process we accelerate, the threat to our way of life, the biggest problem for our younger generations, the destroyer of natural habitats, the often-neglected issue that needs a solution now."

Epizeuxis is emphatic repetition. This is just another way to place emphasis on a word or phrase by repeating it several times (three times is recommended) in succession. For example, a fictitious politician could say: "I know that I don't speak only for myself, but for all of us, when I say that we <u>do not want</u>- <u>do not want</u>- <u>do not want</u> these policies which have left our community behind."

Diacope is placing the same word on opposite ends of an interjecting phrase, which places emphasis both on the intervening phrase and the repeated word. For example, a climatologist could say: "Climate change will most certainly impact <u>our lives</u>, not just other people's lives, <u>our lives</u>."

Parallelism is a technique we've already seen before in some of these examples because it often occurs in tandem with anaphora, epistrophe, and symploce. Parallelism is saying sentences or phrases in succession that have the same (or similar) grammatical structure. Here's a very simple example: "This community is filled with working people of dignity, children of hopes and dreams, families of love."

Here's a less straightforward example: "We shall fight on the beaches, we shall fight on the landing grounds, we shall fight in the fields and in the streets, we shall fight in the hills."

In this case, the parallelism takes the form of (pronoun) (auxiliary verb) (verb) (preposition) (location). We can see that this pattern is repeated: "We (pronoun) shall (auxiliary verb) fight (verb) on (preposition) the beaches (noun), we (pronoun) shall (auxiliary verb) fight (verb) on (preposition) the landing grounds (noun), we (pronoun) shall (auxiliary verb) fight (verb) in (preposition) the fields (noun) and in (preposition) the streets (noun) [this past phrase deviated from the parallel structure slightly], we (pronoun) shall (auxiliary verb) fight (verb) in (preposition) the hills (noun)."

Parallelism is especially obvious when it's accompanied by anaphora, epistrophe, or symploce, because many of the parts of speech end up being the same word. For example, the pronoun in Churchill's speech was always we, the verb was always fight, and the auxiliary verb was always shall. Here's a less obvious example of parallelism from a fictitious politician, in which each of the parts of speech aren't always the same word: "The politicians in Washington tell us we have less and less funding every year. The people of this community show them they lose more and more support every day."

In this case, the parallelism is less obvious, but still creates an elegant symmetry between the sentences. In this case, the parallelism takes this form: "The politicians (noun) in (preposition) Washington (noun) tell (verb) us (object) [entering indirect statement] we (pronoun) have (verb) less (adjective) and (conjunction) less (identical adjective) funding (noun) every (adjective) year (noun). The people (noun) of (preposition) this community (noun) show (verb) them (object) [entering indirect statement] they (pronoun) lose (verb) more (adjective) and (conjunction) more (identical adjective) support (noun) every (adjective) day (noun)."

The parallelism in this previous example by part of speech is as follows: (noun) (preposition) (noun) (verb) (object) [indirect statement] (pronoun) (verb) (adjective) (conjunction) (identical adjective) (noun) (adjective) (noun).

Parallelism creates symmetry between the grammar of the sentences, but contrast between their meanings. In the case of this previous example, the contrast and disconnect between the politicians in Washington and the people of this community is highlighted. This is a strategic point to emphasize for the fictitious politician.

Scesis Onomaton is a (strangely named) form of repetition that repeats different words or phrases with nearly the same meaning to add nuance and emphasis. For example, a politician could say: "The people of this community know what it means to be determined, to have grit, to be tenacious."

Being determined, having grit, and being tenacious all emphasize and provide nuance for one quality of the community that the politician wants to emphasize: that they are hardworking people.

Conduplicatio is the repetition of the keyword or key phrase in a sentence, in a way that places emphasis on that keyword or key phrase. For example, a climatologist could say the following: "Climate change will cause more suffering than most people realize. It will force people to suffer economic hardship, to suffer food insecurity, to suffer unprecedented natural disasters, to suffer massive flooding."

An expletive is an interjection in the flow of speech with a word or short phrase that can add nuance, add meaning, and add emphasis. Here is an example from our politician: "And this community, I assure you, wants to work hard. This community wants to work hard, but as we all know, also wants to be fairly compensated for hard work."

A common use for an expletive is to relate the information back to the speaker or the audience. For example, when stating "I assure you," the politician relates the sentiment to his belief in what he is saying. When stating "but as we all know," the politician relates the information to the shared understanding in the community. In addition to this, expletives add emphasis to the words preceding and following the expletive. Be wary of overusing expletives: they are certainly eloquent in moderation, but overused, they can change from being eloquent interjections to being annoying interruptions.

Litotes create a sense of irony and cynical humor by changing statements like "this is a huge issue!" to "this is no easy problem."

An attached adjective is when a noun is never, or rarely said, without certain adjectives attached to it. For example, a climatologist could always refer to climate change as "Dangerous climate change," or "the danger of climate change." Be careful not to repeat this too much. If the climatologist used the word climate change frequently, it is not a good idea to attach the adjective to it all the time. Attached adjectives cement the quality to the noun. Repeating "dangerous climate change" forms an association that climate change is dangerous. This can be used to re-emphasize any quality about any noun, as long as it is subtle, which means that it needs to be done in moderation.

Antimetabole is a reversal of a phrase. For example: "All penguins are birds, but not all birds are penguins."

An oxymoron attaches two words to each other that seem to contradict one another, but which is still valid. This forms a new way of looking at things. For example: "Climate change will gently shock us soon enough." The words gently and shock seem to contradict each other, but the meaning is still valid: climate change happens gradually, gently, but the effects will still shock us.

There are many so-called "rules of three" in public speaking. One of them is that lists of three are satisfying to hear. The formal name for a list of three is a tricolon. For an example of effective use of tricolon, we return to JFK's "moon speech:" "We meet at a college noted for knowledge, in a city noted for progress, in a State noted for strength, *[Excellent use of the rule of three; also note that he places the key words at the end of the phrases, right before the commas. In this case, he wants the focus to be on the adjectives knowledge, progress and strength].* and we stand in need of all three, for we meet in an hour of change and challenge, in a decade of hope and fear, in an age of both knowledge and ignorance *[We see a rule of three yet again; this time, it's a little less clear. The reason? Each item in the list of three is actually a grouping of two things: (1) change and challenge, (2) hope and fear, (3) knowledge and ignorance. Additionally, each item in the groupings of two that make up the list of three contradicts the item it's grouped with, which is antithesis. Change and challenge, hope and fear, knowledge and ignorance. This depicts the chaos and confusion of a time in which America is torn between opposing impulses].* The greater our knowledge increases, the greater our ignorance unfolds. Despite the striking fact that most of the scientists that the world has ever known are alive and working today, despite the fact that this Nation's own scientific manpower is doubling every 12 years in a rate of growth more than three times that of our population as a whole, despite that *[Another instance of the rule of three: the third item is quite simply "that." Does it still work? Yes. The repetition of despite emphasizes the irony of how little we truly know about the universe even though scientific pursuit is at an all-time high],* the vast stretches of the unknown and the unanswered and the unfinished still far outstrip our collective comprehension."

Lastly, there are "ascending" and "descending" tricolon sentences. An example of an ascending tricolon sentence is: "The worst impacts of climate change will be loss of biodiversity, suffering for people in poorer countries, and a completely fractured economy that will make life harder for all of us."

Let's analyze it closely. I have put parentheses around each item in the tricolon pair, followed by the syllable count: "The worst impacts of climate change will be (loss of biodiversity) [Section 1: 7 syllables], (suffering for people in poorer countries) [Section 2: 11 syllables], and a (completely fractured economy that will make life harder for all of us) [Section 3: 20 syllables]."

On the other hand, a descending tricolon would be: "The worst impacts of climate change will be a completely fractured economy that will make life harder for all of us, suffering for people in poorer countries, and loss of biodiversity."

Sentence structure is one of the most interesting parts of speech writing. It can be very difficult to include these techniques in a speech that isn't prepared in time, or a speech that is delivered around a set of core ideas. In the case of an impromptu speech, don't worry about including these techniques. In the case of a speech delivered around a set of core ideas, you can choose to memorize just one or two groups of sentences, and write those portions using these techniques.

Every aspect of sentence structure falls under the umbrella of one idea: manipulating the positions or expressions of words and grammatical devices to give sentences greater impact. All of the "secrets" of how incredible speakers use their words;

all of their methods of producing incredible eloquence; all of the techniques of Plato, Aristotle, Socrates, and all the other ones, have just been unwrapped for you in this chapter. Some of these techniques are easier to include in an impromptu speech, or one centered around a core set of ideas, than others. Some of them aren't. For those that you find easy to naturally include in your speech, begin to use them when you speak around a core set of ideas. For those which don't seem easy to naturally include, save them for a written speech. Nonetheless, you now have all the keys to eloquence at your disposal.

METAPHOR, SIMILE, AND ANALOGY

Vincent Van Gogh has a little-known saying: "Conscience is a man's compass." It's a nice saying because it is told in the form of a metaphor. It would be a more boring saying had it been "Conscience guides a man." Both forms deliver the same sentiment, but the first one is more vivid because you can easily picture the way a compass guides someone. The same holds true for any statement you could possibly be making. For example, why say "it's hard to find a good man for the job" when you can say "finding a good man is like finding a needle in a haystack"? The second version is clearly more vivid and inventive because you can easily imagine the frustration and tediousness of pawing around a haystack for a tiny needle.

A metaphor is when one thing becomes symbolic of another. In Van Gogh's saying, the compass became symbolic of a man's conscience.

A simile is like a metaphor, but unlike a metaphor, a simile makes use of the words "like" or "as" to aid the description.

Lastly, an analogy is comparing an idea people are familiar with to one they aren't familiar with.

Use metaphor, simile, and analogy often in your speech: they are the seasoning of your verbal kitchen.

DICTION AND WORD CHOICE

Compare these two sentences: "Climate change is a threat to our wellbeing and long-term success as a species," and "climate change is a precariousness to our durability and our longevity of opulence as a variety of life on Earth." This simple example disproves the common belief that using complex words makes one sound sophisticated; the second sentence is far from it.

Many who are composing their first speech fall for the belief that speaking with the most complex words will make them appear more knowledgeable. Using unnecessarily unusual words (which almost always have a simple synonym) is one of the most annoying types of dictions to listen to. Imagine the mind-numbing experience of listening to an entire speech delivered with the diction of the second sentence. Why do that to your audience? The best word to say is the one which pops into your mind first. Following this rule will make for a smooth and natural diction, and leave you uninhibited by mental attempts to seek more sophisticated words.

While you should never speak as shown in the second sentence, there are times when it can be favorable to spruce up the sophistication of your word choice and diction. In a conversational speech, natural word choice and diction, meaning whatever comes into mind first, is the rule to follow. It may be difficult to find these natural phrases and words because, at times, anxiety can cloud what is normally a steady stream of natural words. To "re-center" and regain the ability to speak naturally, clear your head and focus on lifting your inhibitions and letting the words flow out of you. When it comes to formal speeches, certainly do not speak as shown in the second sentence, but do make an effort to find particularly sophisticated, smooth, and flowing language.

Setting aside the first example for now, here is a non-exaggerated comparison between the diction and word choice of a conversational speech versus a formal one: "Hey everyone, how is everybody doing today? Well, I hope. Today I'm going to be talking about climate change. Climate change is technically a natural process that's been happening on Earth forever, but the way we use it today, it's often describing human-accelerated climate change. The biggest question I try to answer in my work is how fast it's being accelerated and by what specific actions humans take."

Now, the same sentiment delivered formally: "Hello everyone. I sincerely hope you are all doing well this pleasant evening. I am here to speak about climate change, a process which has been occurring on Earth ever since the planet's birth, and which has been accelerated through the actions humans take on a daily basis. My work focuses on two fundamental questions: how fast is climate change accelerated, and by what actions."

The difference is subtle, but remember: truly exceptional public speaking is the product of attention to detail and mastery of subtleties.

Note one particular alteration between the two examples of different dictions: the formal one lacked contractions, while the conversational one used them in abundance. Contractions are one of the most overlooked aspects of speech-writing and delivering, and despite their seemingly insignificant presence in sentences, they can make a subtle but significant impact on the way a speech is received.

Using contractions is well suited for informal speeches, while breaking them up is well suited for formal ones. Contractions make speech sound easy-going. Breaking them up makes speech sound methodical, calculated, and polished.

ACTIVE AND PASSIVE VOICE

Not all components of good grammar that is written translates to good grammar that is spoken. The medium is different, and that effects the message. One element of writing that is certainly true for both written and spoken word is the use of the active voice over the passive voice. The names themselves express how each of the different types of sentences sound: the active voice is active, strong, and straightforward. The passive voice is passive, weak, and obscured.

In the active voice, the subject does the verb. The subject is actively doing the action of the verb. In the passive voice, the verb is being done to the object. The object is passively receiving the action of the verb. Here are some examples of the active voice versus the passive voice:

COMPARING THE ACTIVE AND PASSIVE VOICES

ACTIVE	PASSIVE
The man probably wrote five speeches. (The man, who is the subject, is doing the verb, which is the eating).	Five speeches were probably written by the man. (The subject is now the five speeches, and they are receiving the action of the verb because they are being written).
After a long time, she finally mailed the kind letter. (She, who is the subject, is doing the verb, which is the mailing).	After a long time, the letter was finally mailed by her. (The subject is now the letter, and it is receiving the action of the verb because it is being mailed).
Zebras live in grassy plains and sometimes tundra. (The Zebras, who are the subject, are doing the verb, which is the living).	This cannot be changed to passive voice because there is no direct object.

Avoid using the passive voice whenever possible. Many online tools are available to help you detect uses of the passive voice. Many of these tools are free. Just search for "passive voice detector" in a search engine.

SUBSTANCE

I'm going to present to you a quasi-equation: Substance = Information / Words. If you want to increase the substance of your speech, find a way to pack more information into fewer words.

There are two key lessons relating to substance that can be drawn from the world of politics. Firstly, politicians have an astounding ability to, given the right circumstances, pack an incredible amount of information into very few words. Secondly, politicians also have an astounding ability to, given the wrong circumstances, pack very little information into an incredible number of words. Politicians have developed a reputation for being on the wrong end of the "substance = information / words" equation. But they can frequently be on the right side of that equation as well.

It's very difficult to quantify information transferred in a speech. For the purposes of this example, every time a politician makes a complete statement or presents a complete idea, they will gain one "information point." They will gain half a point when they present information that is contextual or tangential but still relevant. They will also gain half a point when they first repeat an idea they already gained a point for, and zero points for further repetitions. Lastly, they will gain half a point when they make introductory statements. This is less straightforward than it seems given the frequent use of emotive, implicative, and evocative language that condenses even more information in fewer words.

First, let's begin with an example of a highly substantive statement from a man named Ben Sasse, a senator from Nebraska who is a self-proclaimed independent that caucuses with one of the major parties. He was making a statement in critique of the functions of congress, which was delivered on September 4, 2018: "[of the current state of congress] How did we get here, and how do we fix it? [+0.5 introductory] I want to make just four brief points [+0.5 introductory]. Number one: in our system, the legislative branch is supposed to be the center of our politics [+1]. Number two: it's not [+1]. Why not? Because for the last century [+0.5 contextual], and increasing by the decade right now [+0.5 contextual], more and more legislative authority is delegated to the executive branch every year [+1]. Both parties do it [+1]. The legislature is impotent [+1]. The legislature is weak [+0.5 repetitive]. And most people here want their jobs more than they really want to do legislative work [+1], and so they punt most of the work to the next branch [+1]. The third consequence is that this transfer of power means the people yearn for a place where politics can actually be done [+1], and when we don't do a lot of big actual political debating here [+0.5 contextual], we transfer it to the Supreme Court [+1], and that's why the supreme court is increasingly a substitute political battleground in America [+1]. It is not healthy [+1], but it is what happens and it's something that our founders wouldn't be able to make any sense of [+1]. And fourth and finally: we badly need to restore the proper duties and the balance of power from our constitutional system [+1]."

So, let's calculate his substance score. This statement was 204 words total, and Ben Sasse earned an impressive 16 information points. 16 / 204 = a substance score of 0.078. This is a very good score.

Now, let's compare this to another statement, this time given by former president Jimmy Carter in a debate against incumbent Gerald Ford on October 22, 1976: "Well I might say first of all that I think in case of the Carter administration the sacrifices would be much less [+1]. Mr. Ford's own uh – environmental agency has projected a 10 percent unemployment rate by 1978 [+1] if he's uh – president [+0.5 contextual]. The American people are ready to make sacrifices if they are part of the process [+1]. If they know that they will be helping to make decisions and won't be excluded from being an involved party to the national purpose [+0.5 repetitive]. The major effort we must put forward is to put our people back to work [+1]. And I think that this uh – is one example where uh – a lot of people have selfish, grasping ideas now [+1]. I remember 1973 in the depth of the uh – energy crisis [+0.5 contextual] when President Nixon called on the American people to make a sacrifice [+0.5 contextual], to cut down on the waste of uh – gasoline, to cut down on the uh – speed of automobiles [+1]. It was a – a tremendous surge of patriotism, that "I want to make a sacrifice for my country [+1]." I think we uh – could call together, with strong leadership in the White House [+0.5 contextual], business, industry and labor, and say let's have voluntary price restraints [+1]. Let's lay down some guidelines so we don't have continuing inflation [+0.5 repetitive]. We can also have a – an end to the extremes. We now have one extreme for instance, of some welfare recipients, who by taking advantage of the welfare laws, the housing laws, the uh –

Medicaid uh – laws, and the uh – food stamp laws, make over $10 thousand a year [+1] and uh – they don't have to pay any taxes on it [+1]. At the other extreme, uh – just 1 percent of the richest people in our country derive 25 percent of all the tax benefits [+1]. So both those extremes grasp for advantage [+1] and the person who has to pay that expense is the middle-income family [+1] who's still working for a living and they have to pay for the rich who have privilege [+0.5 repetitive], and for the poor who are not working [+0.5 repetitive]. But I think uh – uh – a balanced approach, with everybody being part of it and a striving for unselfishness [+1], could help as it did in 1973 to let people sacrifice for their own country [+1]. I know I'm ready for it. I think the American people are too."

Jimmy Carter earned 19 information points over the course of 385 words, earning him a substance score of 19 / 385, which equals 0.049. This is still a very good score, but not as good as Ben Sasse's impressive 0.078.

If it helps make substance scores more intuitive, you can multiply them by a factor of 100. 0.078 becomes 7.8, and 0.049 becomes 4.9. This doesn't change anything aside from making the numbers more intuitive.

What specifically makes Ben Sasse's statement so substantive? What strategies did he use to earn a score of 0.078? He said extremely succinct phrases, such as "Both parties do it [+1]. The legislature is impotent [+1]." Those two sentences alone have a substance score of 0.25. Eight words deliver two complete ideas. Additionally, he presented pieces of consecutive contextual information, as seen when he said "Because for the last century [+0.5 contextual], and increasing by the decade right now [+0.5 contextual], more and more legislative authority is delegated to the executive branch every year [+1]." Furthermore, he used very little repetition, making only one repetitive point. Repetition isn't a bad thing. On the contrary, it can be beneficial. It doesn't do much for substance score, however. Especially when the ideas in a speech are presented as clearly as they were in this segment of Ben Sasse's statement, there's no need for repetition. Lastly, Ben Sasse also presented his information in a very logical way, by listing his main points: "Number one [..]. Number two [..]. The third consequence [..]. and fourth and finally." This strategy not only makes the information easier to grasp and understand cohesively, but increases substance score by preventing words from being spent on transitions.

Using these methods to maximize the substance of your speech is helpful if it's a speech solely designed to inform. Some scenarios require a little more finesse, but these strategies are still extremely powerful. In some scenarios, style is king. In other scenarios, however, efficiency is king.

One final strategy to sound very substantive as a speaker is to remove unnecessary words. For example, consider this segment from Carter's speech: "We can also have a – an end to the extremes. We now have one extreme for instance, of some welfare recipients, who by taking advantage of the welfare laws, the housing laws, the uh – Medicaid uh – laws, and the uh – food stamp laws, make over $10 thousand a year [+1] and uh – they don't have to pay any taxes on it [+1]. At the other extreme, uh – just 1 percent of the richest people in our country derive 25 percent of all the tax benefits [+1]."

This segment uses 86 words to convey three main pieces of information. Therefore, it has a substance score of 0.035. If we take out the superfluous words, and replace certain phrases with shorter phrases or single words, it becomes significantly more substantive:

"We can end the extremes. One extreme is welfare recipients taking advantage of the welfare, housing, Medicaid, and food stamp laws, making over $10 thousand a year [+1] that goes untaxed [+1]. The other extreme is that 1 percent of the richest people in our country derive 25 percent of all the tax benefits [+1]."

This shortened segment uses just 55 words to convey the same three main pieces of information. It has a substance score of 0.054. Some unnecessary words and phrases had to be cut out completely, while others were simply condensed. Without a doubt, it could still be condensed even further. A superfluous word or phrase is one that can be removed or altered without the pieces of information being altered in any way. Of course, it's not always beneficial to aim solely for efficiency, but if you decide that efficiency is the best goal for a certain situation, now you know how to achieve it.

KEY INSIGHT:

Dense Speech Sounds Commanding and Authoritative.

Perfection Is What's Left When You Take Everything Unnecessary Away.

Make Your Point Clearly, Concisely, and Simply: A Straight Line, A to B to C, Wasting No Words, With No Meandering.

REVEALING A COMMUNICATION EQUATION: SUBSTANCE

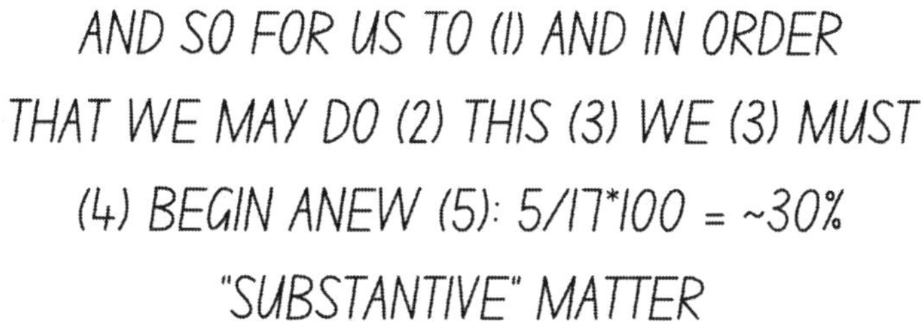

AND SO FOR US TO (1) AND IN ORDER
THAT WE MAY DO (2) THIS (3) WE (3) MUST
(4) BEGIN ANEW (5): 5/17*100 = ~30%
"SUBSTANTIVE" MATTER

FIGURE 74: You can apply the substance equation at the level of any unit of meaning. Divide the number of substantive words by the number of words.

VISUALIZING PUNCHY, FOCUSED SPEAKING

WE MUST START AND BEGIN ANEW
5/6 SUBSTANTIVE

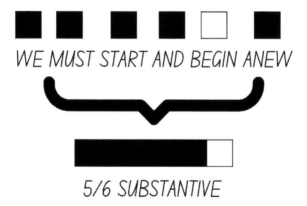

FIGURE 75: This is another way to visualize the concept of substance, or meaning-saturation.

There is a French phrase called *"langue de bois"*, which roughly translates to "language of the woods" because it serves to obscure rather than clarify a message. This phrase has been used to characterize a type of empty, meaningless language that is full of ambiguity and is incredibly vague. The closest phrases we have in English are "empty talk" and "wooden language."

Avoid *"langue de bois"* at all costs. Politicians have been forced to adapt and learn how to maximize substance when speaking with no preparation. This is a skill that comes only with practice, and can be difficult at first. However, it's fairly easy to maximize substance when writing and memorizing a speech. In this scenario, you have the benefit of being able to rewrite, rephrase, and reshape your speech in order to maximize the value of the substance equation.

You shouldn't immediately aim to increase your substance score. Some situations demand a more moderate balance between substance and style, although there is a no-nonsense style associated with highly substantive statements like the one made by Ben Sasse.

NOVELTY

The vast majority of professionally edited, viral YouTube videos have a common characteristic: transitions are rapid, immediately shifting from one scene to another. People who make videos of them speaking even sometimes cut the pauses between their sentences, resulting in a rapid-fire barrage of new information. These are called jump cuts. Don't mistake this lesson for not pausing between sentences. On the contrary, the important lesson to learn from those YouTube videos is to present a refreshing novelty of information.

Why can people scroll for hours on social networking sites such as Instagram? Because with every flick of the thumb, there is a new novelty presented. We always crave new information.

As Donald Draper, the main character of the highly acclaimed show *Mad Men* once said: "the most important word in advertising is new." In public speaking, a powerful gift from you to your audience is something new: something unfamiliar to them, and something you haven't already told them. Everyone appreciates the speaker who gives them the most comprehensive information, especially if it is new and can give them a competitive advantage in life.

Our attention spans (on a micro-scale) have apparently dropped from 12 seconds to 8 since the dawn of the internet age. So, if there's one lesson public speakers can gain from electronic media such as YouTube videos and Instagram feeds, which have experienced astounding success at gaining the attention of a global audience, let it be this: present new and exciting information rapidly.

Take this book, for example. You might have realized that the information being packed into short, succinct, and straightforward subsections makes it more pleasurable to read for prolonged periods of time. Would it be the same if it was just one long, winding narrative? No, nor would it be as effective at giving you the information.

Frequently, public speakers make the mistake of exhausting an idea or train of thought and then continuing to spend time going deeper and deeper, chasing miniscule detail that do not support the big picture. Meanwhile, their audience is growing restless. It's better to properly deliver three points and to convey the big picture idea behind them then it is to fully exhaust one point in the same amount of time. Why? Because the minute detail will be forgotten, and your audience will lose interest if you keep talking about an idea you've already presented sufficiently. Keep it exciting, and keep it new.

There's a theory of diminishing returns with finances: it states that more money will make you happier until a certain point (75,000 a year is the common estimate). After this point, diminishing returns occur: the same amount of money provides less happiness. Adding 75,000 dollars, and doubling the yearly income does not double the happiness. The same applies to information. Up until a certain point, more information does help increase audience understanding of the main message and the big picture idea. After a certain point, more information becomes dilatory and doesn't provide the same return on investment.

A good analogy is this: the information in your speech is a coral reef, and you want to show it to an audience of tourists. Do you take them out on a jet ski and skim the surface of the water above the reef? No. Do you buy a deep-sea drilling rig and dig hundreds of meters into the Earth to show them the different coral layers? No. You take them for a nice scuba dive, moving quickly along but slowly enough for them to take it all in.

Don't spend too much time on one idea: provide a novelty of ideas to your audience, and keep them engaged by doing so.

REFRESHER PHRASES

Depending on the structure, content, and purpose of your speech, you might find it difficult to provide novelty to your audience. Here's the solution: one way to maintain a sense of novelty throughout your speech is to use refresher phrases. Refresher phrases are a special type of transition in your speech that function like jump cuts in videos. They reset your audience's attention spans and are used to segue into a new idea. Here's the thing: I used one previously in the "refresher phrases" section. Can you find it? It's "here's the solution." In fact, "here's the thing" is one too.

The technique of refresher phrases originated when copywriters in charge of writing the sales copy on sales brochures found out that phrases like these can keep someone reading. For example, when I wrote "here's the solution," it's only logical that you read further with renewed attention, because you want the solution.

Since copywriters who worked in advertising found that these refresher phrases worked in sales copy, they have been adapted to other forms of written media as well. Want to know the best part? Using them in a public speech can be very effective as well.

Here's an example of a segment from a climatologist's speech without refresher phrases: "It is now estimated that we have only 12 years to begin to reverse the effects of man-made climate change. Is that a reliable estimate? Yes, it is an estimate produced by several government agencies working together. We can stop climate change if we put our best efforts towards it. If we all make some small changes in our daily lives, like carpooling and recycling, it can make a significant difference. Also, if we begin pressuring our government to restrict the carbon output of factories, we can slowly work towards a healthier, safer planet. We caused climate change, so we can stop it."

Now, here's the same segment with refresher phrases included. You'll notice how the refresher phrases also act as transitions: "Here's the scary part: it is now estimated that we have only 12 years to begin to reverse the effects of man-made climate change.

You might be wondering: is that a reliable estimate? Here's the answer: yes, it is an estimate produced by several government agencies working together. But there's good news: we can stop climate change if we put our best efforts towards it. Here's how: if we all make some small changes in our daily lives, like carpooling and recycling, it can make a significant difference. Also, if we begin pressuring our government to restrict the carbon output of factories, we can slowly work towards a healthier, safer planet. The bottom line is this: we caused climate change, so we can stop it."

VISUALIZING HOW TO CAPTURE ATTENTION WITH EASE

BUCKET BRIGADE

FIGURE 76: Bucket brigades are captivating transitions that serve to "pass" attention from sentence to sentence or slide to slide without dropping it.

Do you see how refresher phrases can keep audience attention spans active by rapidly renewing their interest? In most cases, you don't need to use this many refresher phrases to achieve the desired effect of producing a sense of novelty. If you achieve the right balance between depth and breadth of information, meaning that you cover just the right amount of new information and cover it to just the right level of detail, then refresher phrases are less necessary. However, if there is a big block of your speech that has little natural novelty, it can be a good idea to include refresher phrases.

POSITIVE AND INCLUSIVE LANGUAGE

Another key subtlety for you to master, one tied closely to word choice and diction, is the use of positive and inclusive language. This is an example: "The future can still be bright; we just have to make it so. We can seize control of our planet's future if we seek the right changes in the way we live today."

People will always respond to a speech if it gives them a glimmer of hope as opposed to one which simply lays out an unfortunate situation.

Now what about inclusive language? Inclusive language is saying "we" or "us," instead of "you" or "I." Paint yourself as being in the same boat as your audience members, and they will find you infinitely more relatable. This is particularly important in the case of election related speeches, when it is important to gain people's faith and trust.

An example of inclusive language is instead of saying "You all struggle because of rising taxes," saying "We all struggle because of unfairly high taxes." The second sentence is inclusive because it replaces "You" with "We," and describes the taxes the way the audience in this situation likely perceives them (as unfair) to add another layer of genuine relatability. Using inclusive language goes a long way in portraying yourself as a leader and as someone who understands and empathizes with your audience. Don't use exclusive language, like "me and you," when you can use inclusive pronouns instead.

In a debate between George W. Bush and Bill Clinton, when asked a question regarding how the national debt had affected them in their lives, Bush stuttered in response and answered quite coldly and without emotion, within the one-yard radius around his stool and podium. Clinton, on the other hand, left his podium and advanced towards the audience. He made eye contact, intensely narrowed his eyes, and described with highly inclusive language how the national debt has affected all Americans including himself. This is what happened at the famous debate moment between Bush and the audience, stutters included.

Audience member: "How has the national debt personally affected each of your lives and if it hasn't how can you honestly find a cure for the economic problems of the common people if you have no experience in what's ailing them?"

Bush: "Well I think the national debt affects everybody, uh, obviously it has a lot to do with interest rates, it has –"

Moderator: "She's saying you personally."

Audience member: "Yes, on a personal basis, how has it affected *you?*"

Bush: "Well, I'm sure it has, I love my grandchildren, I want to think that – "

Audience member: *"How?"*

Bush: "I want to think that they're going to be able to afford an education, I think that that's an important part of being a parent – I, if the question, if you're sa – maybe I won't get it wrong, are you suggesting that if somebody has means, that the national debt doesn't affect them?"

Audience member: "Well what I'm saying is – "

Bush: "I – I'm not sure I get it, help me with the question and I'll try to answer."

Audience member: "Well I have friends that have been laid off from jobs."

Bush: "Yeah

Audience member: "I know people who cannot afford to pay the mortgage on their homes, their car payment, I have personal – "

Bush: "Yeah"

Audience member: "– problems with the national debt, but how has it affected you? And if you have no experience in it, how can you help us? If you don't know what we're feeling?"

Moderator: "I think she means more the recession, the economic problems today the country faces rather than the national debt"

Bush: "Well listen, you oughta, you oughta be in the white house for a day and hear what I hear and see what I see and read the mail I read, and touch the people that I touch from time to ti – I was in the low max, AME church, it's a black church, just outside of Washington D.C., and I read in the bulletin, about teenage pregnancies, about the difficulty that families are having to meet ends – make ends meet, I've talked to parents. I mean, you've gotta care. Everybody cares if people aren't doing well. But I don't think, I don't think it's fair to say you haven't had cancer therefore you don't know what it's like. I don't think it's fair, uhh, you know whatever it is that you haven't been hit by personally, but everybody's affected by the debt, because of the tremendous interest that goes into paying on that debt, everything's more expensive, everything comes out of your pocket and my pocket, so it's, it's set, but I think in terms of the recession, of course you feel it when you're the president of the United States, that's why I'm trying to do something about it by stimulating the export, investing more, better education system. Thank you, I'm glad to clarify."

Now Clinton, in response to the same question with stutters included.

Clinton: "Tell me how it's affected you again?"

Audience member: "Uhm..."

Clinton: "You know people who've lost their jobs –"

Audience member: "Well yeah"

Clinton: "And lost their homes?"

Audience member: "Mhm"

Clinton: "Well, I've been governor of a small state for 12 years. I'll tell you how it's affected me personally. Every year, congress – and the president sign laws that makes us – make us do more things and gives us less money to do it with. I see people in my state, middle class people; their taxes have gone up in Washington and their services have gone down, while the wealthy have gotten tax cuts. I have seen what's happened in this last four years, when – in my state, when people lose their jobs there's a good chance I'll know em' by their names. When a factory closes, I know the people who ran it. When the businesses go bankrupt, I know them. And I've been out here for thirteen months, meeting in meetings just like this ever since October, with people like you all over America; people that have lost their jobs, lost their livelihoods, lost their health insurance. What I want you to understand is, the national debt is not the only cause of that. It is because America has not invested in its people; it is because we have not grown; it is because we've had twelve years of trickle-down economics. We've gone from first to twelfth in the world in wages, we've had four years when we produced no private sector jobs, most people are working harder for less money than they were making ten years ago. It is because we are in the grip of a failed economic theory. And this decision you're about to make better be about what kind of economic theory you want; not just people saying I wanna go fix it, but what are we going to do! What I think we have to do is invest in American jobs, American education, control American healthcare costs, and bring the American people together again."

Do you see the difference? It's huge. What happened at that town hall debate connects so many aspects of this book, from the basic public speaking triad to eye contact, facial expression, and so much more you will learn in the Use of Voice, Use of Body, and Aspects of Delivery sections. Let's take a much deeper analysis of the speeches:

Audience member: "How has the national debt personally affected each of your lives and if it hasn't how can you honestly find a cure for the economic problems of the common people if you have no experience in what's ailing them?"

[Audience member is seeking information and a connection to the speaker. She was already connected to the idea; she may not have thought of it this way, but what the candidates were prompted to do by her question was to connect themselves to her and to the idea].

Bush: "Well I think the national debt affects everybody, uh, obviously it has a lot to do with interest rates, it has –"

[Bush starts off on the wrong foot by not directly addressing the question, which the moderator points out. He is lacking a connection to both the idea and the audience member at this point].

Moderator: "She's saying you personally."

[Need of the moderator to clarify emphasizes the broken public speaking triad: the speaker and the audience member are disconnected].

Audience member: "Yes, on a personal basis, how has it affected you?"

[Audience member tries to form the connection to the speaker again and prompts the speaker to connect himself to the idea which she feels connected to].

Bush: "Well, I'm sure it has, I love my grandchildren, I want to think that –"

[Bush struggles to form the connection to the idea, and chooses a very non-compelling example. He doesn't use any inclusive language either].

Audience member: "How?"

[Audience member, once again, tries to make the connection].

Bush: "I want to think that they're going to be able to afford an education, I think that that's an important part of being a parent – I, if the question, if you're sa – maybe I won't get it wrong, are you suggesting that if somebody has means, that the national debt doesn't affect them?"

[Bush continues struggling trying to connect himself to the idea and audience member; the public speaking triad remains broken, and he employs little to no inclusive language to try to reconnect it].

Audience member: "Well what I'm saying is –"

[Audience member tries rephrasing, and Bush interrupts].

Bush: "I – I'm not sure I get it, help me with the question and I'll try to answer."

[Bush, instead of finding a way to connect himself to the audience member and to the idea, asks her to rephrase the question even though she already made it clear several times].

Audience member: "Well I have friends that have been laid off from jobs."

[She tries to prod for a connection here].

Bush: "Yeah"

[Bush attempts a filler word, which doesn't sound good at this particular moment].

Audience member: "I know people who cannot afford to pay the mortgage on their homes, their car payment, I have personal –"

[She continues trying to prod for a connection both between herself and Bush, and Bush and the idea of the national debt and its impact on each candidate].

Bush: "Yeah"

[Another filler word].

Audience member: "– problems with the national debt, but how has it affected you? And if you have no experience in it, how can you help us? If you don't know what we're feeling?"

[Bush still did not find a way to connect himself to the speaker and to the idea].

Moderator: "I think she means more the recession, the economic problems today the country faces rather than the national debt"

[Moderator facilitating the connection between speaker, idea, and audience member emphasizes the broken public speaking triad yet again].

Up until this point, what is most evident is simply a broken public speaking triad. The lack of inclusive, relatable, and positive language becomes more evident once Bush picks a direction:

Bush: "Well listen, you oughta, you oughta be in the white house for a day [Bush attempts a very non-inclusive and non-relatable response: how can the audience member relate to what's going on in the white house?] and hear what I hear and see what I see and read the mail I read, and touch the people that I touch from time to time. [Bush finally begins to describe his personal experiences with the national debt, but once again struggles to make a deliberate connection between himself and the idea, and abruptly shifts approaches] – I was in the low max, AME church, it's a black church, just outside of Washington D.C., and I read in the bulletin, about teenage pregnancies, about the difficulty that families are having to meet ends – make ends meet, I've talked to parents [The audience member is likely thinking "Okay, but what does that have to do with you? You've interacted with people affected by the national debt, but how does that deliberately connect you to it?" This is barely inclusive]. I mean, you've gotta care. Everybody cares if people aren't doing well [Again, the question doesn't have to do with how everybody has been affected, but how Bush has been affected]. But I don't think, I don't think it's fair to say you haven't had cancer therefore you don't know what it's like [Non-inclusive language that alienates the audience member even further from Bush by saying her question was unfair]. I don't think it's fair, uhh, you know whatever it is that you haven't been hit by personally, but everybody's affected by the debt ["Everybody" is a poor substitute for the much more inclusive and personal pronoun "we." Bush was unable to do the most important thing at this point: framing the issue as something directly inclusive (a "we problem") instead of as something remotely inclusive (an "everybody problem")]. because of the tremendous interest that goes into paying on that debt, everything's more expensive, everything comes out of your pocket and my pocket [Instead of emphasizing the separation between "your pocket" and "my pocket," why not say "our pockets"?], so it's, it's set, but I think in terms of the recession, of course you feel it when you're the president of the United States [Very non-inclusive: how can the audience member possibly relate to being the president?], that's why I'm trying to do something about it by stimulating the export, investing more, better education system. Thank you, I'm glad to clarify."

Bush's response suffered from a broken public speaking triad and an absence of relatable, inclusive language. Not only that, but the initial confusion and lack of connection between him, the idea, and the audience member threw him off. When he finally got on track, he was not quite as eloquent as he may have otherwise been. Clinton does not repeat Bush's mistakes:

Clinton: "Tell me how it's affected you again?"

[He starts off on the right foot. Clinton, at this point, was trying to re-identify the connection between audience member and idea, so that he could present to her a similar connection between himself and the idea].

Audience member: "Uhm…"

[Audience member is evidently caught off guard by the sudden connection to the speaker, after a few minutes when it was absent with the previous speaker].

Clinton: "You know people who've lost their jobs – "

[Clinton notices her off-guardedness, and lends a helping hand, bolstering the speaker to audience connection yet further].

Audience member: "Well yeah"

[Clinton gets the audience member agreeing with him, even on a matter of clarification, right off the bat].

Clinton: "And lost their homes?"

[He continues by saying what the audience member was likely thinking. This goes a very long way to developing the speaker to audience connection].

Audience member: "Mhm"

[The speaker to audience connection is complete at this point. Clinton made it clear that unlike Bush, he understands her situation very well. He proceeds, with this clear understanding of her situation, to relate himself to it in an inclusive and relatable way].

Clinton: "Well, I've been governor of a small state for 12 years. [Clinton keeps the background information concise, but also subtly draws attention to his experience]. I'll tell you how it's affected me personally. [He immediately commits himself to answering her question clearly and unambiguously]. Every year, congress – and the president sign laws that makes us [us, not me] – make us do more things and gives us [us, not me] less money to do it with. I see people in my state, middle class people; their taxes have gone up in Washington and their services have gone down, while the wealthy have gotten tax cuts. [This may be misleading: it is indeed a lot of "I." However, it is Clinton describing to the audience member how her situation has been occurring to people in his state for a very long time]. I have seen what's happened in this last four years, when – in my state, when people lose their jobs there's a good chance I'll know em' by their names. When a factory closes, I know the people who ran it. When the businesses go bankrupt, I know them. [This is perhaps the best example of Clinton's mastery of inclusive language. He is saying in a very compelling way, that "I know people just like you in my state. I have spent the past 12 years working to help them. I have, every day, seen people affected by this, and because I am their governor, I was affected by it myself."] And I've been out here for thirteen months, meeting in meetings just like this ever since October, with people like you all over America; people that have lost their jobs, lost their livelihoods, lost their health insurance. [Highly inclusive once again: he makes a clear effort to describe some of the struggles people are facing. Some of the very struggles she identified in her question]. What I want you to understand is, the national debt is not the only cause of that. [He pivots after connecting himself to the speaker and to the idea. This speech is technically one to inform and persuade, and now that he completed the public speaking triad, he begins working to accomplish those goals]. It is because America has not invested in its people; it is because *we* [directly inclusive language] have not grown; it is because *we've* had twelve years of trickle-down economics. *We've* gone from first to twelfth in the world in wages, *we've* had four years when *we* produced no private sector jobs, most people are working harder for less money than they were making ten years ago. It is because *we* are in the grip of a failed economic theory. And this decision you're about to make better be about what kind of economic theory you want; not just people sayin' I wanna go fix it, but what are *we* going to do! What I think *we* have to do is invest in American jobs, American education, control American healthcare costs, and bring the American people together again. [more directly inclusive language, also ending on a very positive note]."

Let's compare Bush and Clinton's approaches. From the start, the audience member was connected to the idea: struggling economically due to the national debt. The sentiment of her question, then, was essentially: "Which candidate can better connect to me and my struggles due to the national debt?"

Bush did not connect to her and her struggles. Clinton methodically connected himself to the audience member, and then proceeded to connect himself to the idea. In doing so, he completed the public speaking triad. Inclusive and relatable language is one of the biggest tools he used to establish these connections.

In the larger segment of Bush's speech, when he finally got his footing, he used *only two* vaguely inclusive and relatable statements: "I was in the low max, AME church, it's a black church, just outside of Washington D.C., and I read in the bulletin, about teenage pregnancies, about the difficulty that families are having to meet ends – make ends meet, I've talked to parents...," and "everything comes out of your pocket and my pocket." Clinton, on the other hand, used 13 highly inclusive and relatable statements. Additionally, Clinton ended on a very positive note: that of bringing the American people together again. Bush didn't end on a negative note, but not on a particularly positive one either.

Above and beyond inclusive language, Clinton was suave, spoke eloquently, had intense stage presence, and made use of at least 57 of the public speaking principles shared in this book.

Who do you think got that lady's vote? Who do you think got the votes of a large group of Americans who felt the same way as her, and had the same question? It was probably the same candidate who won that election by six million votes. Bill Clinton.

SALIENCY, INTENSITY, AND STABILITY

Every single statement has three qualities: saliency, intensity, and stability. Every statement has these qualities in varying amounts, and the most compelling statements have the most of all of them.

Saliency refers to how many people care about a given subject, or in other words, how important a given subject is. It is the portion of the population that cares about something. Intensity is a measure of how strongly people care about a subject. It is a measure of how much energy people are willing to devote towards one topic. Stability is how long people are willing to continue caring about a given subject, or how easy it is to switch the opinions of those who do care about a given subject.

In summary, saliency is how many people care, intensity is how much they care, and stability is for how long they will care.

UNVEILING SALIENCY, INTENSITY, AND STABILITY

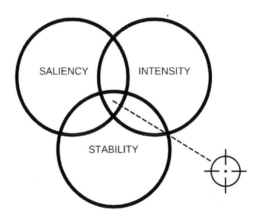

FIGURE 77: Saliency is how many people care about a given subject, intensity is how strongly they care about it, and stability is for how long they have and how long they will continue to care about it. The most powerful messages speak about subjects that are salient, intense, and stable. This is another Venn-diagram framework.

Because saliency, intensity, and stability are not intuitive concepts, here's another helpful way to think about them: saliency is how important a topic is, intensity is how important it is to those who think it's important, and stability is for how long it will be important to those who think it's important.

Every compelling subject or statement is salient, intense, and stable: by combining these three qualities, you can maximize the chance that what you're saying will have an impact on your audience and that they will tune in. In many cases, however, your topic might not be salient, intense, or stable. In this case, the best strategy is to find the most salient, intense, and stable consequences of what you're speaking about and deliberately connect them to your subject.

Everything of impact occurring in the real world has consequences and is connected to other occurrences. Many topics are part of an interconnected web, in which everything impacts everything else in one way or another.

By tapping into and connecting your subject to another one which is more salient, intense, and stable, you gain the very useful benefit of speaking in terms of something which most people in your audience will care about, which they will care about strongly, and which they will continue caring about long after you finish your speech. Stability is particularly important: stability is essentially the longevity of concern, interest, or relevance your ideas have to your audience. If they only care about what you're saying when you're saying it, and not after or even before you've said it, that's obviously not a good situation. Avoid this by connecting your idea to something you know your audience will care about in the long run.

As you can see from the chart, and as any career politician will vehemently assert, the economy is the most salient, intense, and stable issue. People will vote for a candidate who has a disappointing personal track record if they believe that he or she will lower their taxes. People love money. It's that simple. In order for our climatologist to tap into the salient, intense, and stable nature of how the general population thinks about the economy, money, and personal finance, they can say something like this: "To my understanding, people usually don't realize how expensive climate change will be. It's not their fault, of course, but let me illuminate some numbers. The federal government as well as state governments across the country will have to increase taxes in order to deal with the consequences of climate change, so the average increase in taxes per person can be up to $1,000 annually. Similarly, if you live close to a coast, lake, or major river, you might have to pay up to $10,000 to protect your house from flooding caused by climate change."

It might make you cynical to think that money is high on the list of what people care about, but it shouldn't. It makes sense that it is, so use it to your advantage.

Think of these three qualities as a three-way Venn-diagram. In other words think of them as three circles that each overlap each other. Something can be in only one circle, in two circles, or in the center where they all overlap and it is enclosed by all three circles. The more circles your subject and theme are enclosed by, the more interested in your speech your audience will be. If your subject either ends up in the middle of that diagram, or you can find a logical connection that brings it there, then your persuasive power will be maximized.

PERMISSION, CONSENSUS, AND DIVISION

As with all things, there are pros and cons: if your topic is salient, intense, and stable, that's generally a very good thing. But, if this is the case, then you'll find that it might be more difficult to sway people from one side of a debate to another. Here's where the ideas of permission, consensus, and division come into play.

It is said that a topic is "permissive" if it is easy to sway public opinion on that subject.

It is said that a topic has "consensus" if many people agree on it. It is hard to completely sway public opinion if everyone agrees for or against something, and if you challenge the consensus.

It is said that a topic is "divisive" if public opinion is split in half. It is hard to completely sway public opinion in this case, but if a topic is divisive, it generally splits public opinion into two opposing camps, with a small minority of people in the center. In this case, it may be hard to completely sway public opinion, but the goal is only to increase the size of the side you are on.

These three ideas relate back to saliency, intensity, and stability in an interesting way.

If a topic has consensus, it likely has high saliency, intensity, and stability, because the vast majority of people care about something, because they care about it strongly, and because they are willing to care about it for a long time.

If a topic is divisive, it also likely has high saliency, intensity, and stability, because while people are indeed divided into two opposing groups, if they are willing to be divided by a topic, it must be salient, intense, and stable. The opposing sides might disagree with each other on the topic, but they both agree that the topic is important.

If a topic is permissive, this can actually be an advantage. Indeed, a permissive topic likely has low saliency, intensity, and stability, which is normally bad. However, if a topic has low saliency, intensity, and stability, it is a blank slate. This means that it is easy for you to create your own saliency, intensity, and stability in your audience for the subject. Because it is permissive (which it is because it has low saliency, intensity, and stability), you can focus instead on developing those three qualities in your audience, and not only that, but focus on doing so in the direction that you want to.

If something has consensus, you can become very popular by echoing that consensus. It will be more difficult to challenge that consensus, however. Challenge it if you want to, but be prepared to do so with more persuasive calculation.

If something is divisive, be prepared to have some dissenting opinions in the audience. Once again, as with challenging a consensus, don't let this change your course, just plan accordingly.

If something is permissible, however, it is an empty white paper for your audience, and you are the pen. Saliency, stability, and intensity are one form of power. The absence of them, which usually suggests that a topic is permissible, is another form of power.

The power drawn from saliency, stability, and intensity is that the vast majority of the people are interested in the topic you are speaking about, either because they are all in consensus, or because they all have some strong opinion about it because it is divisive.

The power drawn from a permissive topic is that you can focus on inducing saliency, stability, and intensity in your audience, and doing so in whatever manner you want.

If you don't believe that your topic is salient, intense, or stable, rest assured. Maybe people don't think it's important *yet*. Your goal, then, is to make them realize how important it really is.

THEME AND SUBJECT

A theme is what makes a speech impactful. Of course, any given speech has a subject as its focus. A speech about climate change is not a speech with a theme of climate change, however. The subject of that speech is climate change, but there are many possible themes that could match with that subject.

A subject is what a speech is actually about, while a theme is a different perspective from which to view that subject. Think of a speech's subject as what you are photographing, and your theme as different camera angles, filters, and brightness settings. The subject is always the same, but theme is what highlights different aspects of it over others, views it from a different perspective, and changes the overall perception of it. A subject is what you are showing your audience, while your theme is the lens you are showing it through. A subject can often be identified by the title of a speech, while a theme can be found by asking of the title: "what about it?"

Almost all famous speeches have in them, at one point or another, a segment where the theme and the subject are in very strong sync. That's not a coincidence. There's something particularly satisfying and meaningful about a speech that approaches a subject with just the right theme. Keep in mind that while speeches should have one main theme, they can have sub-themes that blur in and out of focus as the speech progresses.

Let's examine a segment from the following speech given by a man named Lou Gehrig. He was a first baseman for the Yankees who was beloved and nicknamed the Iron Horse for his dedication to the sport. At age 36, when he seemed unstoppable, and when he was pushing the bounds of achievement in baseball, he was diagnosed with a crippling disease. On July 4, 1939, there was a ceremony in his honor, at which he gave a speech. This speech would go down in history as one of the greatest speeches ever delivered: "Fans, for the past two weeks you have been reading about a bad break I got. Yet today I consider myself the luckiest man on the face of the earth. I have been in ballparks for seventeen years and have never received anything but kindness and encouragement from you fans. Look at these grand men. Which of you wouldn't consider it the highlight of his career to associate with them for even one day? Sure, I'm lucky. Who wouldn't consider it an honor to have known Jacob Ruppert – also the builder of baseball's greatest empire, Ed Barrow – to have spent the next nine years with that wonderful little fellow Miller Huggins – then to have spent the next nine years with that outstanding leader, that smart student of psychology – the best manager in baseball today, Joe McCarthy! Sure, I'm lucky. When the New York Giants, a team you would give your right arm to beat, and vice versa, sends you a gift, that's something! When everybody down to the groundskeepers and those boys in white coats remember you with trophies, that's something. When you have a wonderful mother-in-law who takes sides with you in squabbles against her own daughter, that's something. When you have a father and mother who work all their lives so that you can have an education and build your body, it's a blessing! When you have a wife who has been a tower of strength and shown more courage than you dreamed existed, that's the finest I know. So I close in saying that I might have had a tough break – but I have an awful lot to live for!"

The subject of the speech is the incredibly unfortunate circumstance that befell him. The theme is what makes it so incredible. There is something truly moving about the fact that he was able to view the subject (the unfortunate circumstance) through a lens of gratitude. That was exactly the theme of the speech: gratitude.

Now, let's examine a segment of William Faulkner's Nobel Prize acceptance speech. In terms of historical context, this speech was given in 1950, when the Soviet Union unlocked the potential of the nuclear bomb. The ensuing intellectual environment in the United States was fearful, cynical, and preoccupied with questions of nuclear death. Pay close attention to Faulkner's acceptance speech, and see if you can identify the subject and the theme: "I decline to accept the end of man. It is easy enough to say that man is immortal because he will endure: that when the last ding-dong of doom has clanged and faded from the last worthless rock hanging tideless in the last red and dying evening, that even then there will still be one more sound: that of his puny inexhaustible voice, still talking. I refuse to accept this. I believe that man will not merely endure: he will prevail. He is immortal, not because he alone among creatures has an inexhaustible voice, but because he has a soul, a spirit capable of compassion and sacrifice and endurance. The poet's, the writer's, duty is to write about these things. It is his privilege to help man endure by lifting his heart, by reminding him of the courage and honor and hope and pride and compassion and pity and sacrifice which have been the glory of his past. The poet's voice need not merely be the record of man, it can be one of the props, the pillars to help him endure and prevail."

The subject is, in a word, humanity. Sure, you can describe it in more than a word: it could be "the current literary discourse," "the nuclear bomb preoccupying literature," "human nature in the face of adversity," etc. There really are multiple possibilities, but sometimes to identify the subject or theme, you have to zoom out and broaden your scope to a single, all-encompassing word. In this case, humanity encompasses each of the previous possibilities. As for the theme, we can see that Faulkner tries to approach the subject (whether it's simply "humanity," or "contemporary literary cynicism") from a place of optimism. That's the theme: optimism and hope. Indeed, the most powerful themes are positive: gratitude, optimism, and hope are all examples of that trend.

KEY INSIGHT:

If You Are Talking About America, Your Theme Is Not "America." Your Theme Is the Conceptual Lens Through Which You Talk About America. It Could Be Opportunity, Change, Freedom, Or Virtue.

DON'T CONFUSE THEMES AND SUBJECTS

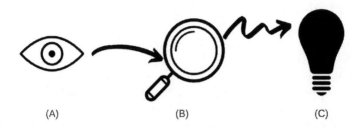

(A)   (B)   (C)

FIGURE 78: People perceive (A), through the lens of a theme (B), your subject (C). The theme is like a lens or a filter, impacting their perception of the subject.

THE SUBJECT, LENS, METAPHOR FRAMEWORK

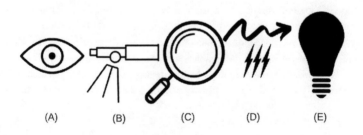

(A)   (B)   (C)   (D)   (E)

FIGURE 79: The subject, lens, metaphor framework adds into the mix a metaphor for the theme. The audience perceives (A), through a metaphor (B), your theme (C), which impacts their perception (D) of your subject (E).

It is important to understand the difference between subject and theme, because one of the best qualities a speech can have is a subject and theme that align beautifully.

KEY INSIGHT:

We Simplify Our Mental Map of the World with Metaphors. They Compress Our Knowledge.

If X Is New to Us, But It Is Like Y In Some Significant Ways, We Deal with X As If It Were Y.

MENTAL MODEL SHIFTS AND REFRAMING

People think of the universe around them through different mental models. Indeed, the subjects taught in school are all different mental models of how the world works. Some are based in language, while others are based in mathematics. Some are based in observations of past events, while others are based in observations of scientific processes. Studies of human nature in Shakespeare's *Hamlet*, a model of parabolic motion described with a quadratic equation, a memorization of the different French Republics, or a study of energy production in plants are all different mental models that describe different aspects of the universe.

A mental model can be built, challenged, and altered in a single speech. Additionally, similar to themes, a mental model can be applied to a new concept in a new way. Let's examine a different segment of John F. Kennedy's "moon" speech: "We meet at a college noted for knowledge, in a city noted for progress, in a State noted for strength, and we stand in need of all three, for we meet in an hour of change and challenge, in a decade of hope and fear, in an age of both knowledge and ignorance. The greater our knowledge increases, the greater our ignorance unfolds. Despite the striking fact that most of the scientists that the world has ever known are alive and working today, despite the fact that this Nation's own scientific manpower is doubling every 12 years in a rate of growth more than three times that of our population as a whole, despite that, the vast stretches of the unknown and the unanswered and the unfinished still far outstrip our collective comprehension. No man can fully grasp how far and how fast we have come, but condense, if you will, the 50,000 years of man's recorded history in a time span of but a half-century. Stated in these terms, we know very little about the first 40 years, except at the end of them advanced man had learned to use the skins of animals to cover them. Then about 10 years ago, under this standard, man emerged from his caves to construct other kinds of shelter. Only five years ago man learned to write and use a cart with wheels. Christianity began less than two years ago. The printing press came this year, and then less than two months ago, during this whole 50-year span of human history, the steam engine provided a new source of power. Newton explored the meaning of gravity. Last month electric lights and telephones and automobiles and airplanes became available. Only last week did we develop penicillin and television and nuclear power, and now if America's new spacecraft succeeds in reaching Venus, we will have literally reached the stars before midnight tonight. This is a breathtaking pace, and such a pace cannot help but create new ills as it dispels old, new ignorance, new problems, new dangers. Surely the opening vistas of space promise high costs and hardships, as well as high reward. So it is not surprising that some would have us stay where we are a little longer to rest, to wait. But this city of Houston, this State of Texas, this country of the United States was not built by those who waited and rested and wished to look behind them. This country was conquered by those who moved forward – and so will space. William Bradford, speaking in 1630 of the founding of the Plymouth Bay Colony, said that all great and honorable actions are accompanied with great difficulties, and both must be enterprised and overcome with answerable courage. If this capsule history of our progress teaches us anything, it is that man, in his quest for knowledge and progress, is determined and cannot be deterred. The exploration of space will go ahead, whether we join in it or not, and it is one of the great adventures of all time, and no nation which expects to be the leader of other nations can expect to stay behind in the race for space."

Do you see what he did? He approached the subject of human progress through the theme of history. This is perhaps the finest example of a theme and subject syncing for great and memorable impact.

Mental models and themes are very similar concepts: both are perspectives from which to view a subject. What John F. Kennedy did is provide a mental model shift to his audience. The climax of this mental model shift was when he said: "no man can fully grasp how far and how fast we have come, but condense, if you will, the 50,000 years of man's recorded history in a time span of but a half-century." What came after that critical turning point in the speech (although it did come relatively early) was a masterful mental model shift. It was a moment when the audience thought: "huh, I've never looked at it like that before, but that makes perfect sense." JFK took a subject, and he applied a theme to it in such a way that he reframed the mental model for his audience members. Therein lies the power of JFK's "let's go to the moon" speech: a new frame through which to view an old subject.

Think about the word frame itself: by taking a picture frame and moving it around, you can change how a picture is seen. Of course, the original picture is still there; reframing just allows it to be seen in a different, new, and exciting way. That's not always the case: just as something can be reframed in a positive way, it can be reframed in a negative way as well.

This might seem abstract, but if you can understand framing on an intuitive, fundamental level, much of successful public speaking will be unlocked for you.

A very contemporary example of reframing was President Donald Trump's 2016 presidential campaign. Regardless of your political stance, two key examples of controlling the frame of a public speaking situation can be drawn from Trump's campaign. You may dislike his presidency and what he said in these specific cases, but try to separate the technique he used from how he used it.

Two of these examples of reframing occurred in a debate preceding the Republican primary elections. One against Marco Rubio, a senator from Florida, and one against Ted Cruz, a senator from Texas. Several Republican candidates battled it out for who could secure the Republican nomination for presidential candidacy.

This is a transcript of what occurred on that Republican primary debate stage, first between Marco Rubio and Trump. Much of this first example actually constitutes a "frame battle," as well as a highly contentious, logical-fallacy filled debate. What's worth learning from, however, is the frame battle.

Rubio: "Well, in fact, I agree we should have won and I wished we would have, but, in fact, you did criticize him for using the term 'self-deportation.' I mean, that's on the record and people can look it up right now online. But, again, I just want to reiterate, I think it's really important, this point. I think it's fine, it's an important point that you raise and we discuss on immigration. This is a big issue for Texas, a huge issue for the country. But I also think that if you're going to claim that you're the only one that lifted this [illegal immigration] into the campaign, that you acknowledge that, for example, you're only person on this stage that has ever been fined for hiring people to work on your projects illegally. You hired some workers from Poland..."

Trump: "No, no, I'm the only one on the stage that's hired people. You haven't hired anybody."

Audience: Cheers and applause.

Rubio: "In fact, some of the people..."

Trump and Rubio: [Crosstalk]

Trump: "And by the way, I've hired – and by the way, I've hired tens of thousands of people over at my job. You've hired nobody."

Rubio: "Yes, you've hired a thousand from another country..."

Trump: "You've had nothing but problems with your credit cards, et cetera. So don't tell me about that."

Rubio: "Let me just say – let me finish the statement. This is important."

Trump: "You haven't hired one person, you liar."

Rubio: "He hired workers from Poland. And he had to pay a million dollars or so in a judgment from..."

Trump: "That's wrong. That's wrong. Totally wrong."

Rubio: "That's a fact. People can look it up. I'm sure people are Googling it right now. Look it up. "Trump Polish workers," you'll see a million dollars for hiring illegal workers on one of his projects. He did it."

Audience: Cheers and applause.

Rubio: "That happened."

Trump: "I've hired tens of thousands of people over my lifetime. Tens of thousands..."

Rubio: "Many from other countries instead of hiring Americans."

Trump: "Be quiet. Just be quiet."

Audience: Cheers and applause.

Trump: "Let me talk. I've hired tens of thousands of people. He brings up something from 30 years ago, it worked out very well. Everybody was happy."

Rubio: "You paid a million dollars."

Trump: "And by the way, the laws were totally different. That was a whole different world."

Moderator: "Thank you."

Trump: "But I've hired people. Nobody up here has hired anybody."

Audience: Cheers and applause.

Do you see how the frame battle impacted the broader outcome of that debate? Do you see how Trump was able to set the frame of the debate to something that favored him? Let's dive into much deeper detail:

Rubio: "Well, in fact, I agree we should have won and I wished we would have, but, in fact, you did criticize him for using the term "self-deportation." I mean, that's on the record and people can look it up right now online. But, again, I just want to reiterate, I think it's really important, this point. I think it's fine, it's an important point that you raise and we discuss on immigration. This is a big issue for Texas, a huge issue for the country. [Up until this point, Rubio was simply wrapping up a previous point. Now, he begins setting a new frame]. But I also think that if you're going to claim that you're the only one that lifted this into the campaign, that you acknowledge that, for example, you're only person on this stage that has ever been fined for hiring people to work on your projects illegally. [That's the new frame set by Marco Rubio: the fact that Trump claims to be hard on illegal immigration, yet he once hired illegally immigrated workers for one of his projects. This is a frame beneficial to Rubio and harmful to Trump's image]. You hired some workers from Poland..."

Trump: "No, no, I'm the only one on the stage that's hired people. You haven't hired anybody."

[Instead of succumbing to the frame Rubio set, namely that Trump hired illegal workers, Trump zooms out and reframes the situation from: "Trump hired illegal workers" to "Trump is the only primary candidate who actually hired anyone in the first place." By taking control of the frame away from Rubio and setting a frame more beneficial to himself, Trump earned a few seconds of much needed audience cheers and applause].

Audience: Cheers and applause.

Rubio: "In fact, some of the people..."

Trump and Rubio: [Crosstalk]

Trump: "And by the way, I've hired – and by the way, I've hired tens of thousands of people over at my job. You've hired nobody."

[Trump set the frame in his previous statement, and immediately afterwards, he reasserts his frame. Reasserting this frame by essentially restating his previous statement might seem repetitive, but at this point it cements the frame Trump set].

Rubio: "Yes, you've hired a thousand from another country…"

[Rubio, instead of reframing the debate again, tries reasserting what has been turned into a sub-frame].

Trump: "You've had nothing but problems with your credit cards, et cetera. So don't tell me about that."

[An ad-hominem fallacy. Trump doesn't reassert the frame again: it's already set to be favorable to him].

Rubio: "Let me just say – let me finish the statement. This is important."

[Rubio is put into a situation of asking for permission to reassert his sub-frame].

Trump: "You haven't hired one person, you liar."

[Trump, in response, reasserts his frame again].

Rubio: "He hired workers from Poland. And he had to pay a million dollars or so in a judgment from…"

[Rubio attempts, yet again, to reassert his sub-frame].

Trump: "That's wrong. That's wrong. Totally wrong."

[Trump flatly claims that Rubio is factually incorrect. He's attacking Rubio's frame instead of reaffirming his because his is winning].

Rubio: "That's a fact. People can look it up. I'm sure people are Googling it right now. Look it up. "Trump Polish workers," you'll see a million dollars for hiring illegal workers on one of his projects. He did it."

[Rubio reasserts his sub-frame yet again. This time, he did it in a stronger way then he had before, and brings his frame back into the forefront of the frame battle. This earns him some cheers and applause].

Audience: Cheers and applause.

Rubio: "That happened."

Trump: "I've hired tens of thousands of people over my lifetime. Tens of thousands…"

[Trump puts his frame back on top].

Rubio: "Many from other countries instead of hiring Americans."

[Rubio, again, as he has multiple times, reasserts a sub-frame instead of reframing the debate].

Trump: "Be quiet. Just be quiet."

[Aggressive debate tactics that somehow earn him some cheers and applause].

Audience: Cheers and applause.

Trump: "Let me talk. I've hired tens of thousands of people. He brings up something from 30 years ago, it worked out very well. Everybody was happy."

[Trump targets Rubio's subframe instead of continuing to assert his].

Rubio: "You paid a million dollars."

[Another sub-frame reassertion].

Trump: "And by the way, the laws were totally different. That was a whole different world."

[Targeting Rubio's sub-frame again].

Moderator: "Thank you."

[Moderator trying to get things under control. This impact might be lost on paper transcript form, but the debate was highly contentious, with a lot of yelling and cross-talking].

Trump: "But I've hired people. Nobody up here has hired anybody."

[Trump gets the last word. What does he do with it? He reasserts his frame yet again. This frame earns him cheers and applause, especially as conveyed with the finality of how he said this past statement].

Audience: Cheers and applause.

This segment of the Republican primary debate was certainly fraught with disappointing debate tactics and yelling. Nonetheless, diving beyond that aspect of it, it constituted a frame battle that was won by Trump. Rubio was able to make nine coherent, substantial statements. One of them was setting the frame, six of them were reasserting his subframe, one of them was asking permission to do so, and the last one was a very weak subframe reassertion. Trump was able to make nine coherent, substantial statements as well. One of them was reframing the debate, four of them were reasserting his winning frame, and the other four were either attacking Rubio's subframe or attacking Rubio himself. Rubio had the first word, but he was "out-framed" by Trump and put on the defensive.

This is a transcript of what occurred between Ted Cruz and Trump during the same Republican primary. Once again, it is a "frame battle," just much shorter.

Trump: "[..]. and it scared the hell out of people, and it said the only way you clear up the violation, essentially, is to go and vote for Ted Cruz. I watched that fraudulent document, and I said it's the worst thing I've ever seen in politics. I know politicians – I know politicians, believe it or not, better than you do. And it's not good."

Cruz: "I believe it. No, no. I believe you know politicians much better than I do, because for 40 years, you've been funding liberal Democratic politicians. And by the way..."

Trump: "I funded you. I funded him. Can you believe it?"

Audience: "Cheers and applause. "

Cruz: "... the reason is – you're welcome to have the check back."

Trump: "I funded this guy. I gave him a check."

Cruz: "Yeah, you gave me $5,000."

Trump: "I gave him a check. He never funded me."

This example is similar to the last one. It is a typical frame battle. Let's look at it deeper: Trump: "[..]. and it scared the hell out of people, and it said the only way you clear up the violation, essentially, is to go and vote for Ted Cruz. I watched that fraudulent document, and I said it's the worst thing I've ever seen in politics. I know politicians – I know politicians, believe it or not, better than you do. And it's not good."

[Trump sets the frame to the fact that he knows how some politicians try to use power to gain more power or preserve existing power. He uses this frame to attack Ted Cruz's past actions].

Cruz: "I believe it. No, no. I believe you know politicians much better than I do, because for 40 years, you've been funding liberal Democratic politicians. And by the way..."

[Cruz reframes the situation to the fact that Trump has funded liberal politicians despite now running as a Republican].

Trump: "I funded you. I funded him. Can you believe it?"

[Trump, instead of reasserting what has now been rendered a subframe, escalates the frame to something that favors him and hurts Cruz. This earns him cheers and applause].

Audience: "Cheers and applause. "

Cruz: "... the reason is – you're welcome to have the check back."

[Cruz can't find a way to escalate the frame. Nor does he reaffirm his frame. Instead, he begins speaking under Trump's frame].

Trump: "I funded this guy. I gave him a check."

[Trump reaffirms his winning frame].

Cruz: "Yeah, you gave me $5,000."

[Cruz, again, can't find a way to escalate the frame. Instead, he begins speaking under Trump's frame].

Trump: "I gave him a check. He never funded me."

[Trump reaffirms his winning frame. After this, the frame battle deteriorates into more ad-hominems and personal attacks. However, the pattern remains the same].

Again, despite the ad-hominem fallacies, there are some useful techniques that can be drawn from the Republican primary debate. The first is a type of reframing known as frame escalation. You've seen it in action in the past two analyzed transcripts. This is what frame escalation looks like.

Subject: Trump hiring workers, some of which possibly illegally.

Frame one: "Trump hired illegal workers" – Frame is good for Rubio, bad for Trump

Frame two: "I'm the only person up here that's ever hired anybody, nobody else has" - Frame is good for Trump, bad for Rubio

The exact quotations that are examples of frame escalation from the previous transcripts are: "Trump: "No, no, I'm the only one on the stage that's hired people. You haven't hired anybody," and "Trump: "I funded you. I funded him. Can you believe it?"

Note that frame one and frame two aren't factually contradicting each other, although the candidates may have been. The frames are not factually contradicting each other because they are simply two different ways of viewing and interpreting the same facts. Another type of reframing is frame specification.

Person A sets frame one: the frame is favorable to person A.

Person B sets frame two: the frame is a response to person A's frame, and is contained within it.

Person A sets frame three: the frame maintains the initial frame, which was favorable to person A

There are different times when frame specification and frame escalation are useful. Frame specification is useful if you have set the frame and your opponent has succumbed to that frame. It is not changing the frame, but making it more and more specific. This is a useful tactic because a debate, argument, or any conflict of ideas is usually won by the person who set the frame that dictates the course of the debate.

Frame specification is essentially the art of keeping the scope of the conflict under the frame that is favorable to you by becoming more and more specific and preventing your opponent from using frame escalation. After a number of frame specifications, any attempt to perform frame escalation by your opponent inherently sounds like them saying "okay, you've won this one. I'm picking a new battlefront to fight on."

Frame escalation is effective if it preempts frame specification. Frame escalation is useful to gain the upper hand at the start of a conflict of ideas. The final word on framing is this: whoever controls the frame of a discourse is the one who comes out on top. Use frame escalation to gain control of the frame, and frame specification to keep control if you already have it.

Of course, we can't forget frame reassertion. This occurs when a speaker sets a frame, and then simply asserts that frame again and again as long as doing so keeps that frame on top. This is a less sophisticated, but still valid approach.

You may be wondering why this type of competitive frame setting technically falls under the topic of public speaking. Well, first of all, many public speaking scenarios are competitive. Still, competitive public speaking is not the focus of this book. The reason that competitive frame setting is worth going over is because when you are giving a speech, it is often in response to another idea, concept, or person. In this case, frame setting may not be directly competitive, meaning that escalation and specification won't be occurring in the moment back and forth between two people. On the contrary, when giving a non-competitive speech, you can be escalating or specifying a frame that is in the back of people's minds, that has been advanced by another speaker in a separate speech, or that is a generally accepted status quo.

For example, in this speech delivered in 1995 in Beijing, to the United Nations 4th World Conference on Women, Hillary Clinton uses a reframing technique despite the speech not being in competition with another speaker. This speech is often known as Women's Rights are Human Rights: "It is also a coming together, much the way women come together every day in every country. We come together in fields and factories, in village markets and supermarkets, in living rooms and board rooms. Whether it is while playing with our children in the park, or washing clothes in a river, or taking a break at the office water cooler, we come together and talk about our aspirations and concern. And time and again, our talk turns to our children and our families. However different we may appear, there is far more that unites us than divides us. We share a common future, and we are here to find common ground so that we may help bring new dignity and respect to women and girls all over the world, and in so doing bring new strength and stability to families as well. By gathering in Beijing, we are focusing world attention on issues that matter most in our lives – the lives of women and their families: access to education, health care, jobs and credit, the chance to enjoy basic legal and human rights and to participate fully in the political life of our countries. There are some who question the reason for this conference. Let them listen to the voices of women in their homes, neighborhoods, and workplaces. There are some who wonder whether the lives of women and girls matter to economic and political progress around the globe. Let them look at the women gathered here and at Huairou – the homemakers and nurses, the teachers and lawyers, the policymakers and women who run their own businesses. It is conferences like this that compel governments and peoples everywhere to listen, look, and face the world's most pressing problems. Wasn't it after all – after the women's conference in Nairobi ten years ago that the world focused for the first time on the crisis of domestic violence?"

Hillary Clinton's 1995 speech unveils yet another framing technique: frame presentation. Even if you are not speaking directly against another speaker in a debate, argument, or discussion, you can still use frame escalation, frame specification, and frame reassertion. How? All you have to do is precede the reframing by a frame presentation, a technique in which you briefly allude to another frame that you are responding to. We can see that Hillary Clinton does this quite masterfully in this particular section of the previous excerpt:

"There are some who question the reason for this conference. *[This past sentence is frame presentation of another frame held by a vaguely defined but still relevant group].* Let them listen to the voices of women in their homes, neighborhoods, and workplaces. *[This past sentence is frame escalation. She now has a frame to escalate off of and challenge because she presented it in the previous sentence].* There are some who wonder whether the lives of women and girls matter to economic and political progress around the globe. *[She expands on her previous frame presentation by exposing another facet of the opposing frame she is presenting and responding to].* Let them look at the women gathered here and at Huairou – the homemakers and nurses, the teachers and lawyers, the policymakers and women who run their own businesses. *[Once again, after presenting another aspect of an opposing frame, Hillary escalates off of it].* It is conferences like this that compel governments and peoples everywhere to listen, look, and face the world's most pressing problems. Wasn't it after all – after the women's conference in Nairobi ten years ago that the world focused for the first time on the crisis of domestic violence?"

Hillary Clinton made the techniques of frame escalation and specification relevant in a non-competitive speech. Make sure you use frame escalation, specification, reassertion, and presentation wisely.

Doing what Hillary did, namely frame presentation followed by frame escalation, makes the audience clearly understand both what you are standing for and what you are standing against. Faulkner's acceptance speech which was recently presented to you is an example of presenting a frame and then escalating the frame as well. Consider why: "I decline to accept the end of man *[presentation of an opposing frame: the frame of viewing the subject of humanity through the frame of inevitable demise].* It is easy enough to say that man is immortal because he will endure: that when the last ding-dong of doom has clanged and faded from the last worthless rock hanging tideless in the last red and dying evening, that even then there will still be one more sound: that of his puny inexhaustible voice, still talking. I refuse to accept this *[presentation of another opposing frame: that humanity will not be wiped out, but that it will barely survive].* I believe that man will not merely endure: he will prevail. He is immortal, not because he alone among creatures has an inexhaustible voice, but because he has a soul, a spirit capable of compassion and sacrifice and endurance *[frame escalation]*."

A basic pillar of Stoic philosophy is this: you cannot control what happens to you, but you can control your interpretation of what happens to you. Similarly, when giving a public speech, you cannot change the basic facts of the subject you are speaking about. To do so would be to lie. What you can do, however, is in an honest way, change the perspective through which you view the basic facts of the subject. That is an awe-inspiring power to have.

KEY INSIGHT:

Reframing Reality Isn't Hiding Reality. Reinterpreting Reality Isn't Denying It.

Frames Neither Deny nor Exist in Objective Reality. They Are What We Bring to the Picture, Altering It Without Distorting It.

Email Peter D. Andrei, the author of the Speak for Success collection and the President of Speak Truth Well LLC directly.

pandreibusiness@gmail.com

WHAT IS A FRAME?

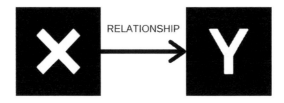

FIGURE 80: A frame consists of two items and a relationship between them: "X [insert relationship] Y."

SECOND-TIER FRAMES VISUALIZED

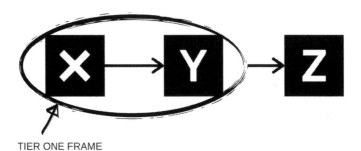

TIER ONE FRAME

FIGURE 81: "X [insert relationship] Y" is a first-tier frame; second-tier frames connect not to either X or Y, but to the first-tier frame as a whole. A second-tier frame is "Z [insert relationship] J" where Z is "X [insert relationship] Y." The expanded form is "(X [insert relationship] Y) [insert relationship] J."

ESCALATION-REFRAMING VISUALIZED

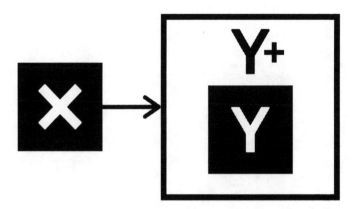

FIGURE 82: "X [insert relationship] Y" becomes "X [insert relationship] Y+." Y+ is an expanded, elevated form of Y; it is Y at a higher level of abstraction or conceptualization. Y is contained in Y+. Y+ does not factually contradict Y.

SPECIFICATION-REFRAMING VISUALIZED

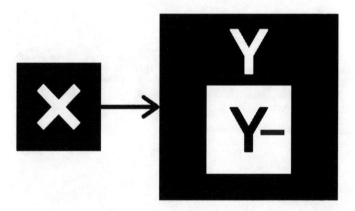

FIGURE 83: "X [insert relationship] Y" becomes "X [insert relationship] Y-." While Y+ was a zoomed-out, elevated form of Y, Y- is a zoomed-in, specified form of Y. Y- is contained in Y and Y+. Y- does not factually contradict Y or Y+.

SOFTENING AND HARDENING

There are different ways to say the same things in a softer or harder way. A softer way is more palatable, while a harder way is more shocking. There may be times when you want to make a statement softer, and in doing so, make it less jarring for the audience. Other times, it's better to make it a hard statement that grabs your audience's attention. Here's an example of a statement by a climatologist: "Climate change will hurt our existence. Climate change will make it harder to get food, harder to build structures, and harder to progress as a civilization. Storms cost money, and the government pays for them through state and federal emergency funds. But, if there are more and more storms, the government will have to tax its citizens more to pay for the damages caused by the storms."

It's fairly neutral. It isn't too soft or too hard. Here's what it would be if it were softened: "Climate change might cause some difficulties. Climate change may make it more difficult to farm, to build, and to progress. Storms can cost communities, and the government funds repairs through state and federal reserves. But, if there are more storms, the government might have to collect more money to pay for the repairs."

This statement is "softer" than the first one. Before we discuss what distinguishes how soft a statement is, consider this final statement, which is the hardened version: "Climate change will destroy us. Climate change will starve us, flood our buildings, and prevent any future progress until we solve it. Storms cost massive amounts of money, and your state governments are forced to pay for them through state and federal emergency funds. But, when there are more and more destructive storms, the government will have to tax you more and more to pay for the huge damages to your communities."

The soft one is soft because it uses a lot of words like "might," and "may," instead of "will." Similarly, it uses more abstract phrases to describe what will suffer because of climate change; our ability to "farm," "build," and "progress." Lastly, it rephrases parts that speak directly to the audience with words like "you" or "your."

Ultimately, all of these techniques used to soften a statement essentially blur out the meaning. They dilute the potency of the information. In some cases, this is beneficial. In others, however, if you want to draw attention to an issue or motivate a certain reaction in your audience, hardening your statements will make them less abstract and more concrete.

The hardened statement was made more shocking because instead of using words like "might," or "may," it used "will." Furthermore, instead of vague phrases like "some difficulties," it used phrases like "will destroy us." When discussing the struggles climate change will cause, instead of making them abstract, the hardened statement was very straightforward. It used words like "emergency" and "destructive."

To get an intuitive sense for a softened statement, a neutral statement, and a hardened statement, compare these three sentences.

HOW TO STOKE A MOTIVATIONAL INFERNO

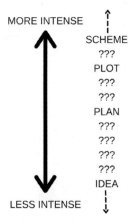

FIGURE 84: You can turn any statement into a more or less intense version of itself. There are potentially infinite positions on the spectrum.

HOW TO EASE THE PRESSURE, HOW TO RAISE IT

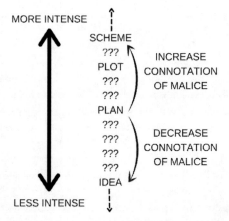

FIGURE 85: Intensity in a broader sense refers to the strength of the qualities the item displays. Terror is more intense than fear; to shred is more intense than to rip; a scheme connotes more malice than an idea.

Softened: "Climate change might cause some difficulties."
Neutral: "Climate change will hurt our existence."
Hardened: "Climate change will destroy us."

SIMPLICITY

There's beauty in simplicity. An idea presented simply is an idea long remembered by your audience. Focus on the big picture before getting into specifics, and make sure that your audience is following the progression of your speech.

WHY LESS IS OFTEN MORE IN COMMUNICATION

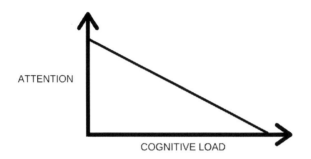

FIGURE 86: As your cognitive load rises, the attention your audience pays to your message drops.

Oftentimes, experts forget that they are speaking to an audience that isn't made up of other experts. What ensues is a situation in which the speaker describes things in the complex jargon of his or her trade, while the audience is left helplessly trying to follow along. If you are presenting a complex topic, don't make your audience feel like they are "mentally running" to keep up with you. Hold their hands and take them for a nice, gentle walk through the information instead.

There a few key considerations to remember when striving for simplicity. Firstly, if you can compress a concept without losing the nuance of it, then do so. Why express an idea in five sentences if you can do it in two or three. Secondly, do not speak in the vocabulary of your trade if you are speaking to people who have nothing to do with it. A climatologist should never say something like "As exemplified by the El Nino-Southern Oscillation and the concurrent Northern Annular Mode, we can clearly see that there's need for greater synthesis between paleoclimatology and paleotempestology." Of course, that's encouraged if the audience is made up solely of climatologists. However, if the audience isn't made up of climatologists, then the speaker shouldn't speak in terms that only another climatologist could ever understand.

Break down your speech until it is simple and easy to follow. Unless you are aiming for evocative, flowing, beautiful language, don't say more than you need to. Furthermore, don't say it in more complex words than you need to. Always keep it simple.

PRIMING

What's the purpose of a table of contents in a book? Sure, it helps you find certain sections, but that's the mainstream interpretation of why a table of contents is important. It's also important because it "primes" a reader's mind for what is coming in the book. It gets them ready to receive the coming information, and helps them identify portions of the book that they might be particularly interested in.

Similarly, priming statements in speeches go a very long way. With a priming statement, you tell your audience members what to expect: you give them a table of contents to your speech, and it builds anticipation for certain portions they might be specifically interested in. A priming statement for our climatologist could be: "Thank you for coming, everyone. Today, we're going to begin by discussing the sneaky beginnings of climate change. Then, we're going to discuss how it will impact our future. After that, we're going to start discussing solutions we can begin using in our lives to stop climate change. Lastly, I'm going to talk a little about my book on climate change."

Do you see how that can prepare the audience to receive the content of the speech? Don't spend too much time on your priming statement, but definitely include a priming statement of the broad topic and subtopics discussed in your speech. It will show your audience that they are in the right place to receive the information they want. Indeed, priming statements are best suited for informational speeches and some persuasive speeches. Speeches to inspire and entertain do not benefit from priming statements. If you are giving an informational speech, but want to build suspense for something within it, then don't give it all away in your priming statement. Instead, you can simply say something like "[..]. and then I'm going to talk about a big secret, that you'll just have to wait to hear."

Just as there shouldn't be a book without a table of contents, there shouldn't be an informational speech without a brief priming statement.

PERSONAL ANECDOTES

The pieces of timeless wisdom that have truly endured the tests of time have been those that were embedded in a story. One of the best ways to foster a connection with your audience is by sharing personal anecdotes that relate to the idea you are presenting to them. A climatologist informing an audience on climate change might say: "I was out in Alaska, and the sun was shining brightly, yet the temperature was still biting through what felt like 15 layers of clothes. My assistant kept asking that we turn back for more hand warmers, but to his dismay, we pressed on. After pawing around in the snow for what seemed like hours, we found the monitors we had planted exactly one year ago. I froze - no pun intended - when I saw the reading. The ice was warming at extreme temperatures, and the sea levels were rising because of it. My assistant kept talking to me, and I would tell you what he said, but in that moment the only thing on my mind was the thought of my coastal home being underwater within the next ten years."

HOW TO GENTLY BRING ANYONE TO YOUR POINT OF VIEW

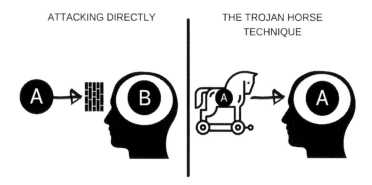

ATTACKING DIRECTLY

THE TROJAN HORSE
TECHNIQUE

FIGURE 87: Instead of approaching your persuasive prospects by flatly stating the core persuasive epiphany you would like them to adopt, embed this persuasive epiphany in a story that will give them the ingredients to experience the belief-shift themselves.

Such an anecdote accomplishes three things. Firstly, it informs the audience on the scientific process of climatology in an interesting and relatable way. Secondly, it expresses how surprising and fearsome the threat of climate change is in an indirect and engaging way because it paints a picture that shows the audience a message instead of just telling it to them flatly. Thirdly, it forms a connection between speaker and audience similar to the one between two friends telling stories about their day.

Many of the best, most accomplished speakers use personal anecdotes. They are certainly one of the best tools at your disposal.

CONTENT CONCLUSION

It's easy to forget the importance of content and words when you're reading about the public speaking techniques that come in the Use of Body and Use of Voice sections. Just remember: at the heart of every truly great speech lies truly great content. Just as a flawed delivery can ruin beautiful content, flawed content can ruin a beautiful delivery. Similar to preparation, if you feel anxious about being able to exert control of the situation when you are actually in the moment giving your speech, you still have 100% control over your content. Take advantage of that and create compelling, meaningful, and powerful content that carries true substance. Remember your toolbox? Well, content is one third of it. Your words are your power. Put your best efforts into developing the best possible content for your speech.

..................................Chapter Summary................................

- Developing your content can be an impromptu affair, or a deeply thought-out process.
- The circumstances will determine the extent to which you must deliberately plan your content.
- The best-case scenario is to master the principles of content so successfully that you can use them without preparation.
- Some elements of content refer to the psychological appeal of your message, seeking to connect it to audience desires.
- Some elements of content refer to the structure of your words themselves, and their rhythm and aesthetic force.
- Some elements of content refer to the orientation of the entire message, and how it seeks to draw the audience in.

KEY INSIGHT:

The Best Impromptu Speech Is the One You Accidentally Spent Your Whole Life Preparing For. The Best Manuscript Is the One Life Wrote on Your Soul.

If You Truly Have Something to Say, If You Spent Time Figuring Out What You Really Believe, Then Speak. Let it Flow Out.

HOW TO MASTER PUBLIC SPEAKING (PART THREE)

1	Background
1.1	Many Public Speaking Books Fail to Teach the Subject Optimally
1.2	This Book Is Designed to Correct Their Mistakes
1.3	Public Speaking is Part of the Foundation of Success
1.4	Public Speaking Will Massively Improve Your Career and Life
1.5	You Will Be More Likely to Get Hired, Promoted, and Paid More
1.6	Starting the Public Speaking Journey Demands Beating Anxiety
1.7	Public Speaking Means to Speak to 10-1,000,000,000 People
1.8	Adopting a Mental Frame of Abundance Will Improve Your Results
1.9	Multiple Opportunities Arise for Practicing the Skill: Seize Them
1.10	Vastly Different Speeches Are Similar at Their Fundamental Level
1.11	The First Type of Speech is Speaking to Inform
1.12	The Second Type of Speech is Speaking to Persuade
1.13	The Third Type of Speech is Speaking to Inspire
1.14	The Fourth Type of Speech is Speaking to Entertain
1.15	All Speeches Share Some Common Fundamentals
1.16	Most Speeches Fulfill More Than One of the Four Purposes
1.17	A Speaker Uses His Words, Body, and Voice to Convey His Message
2	Preparation
2.1	The First Determinant of Speaking Success is Confidence
2.2	Public Speaking Anxiety is Normal, Natural, and Beatable
2.3	There Are Multiple Powerful Strategies For Defeating the Anxiety

2.4	Apply Pre-Speech Relaxation Techniques to Ease the Nerves
2.5	Impromptu and Extemporaneous Speeches Call for Different Styles
2.6	Speeches Prepared Ahead of Time Offer You Time to Practice
2.7	Apply Memorization Tricks and Practice Techniques
2.8	Practice the Skill of Public Speaking Generally, Not Just For a Speech
2.9	Remember the Common Visual-Aid Mistakes
2.10	Choose Your Attire Strategically, As It Communicates Too
2.11	Apply the Principles of Effectively Using Presentation Tools
3	**Content**
3.1	The Three-Point Framework is a Versatile Speech Structure
3.2	The Purpose of the Opening is to Capture Audience Attention
3.3	Transitions Present the Connections Between Units of Meaning
3.4	A Hook is Designed Specifically to Draw People Into Your Message
3.5	The Purpose is to Get Your Audience to Follow the Call to Action
3.6	There Are Three Key Principles of Rhetoric: Ethos, Pathos, Logos
3.7	There Are Six Science-Backed Methods of Persuasion
3.8	Kairos is the Timing of Your Message, And How It Helps You
3.9	Appealing to the Core Human Drives Motivates the Audience
3.10	Using Statistics Can Be a Compelling Rhetorical Strategy
3.11	Monroe's Motivated Sequence is a Five-Step Persuasive Formula
3.12	The Informational Motivated Sequence Uses Monroe's as an Opening
3.13	The Agree, Promise, Preview Method Opens with Influence
3.14	Concessions Make You Seem Trustworthy and Objective

Claim These Free Resources that Will Help You Unleash the Power of Your Words and Speak with Confidence. Visit www.speakforsuccesshub.com/toolkit for Access.

18 Free PDF Resources

12 Iron Rules for Captivating Story, 21 Speeches that Changed the World, 341-Point Influence Checklist, 143 Persuasive Cognitive Biases, 17 Ways to Think On Your Feet, 18 Lies About Speaking Well, 137 Deadly Logical Fallacies, 12 Iron Rules For Captivating Slides, 371 Words that Persuade, 63 Truths of Speaking Well, 27 Laws of Empathy, 21 Secrets of Legendary Speeches, 19 Scripts that Persuade, 12 Iron Rules For Captivating Speech, 33 Laws of Charisma, 11 Influence Formulas, 219-Point Speech-Writing Checklist, 21 Eloquence Formulas

Claim These Free Resources that Will Help You Unleash the Power of Your Words and Speak with Confidence. Visit www.speakforsuccesshub.com/toolkit for Access.

30 Free Video Lessons

We'll send you one free video lesson every day for 30 days, written and recorded by Peter D. Andrei. Days 1-10 cover authenticity, the prerequisite to confidence and persuasive power. Days 11-20 cover building self-belief and defeating communication anxiety. Days 21-30 cover how to speak with impact and influence, ensuring your words change minds instead of falling flat. Authenticity, self-belief, and impact – this course helps you master three components of confidence, turning even the most high-stakes presentations from obstacles into opportunities.

SPEAK FOR SUCCESS COLLECTION BOOK

PUBLIC SPEAKING MASTERY CHAPTER

USE OF VOICE:

Mastering the Little-Known Strategies of Vocal Impact

UNLEASHING THE POWER OF VOICE

A T THE VERY CORE OF PUBLIC SPEAKING IS THE way you speak; the intonations, pitch variations, tremors, and texture of your voice. To deliberately take command of the aspects of how you speak is to achieve mastery as a speaker. To manipulate them to suit your purpose is an undeniable advantage. To do all this effortlessly? A true challenge that takes diligent practice.

VOICE PROJECTION

Everyone respects an effortlessly powerful voice; a voice that is loud without straining itself, and that cuts through all background noise. Properly projecting your voice is the art of making sure everyone in the audience can hear you clearly, as though you are speaking to them side by side instead of across the room. While voice projection gives the obvious benefit of making you heard, it also exudes confidence.

If you have a naturally quiet voice, make a dedicated effort to speak loudly. When you're speaking in a massive auditorium, it indicates that you are omnipresent if your voice is heard as clearly in the back row as it is in the front. While it's crucial that you speak loudly and project your voice, make sure that you're not speaking so loudly that it is abrasive to the audience. Nonetheless, if you're concerned about speaking too loud, keep in mind that it's always better to be too loud than too quiet.

The importance of proper voice projection cannot be understated. Tone, vocal tonality, dramatic pausing, or any other strategy shared in this book will become utterly useless if the audience cannot hear you.

One of the most valuable tips for proper voice projection is taking a deep breath before you actually speak a sentence, and speaking it as you slowly let the air out of you. Speaking through the "mask" of your face is also helpful. The mask of your face is the area around your nose and mouth that would be covered if you put on a surgical mask. Additionally, speaking from your belly can help you make your voice louder. These three tricks make it much easier to project your voice throughout a large auditorium.

Email Peter D. Andrei, the author of the Speak for Success collection and the President of Speak Truth Well LLC directly.

pandreibusiness@gmail.com

THE COMPONENTS OF VOCAL PROJECTION

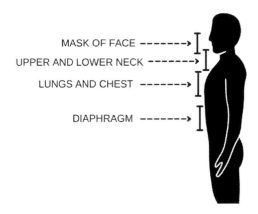

MASK OF FACE -------→

UPPER AND LOWER NECK -------→

LUNGS AND CHEST -------→

DIAPHRAGM -------→

FIGURE 88: This visualizes the components of your body that contribute to vocal projection.

Before you can master the other aspects of successful public speaking, you must master voice projection. Just as one cannot learn to run before they learn to walk, one cannot master the more advanced vocal techniques before they learn to project their voice.

EMPHASIS

Read the sentence "she didn't say he was a bad public speaker," but each time you do, place emphasis on a different word. Doing so will show you the power of emphasis. The sentence "*she* didn't say he was a bad public speaker" implies that while she may not have said so, somebody else did. The sentence "she *didn't* say he was a bad public speaker" places focus on the fact that the subject did not complete the action. The sentence "she didn't *say* he was a bad public speaker" implies the possibility that she may have texted it, typed it, thought it, or expressed it in some other way. The sentence "she didn't say *he* was a bad public speaker" implies that she may have been talking about someone else. The sentence "she didn't say he *was* a bad public speaker" implies that she may still think he is a bad public speaker. The sentence "she didn't say he was a *bad* public speaker" implies that she either said he was a mediocre speaker or a good one. If you master emphasis, and the sentence is spoken about you, it will read "she *didn't* say he was a bad public speaker."

Placing verbal emphasis on a word has the same effect as italicizing it when written. Emphasis highlights the importance of that word relative to the rest of the words in the sentence.

To emphasize a word, say the first syllable slightly louder than the other words in the sentence, make the pitch of the word either higher or lower than the other words in the sentence, say it slower than you normally would, stretch the vowel sound, and make a brief pause after you say it. And, as always, use your body to express the same sentiment as your voice; if you want to emphasize a word, do so with accompanying gestures as well.

What words should you emphasize, and when? It depends on the message you want to convey. For example, let's examine the following sentence: "climate change will affect you; yes, each and every one of you within the next ten years in terrible ways." The words and phrases on which emphasis is best placed are one or more of the following: will, you, each, every, ten years, and terrible. By emphasizing the "will'," the certainty of the outcome is expressed. By emphasizing the "you," the universality and immediacy of the effects will be made clear to the audience. The same is true for the "each and every" phrase. By emphasizing the "ten years," focus will be placed on just how soon the problem will begin to harm us. Placing emphasis on the "terrible" will convey, in a powerful way, how deeply climate change will negatively affect our way of life.

The words you choose to place emphasis on will undoubtedly have an effect on how your message is perceived by the audience. Make a conscious decision as to where your emphasis is best placed. Indeed, some might say that it's possible, even ideal in some cases, to place emphasis on all of those words from that sentence. In speeches delivered with a sense of intensity or emotion, such a strategy can succeed unless it is overdone and becomes tiring to your audience.

A POORLY EMPHASIZED SENTENCE

CONGRESS IS NOT AN EXECUTIVE BODY, IT IS A REPRESENTATIVE ASSEMBLY

FIGURE 89: Equate typography and vocal treatment, and say the sentence out loud. It will show you monotony.

AN ELECTRIFYING AND WELL-EMPHASIZED SENTENCE

CONGRESS IS *NOT* AN *EXECUTIVE*
BODY, IT IS A
R E P R E S E N T A T I V E
ASSEMBLY

FIGURE 90: Equate typography and vocal treatment, and say the sentence out loud. It will show you emphasis and compelling, impactful vocal variation.

Be careful not to inadvertently place emphasis on the auxiliary words of the sentence. From the previous example, the auxiliary words are "climate change will affect you; yes, each and every one of you within the next ten years in terrible ways." These words carry with them no real meaning, and only serve to connect the words that do. Placing emphasis on these words is useless and sounds extremely unnatural and forced. Try saying that sentence, but place emphasis on those four words to see what it sounds like. It is also important to note that "climate change," as the first phrase in the sentence, does not need to be emphasized; it already is by its position in the sentence.

By using emphasis, you can supercharge the vigor of your speech and make its meaning much more vivid.

PAUSING

Dramatic pauses are very powerful tools for a speaker to captivate an audience. Mark Twain once said that the right word may be effective, but no word was ever more effective than a rightly timed pause. If you ever listen to Barack Obama's speeches, you can observe that he uses dramatic pauses often and that it is one of the many reasons his speech sounds so suave, controlled, and intellectual.

When you are speaking, people sometimes passively listen and don't look at you and really give you their full attention. When you dramatically pause for a few seconds, they all tune in completely. Before delivering and after finishing the most important sentence in your speech, inject a dramatic pause to give your listeners a chance to digest it. Doing this will maximize its impact.

As with all of the public speaking tactics shared in this book, make sure not to overdo it. More often than not, you're speaking within a time limit. Overusing dramatic pauses will not only make it difficult to listen, but it will also use your time inefficiently. It's better not to use dramatic pauses at all than it is to use them incorrectly. Obviously, the best-case scenario is to use them well, accomplished by placing them at the right moments: once towards the beginning of your speech, and once before and after an important sequence or the climax of your speech. Shorter pauses can be used with more liberty, but longer pauses shouldn't be used quite as frequently.

Dramatic pauses can act as a way to minimize conversation fillers and fumbles in speech. While a dramatic pause creates suspense within the audience, it also gives you more time to carefully consider what you will say next. Most particularly eloquent phrases are delivered after a dramatic pause because during that pause, the speaker was considering how to word their next sentence. Dramatic pauses lend themselves well to both slow and fast talking-paces.

Pausing is one of the most important, versatile tools a public speaker has. They are even suited to speeches designed to entertain. For example, Trevor Noah, a very popular comedian, uses pausing between segments of jokes, which allows the audience to internalize the humor. In fact, that's a function of pauses that apply to all kinds of speeches: a pause in an informational speech, for example, gives the audience a chance to internalize the information they just received.

AN ELECTRIFYING SENTENCE WITH AN ELECTRIFYING PAUSE

CONGRESS IS *NOT* AN EXECUTIVE
BODY . . . . IT IS A
R E P R E S E N T A T I V E
ASSEMBLY

FIGURE 91: This is an example of a well-enunciated, well-emphasized, and well-varied sentence with an accompanying pause.

Another reason pauses in speech are so effective is that they give you the appearance of being deep in thought for a brief moment. It makes people want to know what you are saying next, because they expect it to be particularly profound, eloquent, or interesting.

Mark Twain was absolutely correct. Pauses make your voice and the sound of silence dance a beautiful waltz together.

TALKING PACE

Everyone has a set of natural speech habits and patterns, and among the plethora of qualities inherent to every speaker is their talking pace. A speaker's default talking pace can either be a challenge to overcome on the road to effective public speaking, or a boost towards that destination. Talking pace is another facet of public speaking which many speakers do not consciously take control of. There are two negative scenarios when it comes to pace: too slow and too fast. Between these two extremes, there are many different paces that have varied effects on you and your audience.

A moderately slow pace creates an air of confidence and control, both in your mind and in the minds of your listeners. If someone is willing to speak slowly in front of others, it shows comfort because they are not rushing back to their seats and are willing to prolong their time in the spotlight. It is also easier to understand people when they speak slowly, and speaking slowly (but not too slowly of course), will guarantee that you can more deliberately modulate your voice and avoid stutters.

Speaking slowly can have downsides as well. A speaker can become unengaging and monotone if they speak too slowly. If executed properly, however, speaking slowly can be very effective at conveying control, calmness, and confidence.

Speaking slowly may show that your heart rate isn't double your resting rate on stage, but speaking fast shows passion. People tune in because if they don't, they might miss something. A slower speaker will have the audience relax, but a faster speaker will usually have them sit up in their seats.

There are some problems with this type of speaking pace, just as there are with speaking slowly. Just as you can speak too slowly, you can also speak too fast. When a speaker speaks too fast, it becomes very abrasive to the audience. Speaking fast can cause syllables to blend together and limit the speaker's ability to enunciate. Make sure, if you speak fast naturally or by choice, that what you are saying is still clear. Additionally, when people are nervous, nine times out of ten they will speak fast. If you speak fast, make sure you still maintain an air of confidence about you through the use of body language. Combine talking pace with tone strategically. For a somber speech, speak slowly. For a speech in which you wish to convey excitement, speak quickly.

You'll have an advantage over most speakers if you carefully consider and strategically choose your talking pace. Most don't.

TONE

Tone refers to the quality of your voice, and what is expressed by the way you speak. The circumstances of the topic you are speaking about should dictate your tone. If you are discussing an emotional topic, speak with emotion in your voice. If you are discussing a sophisticated topic, use an intelligent tone. If you are speaking in condemnation of someone, use an incriminating, or even derisive tone. Regardless of the tone, it should be subtle and seem genuine. The only thing worse than speaking without a tone is speaking with an overdone tone.

Powerful speaking is made up not only of what you say, but how you say it. Emotional words alone will not induce an emotional response, unless they are spoken with what appears to be genuine emotion. Make sure you deliver emotional words with emotion in your voice, just as you should deliver sophisticated words with an air of knowledgeability.

The four common types of speeches all lend themselves to a specific type of tone. The tone for a speech designed to inform should be sophisticated and subtly authoritative, yet not too formal and dry. The tone for a speech designed to persuade should be full of conviction and confidence. The tone for a speech designed to entertain should be conversational and lighthearted. The tone for a speech designed to inspire should be emotional and passionate. Just as one speech can accomplish multiple purposes, one speech can be delivered with different tones at each of its different phases.

A climatologist can give a speech informing an audience about climate change findings, inspiring them to adopt environmentally friendly habits, and persuading them to buy a book on climate change. Each purpose shift should be accompanied by a tone shift. When informing, the speaker should use a knowledgeable tone because they are, after all, an authority on the subject of climate change. When inspiring, the speaker should take up a passionate and emotional tone to move the audience to be more environmentally friendly. And lastly, when persuading, the speaker should use a tone indicating complete confidence in the value of the book.

Tone is important because it allows the function of your vocal inflection to match the ideas you are trying to impart, and the purpose you are trying to accomplish. The process of aligning your voice, posture, and the tone of your presence on stage with what you are actually saying is crucial. If these aspects of public speaking are disjointed, nobody will believe your words. Furthermore, people will grow distrustful because it appears as though you don't believe your own message. This is why it is so important to make sure that your tone fits your words.

VOCAL TONALITIES

Psychology has shown us that one particular type of voice modulation is far more effective than the others, and will make you sound very convincing and confident. A study once reported that 55% of communication is body language, 38% of communication is tonality, and 7% of communication is words. This study may have seriously underplayed the importance of words in communication, but it is certainly not far from the truth: body language and tonality are just as important as words because while your words will impact an audience consciously, your body language and tonality will do so subconsciously.

Anytime someone turns to their friend in the seat next to them and says "something about this guy seems off," it is because of two reasons: that his body language is disjointed from his words, and that his tonality is not modulated properly. Nobody trusts a smile that doesn't reach the eyes and fades quickly. In fact, this has the opposite impact: it builds distrust. This is why the study is likely not far off from the truth. It hits upon the fact that vocal tonality and body language are modes of communication that are layered under words, and that because people can very easily manipulate their words, audiences often look to these two factors instead to determine how they should place their trust. There are three different tonalities, each with several different names.

Raising Tonality / Question Tonality / Seeking Rapport Tonality: This is when someone speaks at a constant pitch, and then raises it upon finishing the sentence. Almost all questions use this. Do not use this unless you are actually asking a question. When you ask a question to someone in everyday conversation, it means that you are unsure of something. It's obviously okay to be unsure of something in everyday conversation, but it reflects poorly on you in a formal setting, in which you are supposed to be an authority figure giving an informative, persuasive, or inspirational speech. When you ask a question, you expect a response. That response is a validation of your question, and when you use this type of tonality in a public speaking setting when you are making definitive statements, it subconsciously suggests to your audience that your statements need their validation. Of course, you can use this tonality for rhetorical questions, but when you are making statements, avoid raising tonality.

Flat Tonality / Neutral Tonality: This is most often used when people are speaking to someone they are comfortable with. While it's not as bad as Question Tonality, it is not as good as breaking rapport tonality. Neutral tonality won't hurt you, but it won't help you.

Downwards Tonality / Breaking Rapport Tonality: This is the most effective tonality and is hugely important. This is accomplished when the speaker ends their statement at a lower pitch than they began. This subconsciously implies that you do not care whether or not you get a response to your statement, meaning that you are very confident in what you are saying and thereby making yourself sound much more convincing. While a question suggests a response is needed, breaking rapport tonality suggests that what you are saying stands alone and that you are completely sure of it. Upon some experimentation, it was found that when cutting into a somewhat loud conversation, breaking rapport tonality is far more effective than the other two at getting the floor. If you think about what it indicates when someone asks a question, and reverse those effects, that's what breaking rapport tonality does. A question, or a statement spoken with question tonality, indicates that someone is unsure of themselves. A statement spoken with breaking rapport tonality, however, reverses that effect: it makes you seem assured.

KEY INSIGHT:

The Master of Vocal Modulation Has an Unbelievably Powerful Ability to Influence, Persuade, and Convince.

THE THREE VOCAL TONALITIES

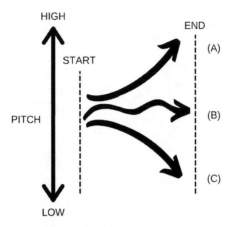

FIGURE 92: Open rapport tonality ends your sentence at a higher pitch than its starting pitch (A). Even tonality ends your sentence at roughly the same pitch as its starting pitch (B). Breaking rapport tonality ends your sentence at a lower pitch than its starting pitch (C).

The importance of using breaking rapport tonality cannot be understated. It can make or break an audience's trust in a speaker without either the audience or the speaker knowing why. Luckily, you will know to use this, and your audiences will always respect you as a figure of confidence, authority, and trust. If you're skeptical about the importance of breaking rapport tonality, let me tell you this: almost all sentences in Winston Churchill's "we will never surrender" speech, and Martin Luther King's "I have a dream" speech, used breaking rapport tonality not only with pitch, but with volume and pace as well.

VOCAL MODULATION

Voice modulation is made up of three main things: volume, pitch, and pace. An experienced public speaker will periodically shift these qualities as they proceed through their speech, making for an interesting, varied listening experience. They will pay special attention to varying their vocal modulation in order to avoid developing a repetitive verbal pattern. Over the course of different sentences, or even within a single sentence, maybe they will speak louder, at a higher pitch, and slightly faster than they previously were. Providing this vocal variance to your audience will make them much more interested in what you have to say as you are saying it.

Consider three consecutive sentences, and their pitch, volume, and pace. Pitch constant then downward at the end of the sentence, volume constant, pace constant. Pitch constant, then up, then down, volume constant, then up sharply as the pitch goes up, and pace constant, and then down when pitch goes up. Pitch constant then downward at the end of the sentence, volume increasing throughout, pace increasing throughout.

At this point, it quite frankly might seem confusing, pointless, and too complex. However, there's a method to the madness. Before I break down exactly why that diagram looks like it does, let me say this: you don't have to be that strategic. Less organized vocal variance is still enough to prevent your voice from becoming monotonous. The vocal calculations I'm going to get into is not always necessary, although it is useful. Let's say that the three sentences are as follows: "Climate change is a pressing problem that demands a solution from us now." "I'm often asked how bad can it really get; let me tell you right now that it can get very, very bad." "These natural disasters that have been ruining lives across the country are just a taste of what climate change can do to us."

Here's exactly how the climatologist is modulating their voice for each sentence: Volume is constant, pitch goes down towards the end of the sentence, and pace is constant. Volume is constant and then goes up sharply, pitch first goes up then goes down in breaking rapport tonality, and pace remains constant before dropping rapidly. Volume increases throughout, pitch goes down in breaking rapport tonality, and pace increases throughout.

Let's examine the purpose of each sentence: A straightforward, relatively calm statement. A frequent question and then the expert answer. A much more emotionally charged and intense statement than the first.

Now, by putting it all together, we can see the method to the madness: "Climate change is a pressing problem that demands a solution from us now"; a fairly objective, level-headed statement of what the expert believes; volume and pace remain constant while pitch goes down at the end of the sentence to achieve breaking rapport tonality.

"I'm often asked how bad can it really get; let me tell you right now that it can get very, very bad"; a question, and then the dire answer; volume and pace remain constant during the question portion of the sentence, while pitch goes up to signal that it is a rhetorical question and achieve question tonality. After the question is posed, volume goes up and pace slows down to accomplish two things: firstly, it breaks out of the question paradigm and into the answer paradigm, and secondly, it places emphasis on the answer to the question. Pitch goes down during the answer to, once again, achieve breaking rapport tonality.

"These natural disasters that have been ruining lives across the country are just a taste of what climate change can do to us"; a very human, emotional, and intense statement of how climate change is threatening our lives; volume goes up and pace speeds up throughout to increase the intensity and emotion of the   delivery, while the pitch goes down to achieve breaking rapport tonality.

Understandably, this is very difficult to achieve at first, but over time it will become second nature. Start small, and work your way towards naturally modulating your voice with highly sophisticated purpose and strategy. It can be done, and it can even be done naturally. It can become second nature. Until then, however, do what is often just as effective: vary your voice in an easier and less organized way. It doesn't always have to be modulated as purposefully as that example, but it must be varied. The example of those three sentences was just a glimpse of how complex it can really be: how pitch, volume, and pace can be modulated to create different effects on an audience.

RANDOM VARIATION

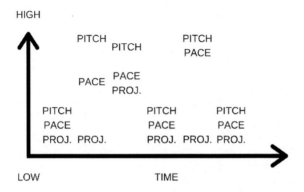

FIGURE 93: Random variation varies pitch, pace, and projection in random, intuitive ways. This beats monotony by a long shot and, even if you include deliberate variation, you will likely default to random variation for some extent of your message. Novices have a monotonous baseline and leap into random variation at select moments. Most effective speakers have a random baseline and leap into deliberate variation at select moments (this is just fine). Masters maintain deliberate variation at all times.

When varying your elements of vocal modulation (pitch, volume, and pace), be careful not to do so too quickly. For example, don't modulate your voice (pitch, pace, and volume) up and down seven times in one sentence.

You shouldn't modulate your voice in this way because too many frequent "ups" and "downs" makes you sound "shaky." Indeed, even "shaky" vocal modulation is better than no vocal modulation, but avoid sounding shaky by modulating your voice in a more smooth, controlled way.

The "shaky" mode suffers from too many variations packed into one sentence. Make sure when you modulate your voice, that you keep it controlled. Make it like the smooth, gentle flowing of a river, not like a rollercoaster.

DELIBERATE VARIATION

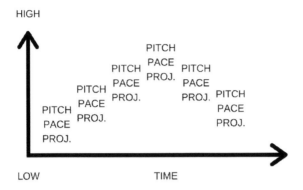

FIGURE 94: Deliberate variation creates specific effects on the audience. For example, this type of variation raises the intensity, and then lowers it.

VERBAL PATTERNS

Many public speakers will develop a verbal pattern that they will use for every single sentence. The ideal vocal modulation is varied and interesting. Whenever you see or hear of a speaker who people tend to naturally enjoy listening to, it often has to do with their voice modulation. Similarly, whenever you see or hear of a speaker who people tend to dislike listening to, it is often because they have a monotonous vocal pattern.

MONOTONY

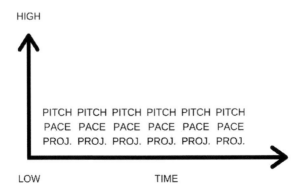

FIGURE 95: Monotony maintains the same pitch, pace, and projection levels. Avoid this.

Sentence one: pitch constant, volume constant, pace constant

Sentence two: pitch constant, volume constant, pace constant

Sentence three: pitch constant, volume constant, pace constan

While the previous example is the stereotypical vocal pattern of the stuffy college professor who puts his students to sleep and doesn't vary pitch, volume, or pace, a much more common repetitive vocal pattern looks something like this:

Sentence one: pitch constant then down, volume constant then up, pace up and down in a bell-curve

Sentence two: pitch constant then down, volume constant then up, pace up and down in a bell-curve

Sentence three: pitch constant then down, volume constant then up, pace up and down in a bell-curve

THE CRUCIAL AND COMMON VARIATION OVERSIGHT

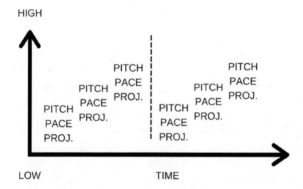

FIGURE 96: While this speaker raises his vocal qualities within his first sentence, he repeats this pattern in his second sentence. Now, some extent of this is fully acceptable. However, too much can become a pattern.

There's variation *within* each sentence, but none *between* them. Make sure that when you are trying to avoid repetitive vocal patterns, you take this into account as well.

VOCAL EXERCISES

Stretching your voice before speaking publicly is the equivalent of stretching your legs before running a mile. When you stretch your legs, they warm up and all the muscles are activated and ready to perform. It is like waking them up from a deep sleep. The same applies to your voice. Vocal exercises make your voice smoother, louder, and improve your articulation. Additionally, vocal exercises will make you better able to command your voice, and will certainly help prevent stumbles in speech. There are several vocal exercises that can be compiled into the following routine:

Hum with high pitch (1 minute): This exercise will warm up the upper vocal pitches which will enable you to speak with pitch variety. You should feel vibrations in your upper throat while performing this exercise.

Hum with medium pitch (1 minute): This exercise will warm up the throat muscles used for your neutral voice pitch; not too deep nor too high. It will help your voice develop a more rich, smooth, and full quality. You should feel vibrations in the middle of your throat while performing this exercise.

Hum low (1 minute): This exercise will warm up the muscles used to produce deeper vocal pitches, and allow you to deliberately lower your voice with greater ease and to a lower depth. You should feel vibrations in your lower throat and even chest when performing this exercise.

Combined pitch hums (1 minute): This exercise will help you deliver smoother tone variances. After performing this exercise, you will be able to modulate your voice much more effectively. To do this exercise, jump from pitch to pitch while humming, as smoothly as possible. This will loosen up all of the muscles in your throat and help you maintain effortless tone variation.

Blow air through lips / flap lips (1 minute): This exercise warms up your lips for articulation. It looks strange, but they should be flapping loudly.

Blow air through lips while humming high, medium and low (30 seconds each): Do the previous exercise while humming, once again high, medium and low in pitch.

Fill mouth completely with air (1 minute): Fill your mouth with air to stretch your cheeks, and then push your cheeks in while continuing to hold the air.

Stick tongue outside of mouth; say a sentence (1 minute): This exercise overworks your tongue so that you can articulate effortlessly later on.

Touch every side of every tooth with tongue (1 minute): This will stretch your tongue and will help you pronounce your words with greater articulation.

Press lips together (1 minute): This will wake up your lips and help with articulation. Press your lips together somewhat forcefully.

There are many vocal exercises; these are just a select few that have been shown to be effective, especially when combined with one another into a complete routine. I even recommend drinking a spicy or hot drink before a speech to clear your throat and to shock your vocal chords awake. You'll notice that after doing this routine, speaking will be much more fluid and effortless, and your voice will sound refreshed. Many people notice that after completing this routine, their voice sounds audibly different and very pleasing to the ear. As always, make sure that you drink plenty of water to prevent your mouth from getting dry, and don't eat anything for two to three hours before speaking. Speaking when slightly hungry gives you an edge, and it's easier to get into a flow.

USE OF VOICE CONCLUSION

In this section, you learned a few key subtleties about public speaking. They might seem obscure to you now, but through practice they will become second nature. One of the greatest pleasures of becoming an experienced public speaker and mastering the art is noticing yourself using some of these techniques without even trying to. You will effortlessly use breaking rapport tonality, vary your voice, and emphasize just the right words. The combination will be thrilling to receive as an audience member, but also thrilling to perform as a speaker. Study the principles in this section many times. The use of your voice is another third of the toolbox you have for constructing a public speaking triad. Own your voice: it is unique, special, and powerful. Use it to its fullest potential.

....................................Chapter Summary...................................

- Your voice often conveys as much crucial information as your actual words do.
- The key to effective vocal modulation is to align the message of your voice with the message of your words.
- There are three principle ending tonalities: breaking, even, and open. They each create a different impact.
- Verbal emphasis is effective at punctuating particular phrases. There are non-vocal kinds of emphasis as well.
- Vocal projection is a prerequisite to using the principles of vocal modulation effectively.
- Employing the various vocal techniques will allow you to project and modulate with greater flexibility and ease.

KEY INSIGHT:

The Persuasive Impact of Vocal Modulations is Entirely Subconscious, Entirely Real, and Entirely Powerful.

HOW TO MASTER PUBLIC SPEAKING (PART FOUR)

1	Background
1.1	Many Public Speaking Books Fail to Teach the Subject Optimally
1.2	This Book Is Designed to Correct Their Mistakes
1.3	Public Speaking is Part of the Foundation of Success
1.4	Public Speaking Will Massively Improve Your Career and Life
1.5	You Will Be More Likely to Get Hired, Promoted, and Paid More
1.6	Starting the Public Speaking Journey Demands Beating Anxiety
1.7	Public Speaking Means to Speak to 10-1,000,000,000 People
1.8	Adopting a Mental Frame of Abundance Will Improve Your Results
1.9	Multiple Opportunities Arise for Practicing the Skill: Seize Them
1.10	Vastly Different Speeches Are Similar at Their Fundamental Level
1.11	The First Type of Speech is Speaking to Inform
1.12	The Second Type of Speech is Speaking to Persuade
1.13	The Third Type of Speech is Speaking to Inspire
1.14	The Fourth Type of Speech is Speaking to Entertain
1.15	All Speeches Share Some Common Fundamentals
1.16	Most Speeches Fulfill More Than One of the Four Purposes
1.17	A Speaker Uses His Words, Body, and Voice to Convey His Message
2	Preparation
2.1	The First Determinant of Speaking Success is Confidence
2.2	Public Speaking Anxiety is Normal, Natural, and Beatable
2.3	There Are Multiple Powerful Strategies For Defeating the Anxiety

4.6	Breaking, Even, and Open Are the Three Basic Ending Tonalities
4.7	Vocal Modulation Conveys Deliberate Meaning with Your Voice
4.8	Verbal Patterns Create Monotony That Bores the Audience
4.9	Vocal Exercises Increase Your Vocal Flexibility and Ease
5	**Use of Body**
6	**Aspects of Delivery**

Email Peter D. Andrei, the author of the Speak for Success collection and the President of Speak Truth Well LLC directly.

pandreibusiness@gmail.com

KEY INSIGHT:

Pitch Up? That Says Something. Down? That Too. A Smoother Texture? That Too. A Raspier Texture? That Too. Volume Up? Down? Same Story. Speed Up? Down? It All Means Something. It All Impacts the Subconscious Mind.

The Brutal Truth is That One Bad Modulation Can Kill a Good Message.

Claim These Free Resources that Will Help You Unleash the Power of Your Words and Speak with Confidence. Visit www.speakforsuccesshub.com/toolkit for Access.

2 Free Workbooks

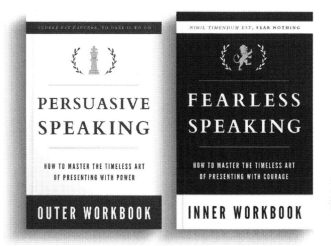

We'll send you two free workbooks, including long-lost excerpts by Dale Carnegie, the mega-bestselling author of *How to Win Friends and Influence People* (5,000,000 copies sold). *Fearless Speaking* guides you in the proven principles of mastering your inner game as a speaker. *Persuasive Speaking* guides you in the time-tested tactics of mastering your outer game by maximizing the power of your words. All of these resources complement the Speak for Success collection.

Claim These Free Resources that Will Help You Unleash the Power of Your Words and Speak with Confidence. Visit www.speakforsuccesshub.com/toolkit for Access.

18 Free PDF Resources

12 Iron Rules for Captivating Story, 21 Speeches that Changed the World, 341-Point Influence Checklist, 143 Persuasive Cognitive Biases, 17 Ways to Think On Your Feet, 18 Lies About Speaking Well, 137 Deadly Logical Fallacies, 12 Iron Rules For Captivating Slides, 371 Words that Persuade, 63 Truths of Speaking Well, 27 Laws of Empathy, 21 Secrets of Legendary Speeches, 19 Scripts that Persuade, 12 Iron Rules For Captivating Speech, 33 Laws of Charisma, 11 Influence Formulas, 219-Point Speech-Writing Checklist, 21 Eloquence Formulas

Claim These Free Resources that Will Help You Unleash the Power of Your Words and Speak with Confidence. Visit www.speakforsuccesshub.com/toolkit for Access.

30 Free Video Lessons

We'll send you one free video lesson every day for 30 days, written and recorded by Peter D. Andrei. Days 1-10 cover authenticity, the prerequisite to confidence and persuasive power. Days 11-20 cover building self-belief and defeating communication anxiety. Days 21-30 cover how to speak with impact and influence, ensuring your words change minds instead of falling flat. Authenticity, self-belief, and impact – this course helps you master three components of confidence, turning even the most high-stakes presentations from obstacles into opportunities.

SPEAK FOR SUCCESS COLLECTION BOOK

V

PUBLIC SPEAKING MASTERY CHAPTER

VI

USE OF BODY:

Mastering the Timeless Principles of Body Language

PORTRAYING NONVERBAL CONFIDENCE

I MAGINE A PUBLIC SPEAKER WITH THE MOST beautiful, soothing yet impassioned, and silky voice. Imagine how pleasing it must be to listen to them. Now, imagine that they stand totally still on stage. Can you picture yourself being engaged? No matter how masterfully you can command your voice, to truly reach your audience, you should throw your entire being into the performance. This includes using your body to help convey your message. Do not be a radio to your audience. Take advantage of your physical presence in the room.

POSTURE

A strong "stage presence" is accomplished by many things, but posture is by far one of the most important. Think of someone you know who is exceptionally confident. Think of the way they stand when they speak in front of people. Emulate it. Stand up straight, face the audience, keep your hands out of your pockets and facing the audience as well, and keep your head held high.

A STEP-BY-STEP PROPER POSTURE CHECKLIST

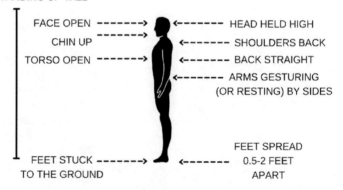

STANDING UP TALL

FACE OPEN ------> <------ HEAD HELD HIGH
CHIN UP ------> <------ SHOULDERS BACK
TORSO OPEN ------> <------ BACK STRAIGHT
<------ ARMS GESTURING
(OR RESTING) BY SIDES

FEET SPREAD
FEET STUCK ------> <------ 0.5-2 FEET
TO THE GROUND APART

FIGURE 97: This image reveals the components of proper posture. Remember, don't take this to an extreme. Don't be a wooden board or a C-3PO-like robot. Maintain relaxation and fluidity. Pay attention to your feet: don't shift them, move your balance from side to side, or otherwise play around with them during the speech. Only use your feet for deliberate stage-movement.

Everyone has one bad physical habit that they subconsciously do when they speak in front of others, such as repeatedly clenching and unclenching fists, shifting feet, constantly readjusting glasses, looking at the clock, or playing with their watch. Find yours and make a deliberate effort to stop. Additionally, make sure not to keep your arms crossed. Having your arms crossed will physically disconnect you from your audience. Maintain open posture to ensure that your audience can connect with you. Certainly do not cover your hands, as that subconsciously indicates to your audience that you are hiding something.

Most of the bad physical habits speakers exhibit have to do with their feet. Many body language experts say that the feet tell all, because people are so used to controlling all of their body language except their feet, which is why shifting feet is such a common public speaking mistake. To help you prevent this, simply plant your feet to the ground. Imagine them stuck there. Don't pick them up and don't shift your body weight from foot to foot. Keep the soles of your shoes flat on the ground until you move from that position.

In the presidential race between John F. Kennedy and Richard Nixon, they had a debate that was both televised and put on the radio. Those who listened on the radio thought Nixon won. Those who watched on television, however, believed John F. Kennedy won. What can possibly explain this? On the radio, it was simply a battle of voices and ideas. In this battle, Nixon had the edge over Kennedy because he brought stronger points to the table and refuted Kennedy's arguments more readily than Kennedy did his. On the television, Kennedy won because the television conveyed not only voices, but posture. Nixon was stiff behind his podium, had what to this day is still referred to as "Nixon's shifty eyes," and was also sweating profusely. Kennedy's posture was much better tuned. He was calm, smiled at the camera, and was fluid and smooth. This example illustrates the importance of posture. Simply seeing the way someone stands and carries themselves can make a big impact on the way they are received, despite what they are saying. When the people of America couldn't see Kennedy's confident posture and Nixon's poor posture, they favored Nixon. When they could, they favored Kennedy.

A strong posture shows a strong person, and someone's posture is usually the best way to read them. The way a person stands can betray underlying nervousness, or reveal boundless confidence. People subconsciously scan the posture of those they are interacting with, and your audience will certainly do so to you. Whoever can master good posture has a massive advantage not only when speaking publicly, but in all aspects of life.

EYE CONTACT

The saying "see eye to eye" means to be in agreement with someone. You should literally see eye to eye with your audience if you want them to agree with you. Eye contact is crucial. This doesn't apply only to public speaking, but in the context of public speaking, it is one of the best tools to become more engaging. A conversation between two people is more engaging if they make eye contact with each other. In a public speaking setting, however, you should only maintain eye contact with one person if you are speaking directly to them. When you are speaking to your entire audience as opposed to just one member of it, make eye contact with all of them. This seems impossible, and has been an age-old challenge faced by speakers.

The way to make eye contact with an entire audience is a strategy known as room sweeping. It's simple: pick one person in each corner of the room (top left, top right, bottom left, bottom right) and one in the middle, and make eye contact with each of them for a few seconds before swiveling to the next. From a distance, people can't tell if you are making eye contact with them or the person next to them. Be careful not to swivel between the audience members too rapidly. Maintaining smooth, consistent, and natural eye contact with your audience is a must-have for forming the speaker to audience connection. One of the concerns with reading a speech off of flashcards or a piece of paper is that doing so eliminates your ability to establish eye contact with your audience.

One other technique which is seen frequently in political debates is narrowing one's eyes and tilting the head slightly up. Bill Clinton did this in what many call the debate which won him the presidency. As opposed to regular eye contact, this conveys much more intensity. Nonetheless, eye contact of any kind with your audience is a requirement when you are speaking.

THE FOUR-CORNER EYE-CONTACT MODEL

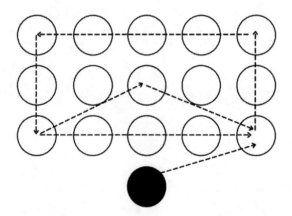

FIGURE 98: Look to the person in your innermost right corner; then the back-most right corner, then the back-most left corner; then the inner-most left corner; then the person in the middle; then repeat.

THE S-PATTERN EYE-CONTACT MODEL

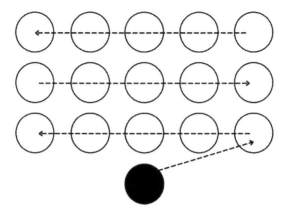

FIGURE 99: Make eye contact with the first row in a line, then jump to the closest person in the next row.

THE REVERSE S-PATTERN EYE-CONTACT MODEL

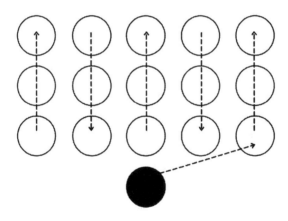

FIGURE 100: This reverses the S-pattern, making it front-to-back instead of side-to-side.

KEY INSIGHT:

Don't "Deliver" a "Speech" to a "Crowd." Just Talk to the People, One at a Time.

THE RANDOM EYE-CONTACT PATTERN

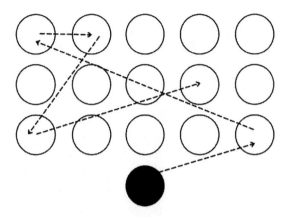

FIGURE 101: Random eye contact simply moves in natural intuitive ways. This is an effective model.

THE X-PATTERN EYE-CONTACT MODEL

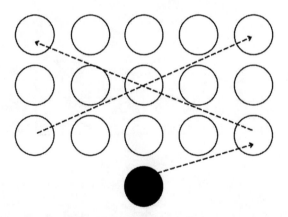

FIGURE 102: X-pattern eye-contact moves from the innermost right corner to the back-most left corner, then the front-most right corner to the back-most left corner.

THE X-PLUS PATTERN EYE-CONTACT MODEL

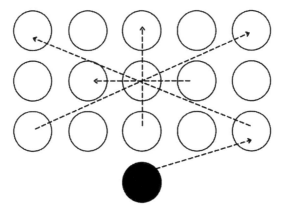

FIGURE 103: X-pattern eye-contact moves from the innermost right corner to the back-most left corner, then the front-most right corner to the back-most left corner. X-plus pattern eye contact includes a "plus sign" pattern in the center of the X.

THE Z-PATTERN EYE-CONTACT MODEL

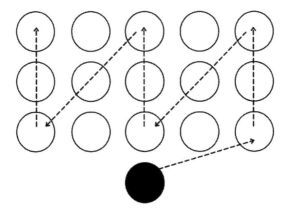

FIGURE 104: Z-pattern eye-contact starts at the frontmost right corner, goes to the back-most right corner to the middle front-most and then to the middle back-most, and finally to the left-most frontmost and the back-most-left-most corner. You truly don't need to know all of these eye contact patterns; they just reveal the depth to which we can analyze eye contact. All of these strategies are designed to spread eye contact out around the audience as opposed to concentrating it in clusters. This ensures equal engagement from all. Most likely, you will end up using random eye contact, but they all work well.

GESTURES

If you want to accomplish something, it's only logical to use every asset at your disposal. Gestures are a true embodiment of that mindset. Why use just your voice to deliver a message when you can accompany your voice with hand motions?

Hand motions are a very useful way to make yourself a more engaging speaker. Benevolent hand motions, palms out facing the audience, as though you're making a physical offering, are best. Don't point or gesticulate too intensely (pointing was one of Mitt Romney's public speaking mistakes in town-hall debates against Obama), and don't jump around the stage waving your arms like a crazy person; keep your gestures calm, controlled, and suave.

In general, open gestures, those that make you appear bigger in the sense that you occupy a larger physical space, are better for two reasons. Firstly, people associate occupying a larger physical space with qualities such as confidence and capability. Secondly, a closed body language; arms crossed, hunched over, chest covered, suggests that someone feels unsafe and unsure of themselves.

This all relates to the inner workings of the human mind. People who cover their chest and torso with their arms appear unfriendly and nervous because the chest and torso are the most vulnerable parts of the body. When you cover them, it subconsciously signals to onlookers that you feel under attack. The opposite of this, which is what you should aim for, is open body language. Keep your chest and torso open with your arms wide and gesturing by your sides. This suggests that you are approachable, capable, and influential.

Keep your gestures in the box between your chest and waist. Going above it makes you seem frazzled, while going below it makes you seem on the defense. The angle between your upper arm and forearm should never exceed 120 degrees.

VISUALIZING OPEN POSTURE

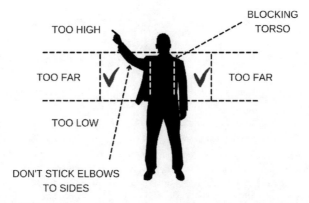

FIGURE 105: This updates our understanding of gestures to account for maintaining open posture. Now, it's not necessary to

always avoid torso-blocking gestures. It's okay to include some. But you must generally leave your torso open.

One gesture used frequently by politicians is the fist of power. This is the gesture with the fingers forming a relaxed fist and the thumb on top of them. As opposed to pointing, this gesture does not feel aggressive and is a good alternative for addressing specific audience members. Additionally, it signals the mind trying to grasp a complex idea, and subtly prompts the audience to try to do so. Use this gesture if you are explaining a portion of your speech that is exceedingly complex.

If any of your gestures point to yourself, this indicates nonverbally that you are talking about yourself. If you want to list anything, hold up your fingers and count with them to correspond to the items on the list. Do this while maintaining eye contact with the audience or else it will seem like you are actually counting on your fingers (which, if you still do, there is nothing wrong with). If you want to indicate something small, hold your fingers together as though you were holding a thumbtack. If you want to grab everyone's attention, hold out your left hand and have it face towards the ceiling, and slap the palm of it with the back of your right hand. Hold your hands in that position for a few seconds. This indicates that you are about to say something important and that you need everyone's attention. The audible clap is an attention grabber as well.

You can also use your hands to represent two sides of one idea, or two separate ideas, groups, or objects that conflict one another. You do this by bringing your hand up in a relaxed fist as you say what it corresponds to, and doing the same with the other hand. Hold them up the entire time you are talking about the two conflicting things, and each time you touch on one specifically give the hand it corresponds to a subtle shake in the air to further cement the representation. If you want to show where these two conflicting ideas meet in the middle, literally bring your hands together as you describe what is common between them.

If you want to convey something stopping, hold out your palm in front of you. If you want to convey intensity, slam the podium once or twice (not full force, just hard enough to make an audible thump). If you want to convey perplexity, wave your arms wide in mock frustration. If you want to convey happiness, cup your hands over your heart. The possibilities are endless. Be creative with them. Just always remember to keep them controlled and fluid, with only a few exceptions to that rule.

Interestingly enough, gestures actually help *you* remember what you were going to say. Much like the technique of hand-writing a speech over and over again, they root your speech in a form of memory much stronger than regular memory: muscle memory. This is especially true when you practice your speech with gestures included.

When it comes to gestures, do whatever you have to do to make the audience truly *feel* your message: a rule of public speaking wisdom that despite its simplicity often makes a massive difference in how successful a speech is.

MOVEMENT

Why is television a significantly more popular form of media than radio? Because it moves. A slow, dramatic, controlled pace across the stage, or across wherever you're speaking, can go a long way by grabbing people's attention and building suspense for what you will say next. Do not speak while pacing, and don't pace too often. Pace once or twice during a ten-minute block of speaking time. The only time you should speak while pacing is if you are transitioning from one point to another. When pacing, keep your torso turned so that you are still facing the audience.

The goal of pacing, aside from building suspense, is to engage everyone in the audience. If you are on one side of the room, speaking from that position will engage everyone on that side of the room because you are closer to them. It is good to pace once or twice because doing so engages more of your audience. If you're speaking from a designated podium, then pacing is obviously not a viable strategy. More often than not, you should be able to decide whether or not you want a podium. If you intend to use the power of movement to engage the audience, skip the podium.

It's important to remember only to pace between three points on the stage or platform: the two ends, and the middle. You should only ever move to a position you haven't been at before. Think of this as your stage, and the three positions: (1 – 2 – 3).

The numbers are the positions on your stage or platform. If you are in position one, you can move to position two or directly to position three. If you are in position two, do not go back to the position from which you just came. For example, if you start in one, and go to two, don't go back to one. Doing so will make the people in the audience closest to position three feel like you forgot about them.

A technique associated with three-position stage movement is that if you structure your message around three main ideas, you should deliver the first one from position one, the second from position two, and the third from position three. If you have more than three main ideas, let's say you have nine, deliver them from these positions: 1, 2, 3, 2, 1, 2, 3, 2, 1. Note that in this case, you deliver four points from position two, three from one, and two from three. It's okay that you deliver more from position two than anywhere else: it's the middle of the stage.

This "one, two, three" technique is useful because it prevents you from looking like you are aimlessly pacing on stage. It adds a clear structure to your movement.

Use your judgement when pacing: positions one and two don't necessarily have to be the corners of the stage, but the corners of your audience. If you have a stage that's ten yards wide, and an audience that's five yards wide, don't go to the opposite side of the ten-yard-wide stage. Stay close to your audience when pacing.

There's an undeniable suspense-building dynamism to a speaker who moves across the stage with a slow, silent walk. It is a dynamism which can captivate an audience, and make the speaker appear confident and in control.

FACIAL EXPRESSIONS

Anthony J. D'Angelo once said "smile, it is the key that fits the lock of everybody's heart." It sounds simplistic, but a quick smile to the audience before beginning your speech can go a very long way. It will make you more approachable, it will make the audience more receptive to your message, and it will even defuse any anxiety you may be feeling.

To share a smile with an audience before you share your speech shows that you are not a robot performing an artificial routine to bolster your personal agenda. A smile shows the audience that you are connecting person to person. It shows warmth, and connects them to the source of your message: you. A smile has a very special psychological affect, and it is contagious. A smiling person makes others smile too. The humanity behind a smile is what makes fumbles in speech and outward anxiety acceptable; your audience can empathize with it and actually relate to you as a person if you smile at them.

VISUALIZING THE IMMENSE POWER OF MIRROR NEURONS

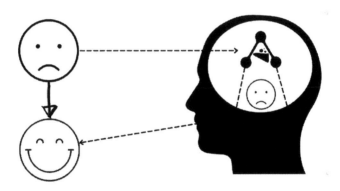

FIGURE 106: When you perceive, for example, an unhappy facial expression, mirror neurons simulate the feeling associated with the expression, revealing to you that it is an unhappy expression. As a result, you can observe the negative state of the audience, and provide the message you think will "turn that frown upside down."

Facial expressions in speeches go beyond a smile, although a smile at the start of a speech is universally effective. If you are speaking about a moment of sadness in your life, let your expression show the pain. If you are speaking about an injustice, let your expression show the anger. If you are speaking about a moment of contentment, let your expression show the happiness. You don't need to be acting or fabricating the emotions. Instead, just let the emotions that are already there be shown on your face. If there are no emotions, then don't fabricate any. Make it genuine by making your facial expression a true representation of how you are feeling.

Public speaking is not accomplished by speaking alone. It goes beyond that, into the realm of using everything at your disposal to convey a message. That includes your facial expressions.

PROPER AND POWERFUL POSTURE VISUALIZED

FIGURE 107: This speaker has achieved open posture. His feet are facing the audience. His feet are shoulder-width apart. His arm is by his side – not stuck up right against his side, not far to the side either – and his torso is open.

A POSTURE MISTAKE THAT LOSES THEIR TRUST

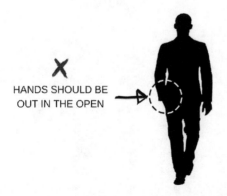

FIGURE 108: The human mind wants to see the hands and palms of those who are communicating with us. Don't hide your hands. This speaker seems like he is hiding something. He seems slightly

sinister, subconsciously at least. Showing people your hands – which is a prerequisite for engaging gestures – shows your trustworthiness.

ANOTHER POSTURE MISTAKE THAT UNDERMINES YOU

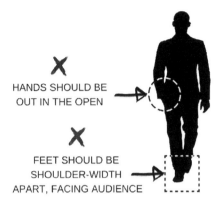

X

HANDS SHOULD BE
OUT IN THE OPEN

X

FEET SHOULD BE
SHOULDER-WIDTH
APART, FACING AUDIENCE

FIGURE 109: Another mistake is positioning your feet poorly. This speaker has his feet aligned with the tip of one shoe pointing at the heel of the other. He should be keeping his feet shoulder-width apart.

HOW TO CORRECT THE TWO COMMON POSTURE MISTAKES

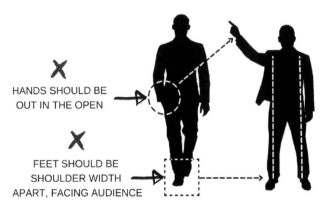

X

HANDS SHOULD BE
OUT IN THE OPEN

X

FEET SHOULD BE
SHOULDER WIDTH
APART, FACING AUDIENCE

FIGURE 110: Look at these two figures. Which one seems more trustworthy? The one who has a hand in his pocket and looks like he is standing on a balance beam, or the one with both hands visible, who is standing up straight, pointing at a presentation slide, and keeping his feet pointing toward the audience, shoulder-width apart?

POINTING CAN ALSO TURN THE AUDIENCE AGAINST YOU

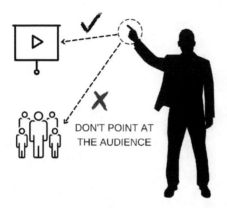

FIGURE 111: Of course, if he is pointing at the audience and not at a presentation slide, then he's making a big mistake. Studies prove that speakers who point at the audience get lower ratings than those who gesture toward the audience in a gentler, less aggressive, palm-up manner.

USE THIS HAND MOTION TO GESTURE TO THEM INSTEAD

FIGURE 112: Go ahead and point to emphasize something on your presentation slides, that's fine. But if you want to gesture toward the audience, do something like the figure on the right: a gentle, palm-up gesture, not a seemingly-aggressive point. This gesture got higher ratings.

THIS POSTURE WOULD COMPLETELY KILL THE MESSAGE

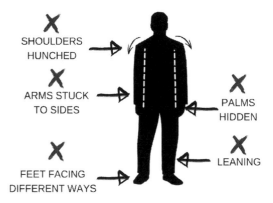

FIGURE 113: People are attracted to enthusiasm. Does this speaker seem enthusiastic? There are five main problems with his posture, and they make him seem disengaged, boring, dispassionate, and otherwise off-putting,

THIS IS HOW YOU CAN FIX IT AND ENGAGE THE AUDIENCE

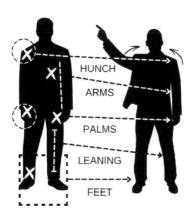

FIGURE 114: Don't hunch your shoulders. Don't tape your arms to your side. Don't hide your palms. Don't lean your weight on one leg – stand up straight – and definitely don't lean back and forth, shifting from foot to foot. Keep your feet facing the audience (keep your feet roughly parallel).

A COMMON POSE THAT TURNS PEOPLE AWAY FROM YOU

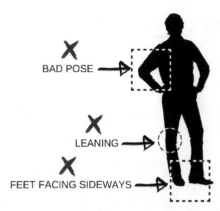

FIGURE 115: The hands-on-hips pose can appear adversarial, authoritarian, defensive, and off-putting. This speaker is also leaning and facing his feet both sideways and in two different directions. This is a bad combination.

HOW TO FIX THREE DESTRUCTIVE POSTURE MISTAKES

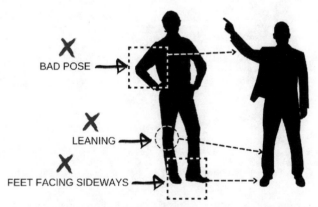

FIGURE 116: Which speaker would engage you more? Which speaker would captivate your attention? Which speaker appears more enthusiastic, pleasant, effective, and impactful? Which speaker seems more charismatic, confident, and compelling? Which speaker seems generally more pleasant to be around?

USE OF BODY CONCLUSION

At this point, you've learned about mastering your words, mastering your voice, and in this past section mastering your body. Your public speaking toolbox is now complete. You know how to use your words, your voice, and your body to convey a message and construct a public speaking triad. It's a skill coveted by many, so make the most of it.

I'm sure you've noticed that there's a wide variety of skills in your toolbox. There are many ways to use your voice to its best impact; some are very simple, and some are exceedingly complex. Nonetheless, it's all yours. The toolbox is unlocked for you.

There are, of course, different aspects of delivery to be mastered in the next and final section of this book. But for now? It's all in your hands. Use your communicator's toolbox often, because every time you do, new opportunities, connections, and accomplishments will be spawned.

Just remember one last thing: with great power comes great responsibility. Never use these skills to manipulate others or to be untrue to yourself. Use them to do good for others, and good will come right back to you.

................................Chapter Summary................................

- Your body language often conveys as much crucial information as your actual words do.
- The key to effective body language is to align the message of your body with the message of your words.
- You must activate (use), control, and align your words, vocal language, and body language.
- Some elements of body language simply prevent a bad outcome, while others ensure a good outcome.
- There are multiple eye-contact formulas, each of them suited for different audiences and different speakers.
- Weak body language can completely undermine a message, no matter how effective the words or vocal modulations are.

KEY INSIGHT:

We Are Wired to Feel Deep Compassion Toward People, Not Abstractions.

HOW TO MASTER PUBLIC SPEAKING (PART FIVE)

1	Background
1.1	Many Public Speaking Books Fail to Teach the Subject Optimally
1.2	This Book Is Designed to Correct Their Mistakes
1.3	Public Speaking is Part of the Foundation of Success
1.4	Public Speaking Will Massively Improve Your Career and Life
1.5	You Will Be More Likely to Get Hired, Promoted, and Paid More
1.6	Starting the Public Speaking Journey Demands Beating Anxiety
1.7	Public Speaking Means to Speak to 10-1,000,000,000 People
1.8	Adopting a Mental Frame of Abundance Will Improve Your Results
1.9	Multiple Opportunities Arise for Practicing the Skill: Seize Them
1.10	Vastly Different Speeches Are Similar at Their Fundamental Level
1.11	The First Type of Speech is Speaking to Inform
1.12	The Second Type of Speech is Speaking to Persuade
1.13	The Third Type of Speech is Speaking to Inspire
1.14	The Fourth Type of Speech is Speaking to Entertain
1.15	All Speeches Share Some Common Fundamentals
1.16	Most Speeches Fulfill More Than One of the Four Purposes
1.17	A Speaker Uses His Words, Body, and Voice to Convey His Message
2	Preparation
2.1	The First Determinant of Speaking Success is Confidence
2.2	Public Speaking Anxiety is Normal, Natural, and Beatable
2.3	There Are Multiple Powerful Strategies For Defeating the Anxiety

KEY INSIGHT:

If You Feel Anxious, "Stand Up Straight with Your Shoulders Back" (Peterson, 2018). The Outer Will Shape the Inner.

Claim These Free Resources that Will Help You Unleash the Power of Your Words and Speak with Confidence. Visit www.speakforsuccesshub.com/toolkit for Access.

2 Free Workbooks

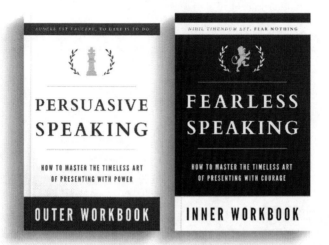

We'll send you two free workbooks, including long-lost excerpts by Dale Carnegie, the mega-bestselling author of *How to Win Friends and Influence People* (5,000,000 copies sold). *Fearless Speaking* guides you in the proven principles of mastering your inner game as a speaker. *Persuasive Speaking* guides you in the time-tested tactics of mastering your outer game by maximizing the power of your words. All of these resources complement the Speak for Success collection.

Claim These Free Resources that Will Help You Unleash the Power of Your Words and Speak with Confidence. Visit www.speakforsuccesshub.com/toolkit for Access.

18 Free PDF Resources

12 Iron Rules for Captivating Story, 21 Speeches that Changed the World, 341-Point Influence Checklist, 143 Persuasive Cognitive Biases, 17 Ways to Think On Your Feet, 18 Lies About Speaking Well, 137 Deadly Logical Fallacies, 12 Iron Rules For Captivating Slides, 371 Words that Persuade, 63 Truths of Speaking Well, 27 Laws of Empathy, 21 Secrets of Legendary Speeches, 19 Scripts that Persuade, 12 Iron Rules For Captivating Speech, 33 Laws of Charisma, 11 Influence Formulas, 219-Point Speech-Writing Checklist, 21 Eloquence Formulas

SPEAK FOR SUCCESS COLLECTION BOOK

V

PUBLIC SPEAKING MASTERY CHAPTER

VII

ASPECTS OF DELIVERY:

How to Deliver with Confidence and Achieve the Mission

BRINGING IT ALL TOGETHER

T HERE WILL ALWAYS BE A TIME AFTER A SPEECH, and there will always be a time before a speech, and these times will not always be particularly interesting. During a speech, however, time is distorted. You are in a state of heightened hyper-consciousness. Before a speech, many will feel anxiety. They are faced with a decision: give in to it, or push through regardless of it. After a speech, most speakers will analyze their performance, and breath a sign of relief. During a speech, however, you will be completely present. This state of hyper-presence positively alters your brain chemistry in an unparalleled way. There are many different ways a speech can be delivered; some chosen deliberately, and others that occur spontaneously. Regardless, you'll find that being in the moment of giving a speech is an incredibly gratifying experience.

CONVERSATIONALISM

A conversation is a bridge between minds. Thoughts transfer freely between them and they experience a sense of true synergy. Performing a public speech in a conversational tone allows you to tap into the magic of a conversation. At its very core, public speaking is the art of connecting with your audience, and imparting ideas through that connection. The stronger the connection between speaker and audience, the more receptive an audience will be to the speaker's ideas.

People naturally feel more connected with someone speaking in a casual, conversational tone, than with someone speaking in a high-minded tone. Speaking in a conversational tone avoids talking down to the audience, but puts them on a plane of equality from which they feel much more amicable with the speaker.

A conversational public speech makes use of everyday language as opposed to overly sophisticated language. Using standard, everyday language in a public speech allows your ideas to be simplified and makes for a more relaxing listening experience. Many people misconstrue this piece of common public speaking advice as "always speak the way I talk to my best friend." While sometimes true, that's not always the case. Speaking conversationally can still mean speaking professionally. It just means speaking professionally without the flourishment of a formal speech.

A conversational public speech is usually not memorized. When you are in a conversation with your best friend, do you memorize exactly what you are going to say? Of course not. You just have the basic ideas in your mind, and the free flow of words conveys these ideas in an understandable, straightforward, and natural way.

A conversational speech should not be memorized with the exception of the opening lines, statistics, and one or two of the most important segments throughout. If you are preparing for a conversational speech, simply write down the main ideas you want to convey, and familiarize yourself with them as best as you can. The words will flow freely, naturally, and effectively, if and only if you know the ideas well. To quote Michael H. Mescon, "the best way to conquer stage fright is to know what you're talking about."

A conversational public speech does not use much intense or emotional vocal modulation. You want to make the audience feel as though they are talking to you over lunch. This illusion is easily shattered if you are too intense or emotional. Some vocal inflection at key parts of your speech is always recommended, but most of it should be delivered in a cool, calm, and collected way.

A guest speaker for a political science class, a scientist presenting findings, or a top-rated salesman addressing the rest of the company are scenarios well suited for a conversational speech. A president addressing a nation in a time of war or responding to a global travesty demands a different approach. This different approach, the opposite of conversationalism, is formality.

KEY INSIGHT:

Huge Mistake: Speaking Conversationally About a Subject Demanding Formality.

Huge Mistake: Speaking Formally About a Subject Demanding a Conversational Tone.

FORMALITY

Put yourself in the shoes of someone at Rice University on September 12, 1962. It's a bright, sunny day, and you hear your president John F. Kennedy start his speech by saying "President Pitzer, Mr. Vice President, Governor, Congressman Thomas, Senator Wiley, and Congressman Miller, Mr. Webb, Mr. Bell, scientists, distinguished guests, and ladies and gentlemen: I appreciate your president having made me an honorary visiting professor, and I will assure you that my first lecture will be very brief." You can anticipate something big coming.

There are some scenarios that demand a palpable sense of intensity, emotion, or importance. The scenarios that demand formality are the history-making scenarios; a new peace treaty, an impending threat of nuclear war, or a commitment to explore space. While a CEO addressing his sales staff after a good fiscal quarter should strike a conversational and lighthearted tone, a general addressing a squad of marines about to be deployed on a mission of utmost importance demands a tone of formality. Don't assume that all formal speeches must be this important. Ultimately, you choose what you prefer. If you feel that formality suits you, go for it. If you feel that conversational speaking does, then do that.

A tone of formality describes most speeches studied in history classes. It is no coincidence that they are all discussing topics of importance. While conversationalism is well suited for speeches designed to inform and entertain, speeches with the purpose of inspiring or in some cases persuading must take up a more formal, intense, emotional, and serious tone.

An appeal by a lawyer in defense of a man that is truly innocent, about to be wrongly sentenced to prison time, demands emotion and intensity to persuade the jury. After all, there is part of a life at stake. A speech to inspire a nation, such as JFK's speech in which he presented the goal of landing a man on the moon must employ a more formal or intense tone. Most speeches given on an everyday basis are well suited for a conversational tone, but the small number of speeches that define the course of humanity are well suited for formality.

How do you deliver a formal speech? First and foremost, a formal speech is characterized by sophisticated and potent language; words that aren't used on a daily basis, but that don't require a dictionary to understand; words that are potent and powerful, but that don't come off as high-minded or pretentious. Beautiful and flowing sentence structure, diction, and word choice are all crucial aspects of a formal speech.

While a conversational speech might open by saying "Hey everyone, it's nice to be here today, and I'm excited to be speaking with all of you," a formal one should open by saying "Hello, it is an honor to address you all this evening, I greatly cherish the opportunity to speak to you about a topic of great importance to myself, all of you, and all of humanity."

A formal speech should be completely and thoroughly memorized, because the beautiful, flowing language of formal speeches can't be delivered off the top of your head. If you feel completely confident that you can deliver a speech with this complex, flowing, beautiful language, then do it. But most people can't. Thorough and complete memorization is usually necessary to deliver a formal speech. You should be able to recite the entire speech by memory, without any stumbles. It is also worth practicing the delivery to memorize when you should grow louder, quieter, faster, and slower to achieve the desired effect on your audience.

A formal speech should be intense, emotional, and full of conviction. The more important an idea, the more intensity must be used to convey that importance. The more intrinsic an idea is to the life of a speaker, the more emotion must be used to effectively convey that passion to the audience.

Give the choice between a formal or conversational approach a lot of thought: one of the biggest mistakes a speaker can make is choosing the wrong approach, and being conversational when they should be formal, or formal when they should be conversational. I don't say that to scare you, just to let you know that it's a very important decision that will impact your entire speech.

FORMAL AND CONVERSATIONAL DICTION

One of the key aspects of what differentiates a conversational speech from a formal one is the diction used by the speaker. This chart shows you some examples of the conversational version of a word compared with the formal one:

COMPARING TWO STYLES OF DICTION

CONVERSATIONAL	FORMAL
Ask	Inquire
Tell	Inform
Say Sorry	Apologize
Start	Begin
Try	Attempt
Afraid	Fearful
But	However
Wrong	Incorrect
Go up	Ascend
Lucky	Fortunate
Smart	Intelligent
Cheap	Inexpensive
Say no	Reject
Right	Correct
Log	Record
House	Dwelling
Build	Construct
Insult	Affront
Nice	Kind
Funny	Humorous
Sad	Upsetting
Happy	Joyous
Loving	Affectionate
Jump	Leap
See	Perceive
Think	Consider
Get	Receive
Write	Transcribe
Now	Currently
Gift	Present

Good	Positive
Bad	Negative
Place	Location

THE INFORMATIONAL APPROACH

We've gone into the four main public speaking triads early on in this book. Now, I'll give you my best advice on how to ace each kind of speech and build each kind of triad. When you're giving an informational speech, a very good way of thinking of it is taking yourself out of the picture and thinking only of the information and of your audience. View yourself as simply a vessel through which the information can reach the audience. Everything you say, as well as the way you say it, should maximize the effectiveness of your function as a vessel for the information. This is a selfless approach because you're taking yourself out of the picture.

Keep an eye on your audience, and before moving from one of your subtopics to another, ensure that your audience understood it. Many teachers and professors make a habit of saying a certain word to see if everyone is on the same page. One of my favorite teachers, a European history teacher, used to say "okay?" followed with a pause, every time he completed explaining an idea. That became a habit for him, and it would give us a chance to reflect on what he just told us for a few seconds, and ask any questions before he moved on. He was an excellent public speaker. It is no surprise that the vast majority of students enjoyed his class and learned extremely well.

If your audience seems to be grasping something quickly, don't spend much more time expanding on it. If your audience sees you continually expanding upon something that they already understand, they'll start daydreaming.

Much of effective public speaking is balancing different, sometimes opposing qualities. For example, to ace an informational speech, you have to carefully find the balance between going through the ideas too quickly and spending too much time on just one aspect of your subject. Make sure that you go through the information quickly enough to keep your audience engaged, but slowly enough that they truly grasp it.

KEY INSIGHT:

Aristotle's Philosophy of the "Golden Mean" Applies to Public Speaking Too.

HOW BALANCE PUTS YOU IN THE GOLDEN RANGE

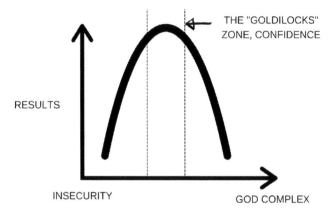

FIGURE 117: Making this mental shift tends to place you in the golden range of most quality-spectrums. On the spectrum of self-belief, both insecurity and a God complex represent different forms of inhibition that produce weak results. In the center, what we call "confidence" produces the best results.

The style I've identified as most effective (for an informational speech) is speaking in a calm, measured, and controlled manner but also being very personable and humorous when appropriate. Being in control doesn't mean being stiff: it means being able to use humor in a non-dilatory way.

Teach, don't preach or advocate your own opinion, and if you do, provide the opposing viewpoint as well. Even when you're persuading or inspiring, don't preach. If your audience expects unbiased information but then they begin to sense that you are injecting your own bias into the speech, they will distrust you. It's okay to explain your own opinion, as long as you acknowledge the opposing side as well.

When you teach, teach with humility: not "I know this and you should too," but "I am thankful that I was able to become an expert on this, and I think you could really benefit from some of the information I have for you." One of the most off-putting qualities to see in a speaker is arrogance. Indeed, that's one of the most off-putting qualities to see in anybody, anywhere, anytime, and under any circumstances.

A good piece of advice for delivering an informational speech is to organize it in "information bundles" and to build it up in a "pyramidal structure." An information bundle is one complete sub-point of your main point and everything else attached to that sub-point. By organizing your speech into these sub-points and having a clearly organized hierarchy of information, you will make your job much easier, and make your audience much more likely to actually learn. Information bundles help you break up the information and help you mentally organize it. They also help you memorize your speech. You can even have more information bundles than you need, and interchange them based on your audience. If you are a business consultant presenting new business trends or innovative processes to clients, you can have ten information bundles, and present the most relevant three to your current audience. You can also have a set of PowerPoint slides specifically devoted to one "information bundle," or a separate flashcard for each of your different information bundles. In some ways, the subsections of this book are individual information bundles. Each of them present one complete idea thoroughly. They each stand as individual units of information. I can give one subsection to someone and it, by itself, is complete.

With regards to pyramidal structure, it's very useful to map out the hierarchy of information in your speech. Any amount of coherent knowledge on a subject is made up of the background a person knows on that topic and then increasingly more complex and difficult concepts that build on each other just like the layers of a pyramid do. Start with easy information, build up a base of knowledge, and then move on to more complex areas of knowledge that you want to teach your audience.

When it comes to informational speeches, structure is very, very important. Yet again, we have a balance that needs to be struck: it's important when trying to inform an audience that you balance structure with a free-flow of information. Know your map of the speech by heart, but also leave room for yourself to go outside of the structure and speak naturally about specific interesting things relating to your topic. Give yourself a chance to speak about information bundles that weren't part of your planned structure, but that you know are interesting. An important part of striking this balance is responding to audience questions. Any time you give an informational speech, you should allow your audience to ask questions. Depending on the formality of it, either let them ask the question whenever they want or only at the end. When they do ask a question, don't be afraid to spend 60 seconds on a tangential line of information that does relate to the main topic, just doesn't specifically relate or fit into the structure of your speech. If someone is asking about something, they clearly are interested in learning more about a specific aspect of the topic. Even if the question doesn't directly fit into the framework of your informational speech, definitely spend some time answering that question. Part of your job as an informational speaker is to make your audience interested in the information. Indeed, that's a crucial part of the public speaking triad. So if someone asks a "fringe" question that still relates to the main topic, then satisfy their curiosity and nurture their interest because, after all, that's part of your job as an informational speaker.

Another helpful mental model for how to view giving an informational public speech is this: you are not necessarily there to lecture, but to take the audience on an adventure and to tell them a story. If you are informing an audience about history, don't just relay what happened, but take them on an adventure through the twists and turns of the events. If you are informing an audience about climate change, tell them a story of how industrial progress and the proliferation of cars sowed the seeds for a challenging fight to re-stabilize our climate.

Lastly, keep in mind that people are pattern recognizing creatures. Show them patterns that support the details. Don't lose the forest by being too focused on the individual trees. Explain to your audience how each individual "tree," or detail, connects to the broader "forest," or broader pattern. Your audience might not remember specifics. In fact, you're lucky if they do. What you should aim to have them remember are patterns and big picture ideas.

THE PERSUASIVE APPROACH

Before we begin this section, let's review some of the methods of persuasion presented previously: reciprocity, scarcity, authority, consistency, likeability, consensus, ethos, pathos, logos, Kairos, as well as invoking the desires of getting, bonding, learning, defending, feeling, improving.

Now, let me add some things to your list of persuasive methods. Firstly, as we've briefly discussed before with the fable of the wind and the sun, people are generally wary of salesmen and saleswomen because they have developed a reputation for the "hard-sell." It's a stigma that has long endured partly because it is a practice that has long endured.

When it comes to persuasion, aggressive, over-confident, and "straight-to-business" persuasion is level one (hint: that's not the level you want to be on). It doesn't take much skill to say "I promise you this is the number one solution to your problem and for this price it's incredible! You need this now. There's no possible reason that you don't need this. Trust me. Just trust me. Are you ready to buy? Sign here and here. Wait, why are you leaving?" True persuasion that is sophisticated and effective avoids such a direct approach, at least at first. True persuasion is much gentler, and makes use of many more psychological principles than the "hard-sell."

Perhaps what's worst about the "hard-sell" is that it comes off as just plain *needy*. It comes off as though someone is *chasing* a desired outcome. It makes the audience feel on edge. Let me put it this way: you've achieved masterful persuasion not when you're convincing your audience, but when you've gotten your audience to convince themselves. A common saying is that nobody wants to be sold to: people just want help buying.

It's helpful when attempting to persuade an audience that you not only speak your mind, but that you speak your audience's mind. If you are selling a solution to a problem, don't just speak your mind about why your solution is the best, but speak your audience's mind: explain the problem and how it impacts them. Show them that you understand their situation. This is an effective persuasion technique because it shows your audience that you understand their problem, and the logical conclusion is that someone who understands a problem is likely more able to solve it than someone who doesn't. Additionally, speaking your audience's mind builds immense relatability. Thoroughly explaining the problem you are selling a solution to will make you more likely to actually sell your solution. Why? It makes your audience go "wait a minute, this guy actually understands my situation." The vast majority of people deeply desire to be understood.

THE ULTIMATE ACT OF RADICAL EMPATHY

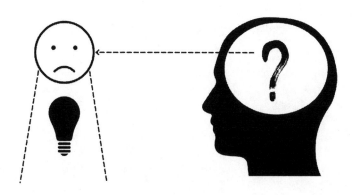

FIGURE 118: The ultimate act of radical empathy is projecting yourself into their consciousness, and seeing the world through their eyes.

An effective persuasive approach is addressing your audience, whether they are a single executive you are selling to, or one thousand people you are convincing to be more climate friendly, with this mindset: "I am here to understand your situation and try to provide a solution to it. I am first going to ask you questions so that I can understand where you're coming from, and then I will try to use my expertise to answer them and to make you a more informed person. Hopefully you will appreciate my help, because it is no-strings-attached. If you decide that whatever I'm persuading you to buy or do isn't for you, then that's fine. Get up and walk out of this room, and that's fine. No matter how important I think what I'm selling is, if you don't agree, then I accept that outcome." Do you see how detached from the outcome this type of mindset is? Do you see how it focuses on helping the audience instead of helping oneself? That is a winning mindset. It produces a presence of reason and exudes confidence.

Many misconstrue detachment from outcome as being apathetic. These people are wrong. Detachment from outcome is still giving an endeavor your all, just not relying on it succeeding for gratification. This mindset is often the key difference between speakers who have identical technical skills. One of them comes off with a needy, chasing tone, and overconfidence that borders on arrogance. The other comes off as level-headed, respectful, and trustworthy.

Compare the winning persuasive mindset to this common losing persuasive mindset: "I'm an expert and I expect you to listen to me when I say that this product or idea is what you need now. I'm going to be very direct and tell you that you need this without even asking you any questions or trying to understand your situation. I need this sale and I'm going to get this sale. If I don't get this sale- well, that won't happen. I'm getting this sale." Do you see how self-preoccupied it is? It is focused not on helping the audience, but making a sale.

Much like when you are trying to inform an audience, when you are trying to persuade them you should be selfless. Once again, you are a vessel. This time, you are simply transporting a solution to your audience instead of information (but oftentimes both, because it pays to make your persuasive prospects more informed).

Trust is obviously a crucial aspect of persuasion, and a counter-intuitive way to build trust is to make an honest and slightly harmful admission about a product or idea. This actually builds trust because when your audience sees that you are willing to admit to a small defect in your product or idea, they believe all the good things you were saying with greater certainty. Making a small concession breaks the image of something being "too good to be true." For example, imagine that someone is trying to sell a product and lists ten substantial good things about it. Many audience members will only half-believe those ten things. However, when the speaker makes a small concession, they suddenly become much more trustworthy, and the audience's belief in those main selling points is reinforced. Making a small, strategic concession is the difference between an audience only semi-believing ten good things about a product or idea, and an audience fully believing one minor defect but nine strong points of a product or idea.

AN UNBELIEVABLY GREAT IDEA OR A CREDIBLE ONE?

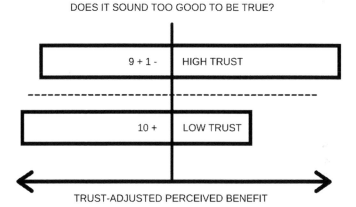

FIGURE 119: A policy with nine benefits and one openly revealed flaw garners high trust. The revelation of the one flaw garners an outsized increase in trust. A policy with ten benefits tends to earn significantly less trust. "It sounds too good to be true: What is the tradeoff? What is he not telling me?" It is not even necessarily the case that policies with ten benefits garner low trust, but that the irrelevant damaging admission gains a great deal of trust.

THE MAGIC OF A DAMAGING ADMISSION

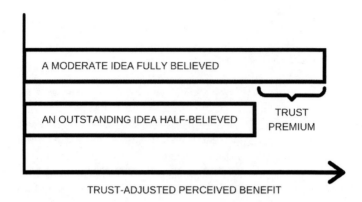

FIGURE 120: A moderate idea fully believed carries more perceived benefit than an outstanding idea partially believed. This is known as the "trust premium."

Another useful mental model for how to view a persuasive speech or presentation involves four things. Number one is your audience. Number two is your audience's decision to buy your product or adopt your idea. Number three is a long road between your audience and their decision to do whatever you want them to do. This road is very perilous and covered with obstacles. Number four is you. Your job in this paradigm is to gently guide your audience down that road, removing the obstacles or objections along the way. This mental model plays well into the concept of gentle persuasion versus the "hard-sell." A "hard-sell" would be you putting your audience into a car and trying to drive them down the road at 120 miles per hour. It won't work: you will run into an obstacle, or they'll pull the safety brake, bring the car to a grinding halt, and walk away. Gentle persuasion, on the other hand, is you taking them for a pleasant walk down the road filled with exchange of useful information, pleasant conversation, and friendship.

THE INSPIRATIONAL APPROACH

Much of Freudian psychology is based around the theory of the tripartite personality : that the human psyche is made up of an id, ego, and superego. The id is base desires, and the superego is the morals society imprints upon us. The ego is reality. It is who we are, and it is sandwiched between our base desires and societally informed morals. The id is primitive, impulsive, biological, and instinctual. A child is all id before society forms the child's superego. The id is where self-preservation comes from, and is based on the "pleasure principle": namely that every desire should be satisfied immediately regardless of consequence. The ego operates to satisfy the demands of the id without creating unpleasant consequences. It operates to satisfy the id within the bounds of socially imposed norms and morals (the superego). Lastly, the superego is the conscience and the conception of the "ideal self." It is an image of accomplished self-actualization. People feel guilt because they go against their superego. The superego is like the angel on our shoulders, guiding us towards moral lives of virtue and principle.

Effective inspiration is empowering the ego and superego to overcome the id. Consider Winston Churchill's "we will never surrender" radio broadcast. The people of his nation were struggling in every possible way: German air raids were destroying homes, claiming lives, and maiming innocent civilians. The collective id of Great Britain was screaming "surrender" out of self-preservation. The pleasure principle was at work, degrading the will of Great Britain's people and making surrender seem like the better option.

What did Winston Churchill's speech really accomplish? What impact did it have on the psyches of his listeners? Through the superego, it strengthened the ego and weakened the incessant demands of the id. The superego was telling the ego not to surrender, to keep fighting against an oppressive force, and to preserve their homeland. The id, more convincingly, was telling the ego to end the suffering and accept surrender. The scale was tipping towards the side of the id, as it often does. It took inspiration from Winston Churchill to tip it back the other way.

To effectively inspire is often directing people towards doing what is right: towards doing what the superego wants the ego to do, instead of what the id wants the ego to do.

How can you accomplish this? The superego is already ingrained in people. You don't have to put it there: it already is. You simply have to strengthen it by appealing to a higher motive, drawing out people's sense of duty, and making clear the consequences of not doing what is right.

As negative as this might sound, guilt and shame are powerful motivators that can instill lifelong habits in people. There are two types of persuasion and inspiration: negative and positive. There should be more positive inspiration than negative, but having some negative inspiration is effective as well. There's a simple distinction between the two. Positive inspiration is: "together, we can save our country and fight for what is right." Negative inspiration is: "if we don't bring ourselves together now, we will lose our country and what we stand for." Positive inspiration is illustrating the good that will happen if people do what you want them to. Negative inspiration is illustrating the bad that will happen if they don't. Contrast inspiration is useful as well: it is negative inspiration followed by positive inspiration, or the other way around.

KEY INSIGHT:

Paint a Picture of a Noble Ideal. Let Its Image, Impressed on the Audience's Conscience, Do the Persuading.

HOW TO CAPTURE COMPLETE AND INSTANT ATTENTION

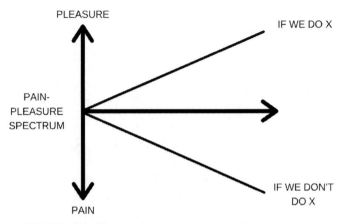

FIGURE 121: Present the moment and your message as a moment of decision; as a fork in the road, with one read leading to immense pain and one leading to immense pleasure.

Positive and negative inspiration both appeal to different human drives. Maybe even by reading the two previous examples you can feel a different gut emotion. There should be at least a 2:1 ratio between positive inspiration and negative inspiration. People prefer to work towards achieving a positive result more than they prefer to work towards preventing a negative result. Nonetheless, both modes of inspiration should be present in an inspirational speech. The principle of negative persuasion or inspiration is powerful because it appeals to human's natural loss aversion : we don't always play to win, but just not to lose. We hate losing things, which is why so many of us are risk-averse.

By understanding how to unlock the driving psychological forces behind why people do what they do, you can inspire any audience towards achieving any goal.

THE ENTERTAINING APPROACH

Detachment from outcome is crucial for all speeches, but even more so for a speech to entertain. Someone who wants to be funny needs to seem like they don't care whether or not they are. They need to seem like they have an "I don't care if you laugh at what I'm saying because I think it's funny so I'm going to say it and laugh at myself" attitude. Not only do they need to *seem* like that's what their thinking: it's even better if it actually is.

Don't be afraid to draw humor from your own life. As long as it's not too personal, you should be willing to expose some mildly embarrassing stories. A very effective model for a joke is saying the first half of a phrase which suggests a logical second half, and then blowing away that expectation. Make your audience think you will say something, and then don't say it. Build a pattern, and then break it. Confound their expectations. It's important when using this technique that the logical conclusion that would follow from the first half of your joke is assumed by most of the people in your audience. Make it very clear.

As with any speech, it's important to limit the number of words you're saying. Brevity is key. Don't delay unnecessarily: build up a joke only as much as it needs to be before getting to the punchline. It's important when giving a speech to entertain that you are natural, easygoing, and are having fun yourself. Your audience will take that cue from you and begin having fun themselves.

Timing is everything when it comes to humor. Build suspense before giving your audience the punchline, and let them process it by pausing after you deliver it. Be energetic, and make your audience energetic by simply being extremely energetic yourself. Unusually energetic. Concerningly energetic.

Be authentic and don't try to get into an avatar that isn't you. Be genuine to who you are when you're trying to express a funny persona, and you'll find it much easier to get into a flow. There are many principles of comedy which are beyond the scope of this book, but which are worth learning nonetheless. Believe it or not, there are actually joke structures and molds that have proven to be effective.

Lastly, use metaphors, analogies, and exaggerations, and paint a picture in your audience's minds of what you want them to imagine.

If you want to learn more about speeches designed to entertain, watch successful comedians do their work and closely observe their techniques.

KEY INSIGHT:

Trying to Adopt the Avatar of a Speaker You Admire Is Not Always a Bad Strategy. Don't Use the Avatar to Replace Your Natural Delivery, But to Shape It, to Help You Adopt the Strengths of the Speaker You Admire.

TIMING

Just as society and everyone in it revolves around time, a public speech will fail if it was not crafted with time in mind. Every speech ever delivered had a time limit whether it was a strict allotted time, or an informal time limit on the audience's attention span. Even the most captivating speaker cannot engage an audience forever.

If you are a guest speaker, ask if there is an allotted time to speak. If there's no set time limit, make sure not to let your speech run on too long because no matter how brilliant a speech might be, its brilliance fades with time. If you see your audience start to seem restless; if you see them shifting in their seats, muttering amongst themselves, or checking their watches, gracefully cut your speech short. If you can accomplish the same goal with the same quality in a shorter speech, then do so.

Timing also refers to how much time you spend on each portion of your speech. For a ten-minute speech, you should spend one minute on introductions, one minute on the hook, six minutes on the content, and two minutes on the call to action. This is obviously up to your judgement. You can split your speech however you see fit.

When deciding how long the total time should be, just remember that nobody has complained about a speech being too short, but plenty of people have complained about a speech being too long.

CONVERSATION FILLERS

Imagine if instead of saying "this is a day that will live in infamy," Franklin Delano Roosevelt said "this is, uh, a day that will live in, um, infamy." Not as powerful, right? We all do it. Uhh, umm, hmm, and like, are all examples of common conversation fillers. Try your best to eliminate them. While acceptable in moderation, if done excessively and obtrusively, they can really blur the clarity of your voice and obscure your message.

Conversation fillers occur when, in the heat of the moment, you're briefly unsure what to say next and pause to think of the next sequence in your speech. In that pause, your subconscious mind feels the urge to fill the silence by injecting a conversation filler. An "um" usually indicates that a longer pause in speech is coming, perhaps that the speaker is trying to formulate the next two or three sentences, while an "uh" usually indicates that the speaker is stumbling on the next two or three words. Either way, both of these conversation fillers are dilatory and detract from your ability to captivate the audience.

There are several strategies for limiting the number of conversation fillers that remarkably, out of nowhere, pop into your speeches. When you feel a conversation filler coming, just pause, recollect yourself, and continue. This is also a natural way to include dramatic pauses in your speech, which are always better than an "ummmmm."

The best way to eliminate conversation fillers is to simply make yourself notice when you use them. Once you are aware of how often or how little you use conversation fillers, and where, it is far easier to stop inadvertently injecting them in your speech.

Additionally, to eliminate conversation fillers, be very familiar with the content of your speech, whether it is completely memorized word for word or centered around a set of core ideas. This will limit the chance of needing time to think about what comes next because, after proper preparation, what comes next in your speech will be crystal clear.

Another strategy is speaking slower, which reduces your chances of having to rely on conversation fillers because you give your mind more time to formulate your next sentence. Lastly, being confident in yourself, your public speaking ability, and your preparation helps tremendously in cutting down your filler words. Once again, confidence is key.

Conversation fillers often occur when you are trying to say something in an unnatural way, which means a way that is deliberately different than the way you first thought of it. Thus, another way to remove conversation fillers is to let words naturally flow out of you.

Speech unmarked by conversation fillers signifies a truly experienced, capable public speaker. Make eliminating conversation fillers from your speech one of your goals as a speaker. They are one of the biggest barriers to eloquence.

FUMBLES IN SPEECH

One of the most feared scenarios that holds people back from speaking publicly is stuttering on a phrase or fumbling words. Everyone has, at one point, painted a picture of this scenario in their heads. It's usually along the lines of: they prepare a speech, they get up on stage in front of their audience, they start, and several seconds in they begin to fumble their words uncontrollably. Scary, right? In reality, it's not that bad if it happens and is easily preventable in the first place.

Dealing with fumbles in speech has to do with what you can do to prevent them, and what you can do once they happen. Yet again, confidence is crucial because the fear of fumbles in speech is what makes them happen.

To prevent fumbles in a memorized piece, practice delivering it time and time again until you eliminate the fumbles. Usually, they occur in the same place, so isolate where they occur, and practice those segments until they are gone. To prevent fumbles in a speech delivered on the spot or around a core set of ideas, let the words flow freely and with no inhibitions. As with conversation fillers, speaking slowly also minimizes the risk of fumbling.

That's what you do to prevent fumbles in speeches, but what if they happen anyway? If you fumble on your words, just pause for two or three seconds, recollect yourself, and continue speaking. Everyone fumbles on their words occasionally. It's no big deal. If you fumble on a set of words, you should not try to repeat the phrase again. Instead, move on to the next sentence. What says more about a speaker than whether or not they stumble is how gracefully they react to a stumble.

AVOIDING A MAJOR AND COMMON PRESENTATION MISTAKE

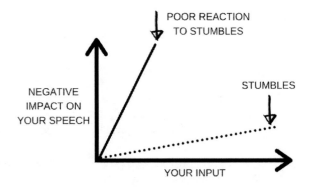

FIGURE 122: Stumbles have a much less extreme negative impact on your speech than poor reactions to stumbles do.

Fumbling in a public speech scares many away from public speaking, but in reality, it's not as scary as it seems.

INDIVIDUAL STYLES

The key to success in public speaking, as well as the rest of life, is figuring out what you naturally are, and becoming more of it. Everyone has their own natural voice. Your voice can be deep and booming, quiet and timid, or loud and high pitched. No type of voice is better than another. What actually matters, however, is how well you master whatever kind of voice you were born with. Deep and booming voices, while sounding powerful, make it harder to enunciate syllables. Quiet and tremorous voices, if used properly, are the most soothing to listen to. Loud and high-pitched voices cut through the air and are very easily heard.

Every speaker, over time, develops their own individual style. Some are calm, measured, and in control." Such a style consists of speaking slowly, clearly, and with depth of voice. Another style is passionate and excited. These speakers speak rapidly and excitedly, often making impassioned gestures and motions on the stage. Such speakers can be very influential and energizing to listen to. Another style is relaxed. This style is exemplified by a laid-back posture and more casual language. While this might make a speaker appear aloof, it can also make them more personable to the audience. Another style is sophisticated and knowledgeable. Such a style consists of using complex phrases and diction that grant authority to oneself.

The number of individual public speaking styles is just as limitless and unique as the number of people who pursue public speaking, and the kinds of people that they are. The challenge lies not with choosing an individual style, but in developing and refining the one you naturally revert to. Find out what kind of speaker you are, and go all in on it.

RESPONDING TO CHALLENGES

Paulo Coelho once said "If everybody loves you, something is wrong. Find at least one enemy to keep you alert." In many public speaking scenarios, such as a formal debate or even in a boardroom, your ideas will come under attack. Keep in mind that when people point out flaws in your stance, they are unknowingly giving you an opportunity to improve it.

There will be competition in many public speaking situations. People will strive to get ahead by pushing their idea or agenda over yours, and will try to undermine your idea. Don't worry: you're being called out because you are a strong, influential person, who is more than a worthy match for any opponent.

No matter how panicked you may feel in such a situation, do not let your face show it. Keep your face a mask of courage, even if you're unsure of yourself. As your opponent is speaking to you and ridiculing your argument, maintain a straight face and make eye contact. Smile. Sounds out of context, but a smile to the person who wants to verbally attack you is scary for them. Then, think about your opponent's argument, its strengths and weaknesses, and try to formulate a rebuttal as fast as possible. Do not wait too long. If someone challenges you, do not let ten minutes go by before you respond to the challenge. Deliver your rebuttal as soon as possible, so that it is still relevant.

There are three major ways to form a rebuttal. Firstly, you can challenge their challenge. State that their argument as to why you're incorrect is incorrect itself, and then explain why.

Secondly, you can sidestep the challenge by strongly restating your initial point and arguments, and then undermining their stance. This essentially shows that "sure, my stance has flaws, but yours has more."

Thirdly, a less favorable response, is a concession. If you state that climate change is bad for three supporting reasons, and your opponent argues against one of your three, then you can concede. Do not ever state that your main argument is wrong. If you say "climate change is bad because it kills crops, is bad for the economy, and hurts people's health," and an opponent successfully challenges your claim that it directly hurts people's health, then say "okay, you may be correct that climate change does not hurt people's health, but my main argument is still valid because climate change does hurt the economy and kills crops, which may indirectly harm people's health."

The only way for an opponent to challenge your point is to challenge the evidence you use to support that point, or the logical steps (otherwise known as logical warrants) connecting that evidence to your main point. Oftentimes, they will focus on undermining the weakest piece of supporting evidence upon which your stance is built. In this case, if they manage to undermine that point in a way that you cannot argue against, then simply say "okay, that piece of supporting evidence was faulty, but the other two of mine were not. Therefore, my point that climate change is bad is still completely valid." While you do have three possible responses, challenging your opponent's challenge is the best way to preserve the validity of your ideas. Understanding logical fallacies and being able to point them out in your opponent's rebuttal is helpful as well.

CHALLENGING OTHERS

It can be fearsome to respond to challenges, but for some, it can be even more fearsome to present challenges to others. There are times when it will be beneficial for you to challenge another speaker's ideas. When doing so, there are some things to keep in mind.

Firstly, don't use an ad hominem, the logical fallacy in which you target not your opponent's argument, but your opponent as a person. Not only is this a fallacy, but it pulls you off of the moral high ground and makes it seem as though you are disagreeing for personal reasons.

Secondly, don't be too derisive. In certain cases, it is okay to inject a drop of derision or condescension into your refutation, but be very careful not to overdo it. Moderate derision can be effective at portraying the absurdity of your opponent's argument. Too much will really harm you in the eyes of the audience.

Thirdly, and most importantly, clearly explain where your opponent's line of reasoning is faulty. Make sure that the entire audience knows why they are wrong and you are right. To achieve this, be specific in exposing the flaws in your opponent's argument, and deliberate in explaining why they are wrong. Don't be afraid to challenge others, just don't make it your main priority. In most cases, it is much more rewarding to build your own arguments up than it is to put other arguments down.

PLEASANTRIES

Politeness between people is what makes endeavors between people succeed. To invest respect, kindness, and good faith in the people around you is to invest in your future as well as theirs. Pleasantries make the audience like you and connect with you on a personal level. Pleasantries fall under the formal and conversational distinctions. Conversational pleasantries typically sound like "Hey everyone! How's everyone doing tonight?" They are warm, light hearted, and friendly. Formal pleasantries typically sound like "Fellow delegates, esteemed observers, honorable colleagues." They are sophisticated and decorative.

Whether formal or conversational, pleasantries are the polite words at the start and end of your speech that show your audience respect. Start with brief opening pleasantries instead of getting right into your speech. Ten seconds of pleasantries is a small commitment that will have a subtle but significant impact on the audience. Conversational pleasantries can be a brief anecdote about how you forgot your keys and had to rush to the venue, or even a brief synopsis of where you grew up, what school you went to, and what hobbies you have. Formal pleasantries can be along the lines of "it is my absolute honor to publicly address such an esteemed audience of accomplished people."

For closing pleasantries, "I hope you all enjoyed hearing about this new idea. If you have any questions, feel free to approach me with them," can go a long way. All pleasantries, whether opening or closing, demand brevity. To truly make an audience connect with you, pleasantries must be genuine. Long, drawn out pleasantries seem ingenuine, and will have the reverse effect on your audience. Keep these tips in mind, and pleasantries will make any audience like you as a speaker and as a person. Here's an example of a speech in which Hillary Clinton used excellent formal pleasantries. Once again, this segment is from her "Women's Rights are Human Rights" speech. In fact, it directly precedes the last excerpt presented from her speech: "Thank you very much, Gertrude Mongella, for your dedicated work that has brought us to this point, distinguished delegates, and guests: I would like to thank the Secretary General for inviting me to be part of this important United Nations Fourth World Conference on Women. This is truly a celebration, a celebration of the contributions women make in every aspect of life: in the home, on the job, in the community, as mothers, wives, sisters, daughters, learners, workers, citizens, and leaders."

Do you see how decorative and honorary it is? Now, here's an example of conversational pleasantries. This excerpt comes from a speech called "Afraid of the Dark," a comedic speech by world-class comedian Trevor Noah: "Wow. Wow. Oh, wow. What's happening, New York? Yeah! Oh, this is amazing. Thank you for coming out. We're gonna have fun tonight. Welcome to it, people. This is us. Can I tell you for a second? This has been my dream since I started stand-up comedy, doing a special in New York City. This is it! This is it. New York, New York! [New York accent] Yeah! New York! I'm walking over here! [audience laughing]"

Do you see how informal, relaxed, and humorous it is? For both formal and informal speeches, it is also worth knowing the principles of winning friends and influencing people from Dale Carnegie's *How to Win Friends and Influence People*, especially the following ones which can be directly used in a public speech:

"Don't Criticize, Condemn, or Complain:" Anybody who intends to convince others of something must avoid these three harmful habits. If our climatologist went up on stage in an effort to get people to live more climate friendly lives and said "You people are ridiculous. Don't you know that you need to recycle? It's literally so easy. The bins are right next to the trash cans. It's because of the things you all do that our planet is dying," do you think he'd get anywhere? No. Absolutely not. Even if the things being said are true, people will by no means respond well to criticism, condemnation, or complaints.

"Give Honest and Sincere Appreciation:" If our climatologist went up on stage, but this time said "Hey everyone. I want to begin this talk by acknowledging the fact that you are all here. Your presence here is clear evidence that you care about our planet and are mindful of the threat of climate change. I'm sure that you all are trying to reduce your impact on the climate, but there's some key ways to do so that you might have just not come across," what do you think would happen? He would receive a very warm reception and people would be glad to listen to him.

"Arouse in the Other Person an Eager Want" / **"Make the Other Person Happy About Doing the Thing That You Suggest:"** People will do tasks much better if they want to than if they don't. If you want to get the best results out of an audience, make them want to do something. Our climatologist could say "don't you want to keep the planet clean for your kids and your kids' kids?"

"Talk in Terms of the Other Person's Interests / Be Sympathetic with Their Desires and Ideas:" This is similar to principle three. If you want people to follow your advice, then frame it in terms of what interests them. Most people are interested in saving money, so our climatologist could say "Money is great. Unfortunately, a great deal of it will have to be spent if we don't make small changes now to prevent climate change later on. Small expenses today will save massive expenses ten years from now. This is a coastal community. Imagine how much a giant flood wall in front of your house is going to cost!"

People respond much better to those who speak in terms of their interests. For example, a climatologist might pursue their work because they are disdained by the impact climate change has on animals. However, not everyone might share that interest. You should always try to find what interests your audience and speak in terms of it. Our climatologist could even interact with the audience, like so: "The gentlemen in the blue blazer in the first row, what is something you like to do on the weekends?" The gentleman might respond "I like to go on hikes with my son up by the creek trail." The climatologist could then incorporate this interest into his speech and say "I really enjoy hiking up that trail too. It's really saddening to me that the trail I've been hiking since I was a kid is going to be flooded soon due to climate change related rising sea levels."

"Get the Other Person Saying 'Yes, Yes' Immediately:" This is an interesting psychological technique that can persuade people into accepting more controversial ideas later on in a speech. When somebody thinks "no" to themselves, then that's it. They've chosen to adopt a mindset of resistance to any new ideas or information that you present them with. When somebody thinks "yes" to themselves, they begin to open up to new ideas with a much more receptive mind. Incorporate this into a speech by first asking basic background questions that anyone would respond yes to. This is essentially the principle of persuasive consistency.

Our climatologist might ask "you all don't want your favorite place to be underwater, right?" to which everyone will think "yes, you're right. I don't want my favorite place underwater." Then they might ask "you are all aware that climate change is caused by greenhouse gasses?" to which everyone will once again likely think "yes, I believe I heard that somewhere." By getting the audience to say yes to themselves twice, when the climatologist begins to challenge the intellectual status quo, the audience will be in a much more receptive state of mind. They will be in a "yes" mood as opposed to a "no" mood.

"Appeal to the Nobler Motives:" This principle is quite self-explanatory. To achieve this, our climatologist could say something along the lines of "think about it: don't you want your grandchildren to have the same beautiful Earth you grew up in?" thereby appealing to the noble motive of preserving things so that they can be enjoyed by future generations.

"Dramatize Your Ideas:" Sometimes, it doesn't hurt to do something bizarre. Our climatologist could take a water gun and spray the people in the front row, saying "the water from this water gun is the rising sea levels, and you in the front row are the coastal communities."

"Throw Down a Challenge:" Make a game out of it. Playfully challenge people to do a certain thing. Our climatologist could say "I challenge each and every one of you to carpool from now on every chance you get. It's not easy and not everyone can do it, so I'll just have to wait and see if you guys have it in you."

"Talk About Your Own Mistakes Before Criticizing the Other Person / Call Attention to People's Mistakes Indirectly:" When advising an audience to make changes to their lifestyle, a speaker can risk making themselves seem high-minded and above the audience. This is easily corrected if our climatologist were to say, for example, "Believe me everyone, I know how difficult it can be. The little changes seem to just slip through the cracks. Before I was a climatologist, I don't think I recycled a single piece of paper." Doing this builds immense relatability.

"Use Encouragement and Make the Fault Seem Easy to Correct:" If someone believes a situation is so dire that nothing they do can alleviate it, then why would they do anything at all? Let's take our climatologist again, for example. If he were to say "Climate change is pretty much irreversible at this point. I don't think you all want to completely change your lifestyles to mitigate it, so it's kind of hopeless," then that will become a self-fulfilling prophecy.

On the other hand, if he were to say "Climate change may seem daunting, but there are a few easy lifestyle changes that can be made any day to start reversing it. I'm sure you all have it in you because you all seem like smart people and because the lifestyle changes are quite minor," then the results would be much better. Because the fault is painted as easy to correct, many more audience members will pursue the solution.

EMOTION

People are very receptive to emotion. An audience can relate to emotion much more than logical arguments and snippets of unfeeling empirical evidence. People are not driven by cold, calculated logic, but by emotion. As you know, the vast majority of the decisions people make are based on emotion, not hard logic.

By tapping into a reserve of emotion when you speak, your words will resonate with your audience in a very memorable way. This doesn't mean, however, that you should cry or throw a fit in front of your audience. Emotion, concentrated and channeled in a specific direction, is one of the most powerful motivating forces known to humankind. If you decide to speak with emotion in your voice, make sure to channel it towards a specific goal, keep it in moderation, and keep it genuine. Raw emotion doesn't appeal to an audience, tempered emotion does.

To successfully use emotion in a public speech, the topic of the speech must be emotional. If you want to unlock the power of emotion in public speaking, you have to be willing to show vulnerability to the audience. By showing honest vulnerability, you show your humanity, and therefore increase the speaker to audience connection.

Using emotional language is a necessity for delivering an emotional speech. Consider the sentence "Climate change will begin affecting three out of every four people by 2030." It is an entirely unemotive phrase. Now consider the sentence "The impending threat of climate change will be destroying our pleasant way of life in 12 short years; one out of every four people will have to say goodbye to food security"; a very emotive phrase. Which is more powerful? Which makes you feel something? Hopefully the second one. Words like "impending," "threat," "destroying," "short years," and "say goodbye to food security" carry emotional implications because they add a human element to the picture.

The third step of delivering an emotional speech is using an emotional vocal inflection, one that exemplifies the emotional quality of the subject. Be resolute for most of the speech, but tremorous at a few key portions of it. The power of emotion in public speaking is unparalleled if used correctly. To quote Carl W. Buechner, "they may forget what you said, but they will never forget how you made them feel."

Emotion is not always appropriate. In business settings, for example, be wary of overusing it. If you are in a situation in which emotion is appropriate, and you do use it effectively, it will add another layer of meaning to your speech. Just make sure the situation calls for it.

KEY INSIGHT:

Let the Emotions You Feel Toward Your Subject Reveal Themselves.

This Is the Key: Don't Fabricate, Reveal. Release. Express. Authenticity Is Irreplaceable.

INTENSITY AND DYNAMISM

Consider Martin Luther King's "I have a dream" speech, in which he galvanized an unwavering determination in his audience. What made his famous speech so powerful? It was the dynamic intensity with which he delivered it. Intensity is a quality heard in the voices of people who are passionate about an idea or cause. Their voice resonates with their audience, and they become a leader who can energetically achieve goal after goal by rallying people to their cause.

Intensity appears when someone is so involved in the idea they are presenting to the audience, and have staked so much on its success, that the speaker's passion about the idea is transmitted into the hearts and minds of the audience. Intensity pushes the audience into action. It pushes people forward. Excitement, intensity, dynamism, charisma, or whatever you want to call it, is contagious. An audience that sees an excited figure will grow excited themselves and associate that excitement with the speaker.

To deliver a speech with intensity, you should speak at a volume that forces every single person in the audience to lend you their ears. This goes beyond the confident voice projection that should characterize all speeches. Intense voice projection has a fiery quality that doesn't belong everywhere. To deliver a speech with intensity, you should speak somewhat fast. A moderate talking pace is not as intense as a fast-talking pace. Speaking fast grants you the appearance of excitement and passion, two qualities that are closely tied to intensity. To deliver a public speech intensely, use strong physical gestures. There is also a specific vocal inflection pitch escalation strategy that can produce an intense, escalating affect.

Sentence one: pitch constant, then sharply up, then slightly down again.

Sentence two: pitch constant, starting where sentence 1 ended, then sharply up, then slightly down.

Sentence three: pitch constant, starting where sentence 2 ended, then sharply up, then slightly down.

Doing this will maintain breaking rapport vocal inflection but also raise the pitch of your voice in an intense and powerful way over the course of a few sentences. The repeatedly raised pitch will build intensity and excitement. Accompany the raised pitch with a raised volume. The final tip to take note of is that after building intensity through this pitch escalation strategy or any combination of intensity-creating techniques, stopping and becoming eerily calm for a few seconds of your speech will chill your audience and place incredible emphasis on what you are saying in that moment.

When your speech reaches its most important segment, throw your entire being into it. You should be out of breath by the end of an intense speech, because you were speaking so fast, so loudly, and gesturing so energetically. Intensity is dynamism; the attribute that allows some people to catalyze extreme change and progress. To quote D.H. Lawrence, "Be still when you have nothing to say; when genuine passion moves you, say what you've got to say, and say it hot."

CONVICTION

T.F. Hodge once said that "you cannot build a dream on a foundation of sand. To weather the test of storms, it must be cemented in the head with uncompromising conviction." Conviction is an internal quality, so how do you manifest it outwardly? In a speech, conviction can only be truly accomplished when the speaker is completely convinced in the validity or importance of their idea. A speaker with conviction will transmit their doubtless belief into the minds of the entire audience. Conviction cannot be achieved if the speaker doesn't believe in their idea: in fact, the closest thing would be fake conviction, which is even worse than no conviction.

Conviction is power. The statement "I believe that this new plan might be one of the solutions to our economic difficulties" lacks conviction. The same statement with conviction is "I know that this extensive plan is the solution to our economic difficulties. This plan will result in each and every one of you having a better life. I know that to be fact." Clearly the one with conviction is stronger.

To harness the power of conviction in your speeches, the first and most important step is to make excessive use of breaking rapport tonality. This will subconsciously express your belief in the idea to your audience. Your words will make a conscious impact on your audience, but the tonality you say them with will make a subconscious one.

As with intensity, there is a vocal inflection technique designed to produce a sense of conviction. It can be performed by asking a rhetorical question to the audience accompanied by raising tonality, and then answering it with almost excessive breaking rapport tonality:

Sentence one: rhetorical question, raising tonality.

Sentence two: answer to question, with massive, clear, and decisive breaking rapport tonality.

This technique is actually called anthypophora, but that refers solely to the rhetorical question and answer, not the accompanying vocal tonalities.

The second step is to speak in absolutes. This means that instead of saying "*I think* this might be the solution," you should say "*I know* this is the solution," or better yet, simply "*this is* the solution." Additionally, place much vocal emphasis on the absolute phrases. Emphasize the fact that *this is* the solution, and that you don't just *think* it is the solution.

The last step is to gesture sharply when you say the absolutes to emphasize them non-vocally. The ideal gestures for emphasizing the absolutes are downward gestures, as though you are placing your hands on the surface of an invisible medicine ball and pushing it down.

By speaking with conviction, you can replicate your belief in an idea in the minds of your audience. That's a very useful, and very powerful ability, and it is what many public speakers seek as their end goal.

PAST, PRESENT, AND FUTURE

Another technique is asserting your beliefs in the past, present, and future. Maybe this seems crazy, but it's not. For example, if you are advocating for a solution, you can say "This was, is, and will continue to be the best solution." You can also stretch it out and add more substance by saying "This was the solution when [insert a time when this would have solved a past problem]. This is the solution now because [reason why this is the solution now]. Most importantly, this will continue to be the best solution because [reason why the value of this solution will not diminish with time]." An example of a politician using this technique is this: "During the Great Depression, government job programs were absolutely critical to revitalizing the economy. The complaints my opponents have didn't happen then, so they won't happen now. Government job programs now are the solution because they will help people who rely on dying industries for their livelihoods, without holding the rest of us back. This solution will always continue to be valuable because every government worker is not only a mouth and family fed, but someone who contributes to this country."

Combining conviction with asserting your ideas in the past, future, and present is an extremely powerful technique. By speaking about the solution in the past, the politician shows that it is tried and true, and that it is reliable. By speaking about the future, the politician shows that the solution is not going to need a replacement any time soon. Regardless of what happens in the future, every government worker will always be someone who contributes to this country, which is why the solution will always be valuable. The relevance to the present is always the most important part of this technique, but by spanning all timeframes, the politician is able to deliver a significantly more thorough and convincing speech.

PODIUM OR NO PODIUM

The question of whether or not to use a podium when speaking has been debated for some time simply because both options have so many pros and cons. Using a podium gives you a place to put your manuscript and notes, lends you a sense of authority, and makes you feel a little more confident and protected. These things, however, come at the caveat of hindering your speaker to audience connection.

Think about it: your body is hidden behind a big wooden block. None of the techniques you learned in the Use of Body section can really apply, and if they do, not as well. Speaking from a podium reduces your physical presence and engagement. It can help you prioritize using your voice at the cost of completely sacrificing your physical presence, and while this may sound beneficial, it could harm your engagement. On the other hand, not using a podium will allow you to use gestures, movement, and all of the other physical techniques shared in this book to maximize engagement.

A podium is well suited for a formal speech due to the amount of authority it lends to the speaker, while a conversational speech most certainly does not benefit from a podium. In many cases, the best use of a podium for a conversational speech is as a place to put a water bottle, like Marco Rubio did in his State of the Union Republican Party Response. The only time a podium is absolutely recommended is in a very formal setting when you have to give a speech word-for-word from a manuscript, but you haven't memorized it yet. In this case, you can use the podium as a place to keep your papers.

MIC OR NO MIC

I will preface this section by saying one thing: if you do use a microphone, do not make the same mistake I've made time and time again. Keep it an appropriate distance from your mouth. Over and over, I would keep the microphone far too close to my mouth. Every "P" sounded like an explosion to my audience. An appropriate distance is anywhere between six to twelve inches away from your mouth. Experiment with it until you find the balance between "what did you say?" and "stop destroying my ears." It's always okay to ask your audience if they can hear you well enough or if you are too loud. The decision to forgo a microphone is a brave one. What if people can't hear you? It all depends on your natural voice. If even after you project your voice to the maximum, meaning just before you begin to yell, your audience still can't hear you, then a microphone is a wise choice. However, if you are one of those speakers with a voice loud enough to fill a large auditorium, there's a certain power that comes with doing so.

If you are speaking in a small room or to a small group, definitely do not use a microphone. If your venue is a large auditorium but less than one third of it is filled, tell everyone to gather in the front set of rows. Putting your audience close together makes them more of an "audience." You and your audience both perceive forty people scattered throughout an auditorium differently than forty people in a close-knit group up in the front rows. If you can, choose the latter. Tell your audience to clump together in the front and don't use a microphone.

Regardless of what you choose, there's no need to burn the bridge: have a microphone on hand and make sure it's working. You'll thank yourself if you decide you need to use it. You can always use it if it's there, but you can't use it if it's not. Leave yourself the option.

POWERPOINT OR NO POWERPOINT

A well-made PowerPoint is a useful advantage. It provides a significant structure to your speech or presentation and dispels any beliefs that you might be winging it. Much like a podium, having a PowerPoint grants you additional authority.

If you are using a PowerPoint, make sure you have a slide clicker so that you can move around the room instead of having to return to the projecting laptop and change slides manually. If you don't, you can always ask someone in attendance to change the slides for you on your command. Laser pointers are useful as well: you can use them to point to key elements on the slide. Clickers with laser pointers in them are a worthy investment if you need to give many PowerPoints.

PowerPoints are useful if you are giving presentations to groups of ten people or more. If you're trying to inform or persuade anywhere between one to five people, a PowerPoint seems overkill. In that case, you can develop a much more personal connection with them by speaking directly to them. Indeed, this isn't an all-encompassing rule. You should know your audience, and you should therefore know if an audience will prefer a PowerPoint even if it is a small audience.

If you have a smaller group and you want to give them some sort of physical information, you can print out small packets and hand them out. Your audience can use them to follow along with your talk or read through them later as a refresher. Doing so can be greatly appreciated in a professional environment, especially if the information is genuinely valuable, actionable, or otherwise obscure. You can even print out your slides and hand them out instead of projecting them if it's a smaller group.

In most cases, using a PowerPoint or other presentation tool such as google slides, or even Prezi (which is more fluid) is very advantageous provided one assumption: that you use it correctly, as shown in the presentation tools section.

KEY INSIGHT:

Most Slide Decks Hurt the Presenter. They Distract, Diminish, and Weaken.

If You Feel Like You Need Your Slide Deck to Present, It's An Attempt to Hide Unpreparedness.

PROPS OR NO PROPS

Another debated question is whether or not props have a place in public speaking. Many people assume props are always a detriment due to their inherent tackiness. These people overlook how props can actually be used in an un-tacky and tasteful way. A writer speaking to an audience about his craft can open by pulling out a pen, holding it in front of him, focusing intently on it with his body language, and saying "three years ago I knew that my ability to find happiness in my life hinged on this plastic thing." Undeniably powerful and memorable. Someone speaking about suffering through difficult circumstances can use a rose throughout their speech as an analogy to a person; they can fold it and then bend it back into place to represent repairing oneself; they can stomp all over it and then show how it is still in one piece; they can hold it above their heads to represent rebirth. The possibilities are endless.

Props are not inherently tacky, but they become tacky when they are overt. There is nothing tacky about using a small pen as a prop, or a rose, or an onion to represent a concept with many layers. It can create pleasant visual unity and give the audience a visual focal point.

If the speaker discussing the process of going through difficult circumstances went through them, they could wear an outfit that is the same color as the rose. Once again; undeniably powerful content that creates a visually united image. They can say: "in the scenario I'm about to show you, I represent life, and the rose represents me" before proceeding to stomp on it. Clever, cynically humorous, and meaningful.

One consideration is that having props can diminish your ability to use hand gestures, which is why many speakers who use props pocket them at a certain point in their speech or lay them down on a podium. Regardless, props are clearly not tacky if used correctly.

READING THE AUDIENCE

Some might believe that a public speech is a form of one-way communication. Rest assured; it's not. It is not only you communicating with your audience. If you are attentive enough, you'll notice that your audience is subtly communicating back to you. Many speakers don't pick up on these subtle forms of communication, and in some cases, the audience doesn't even notice they are performing them. This is simply because of how subtle these signals really are. They take the form of slight, subconscious shifts in body language, and to perceive these shifts in your audience takes a great deal of clairvoyance, presence, and attentiveness.

To pick up on what your audience is telling you is an indisputable advantage. It allows you to know when to speed up, slow down, be louder or quieter, and even cut off your speech if necessary.

What are the actual, physical, observable signs an audience gives off? It can vary widely. They can sit forward in their seats, or lean back. They can look directly at you, or off to one of your sides. They can be fidgety, or they can be still. They can murmur to each other, or be totally silent. They can sigh or check their watches. They can either be responsive to your humor or not. They can show varying facial expressions, or be completely expressionless.

Each of these signs communicate a different sentiment. If your audience is sitting on the edge of their seats, it can mean that they are highly attentive and engaged, but also that you may be speaking too quietly or too quickly and they need to sit forward to hear more clearly. If you are sure it is not the latter, then this is a very good sign that your speech is a success. If they are looking at you, and returning your eye contact (which you should always have with your audience), it means that you have achieved an audience to speaker connection and that they are engaged with your speech. On the contrary, if they are looking to your sides or somewhere behind you, that means that they are distracted by something and you need to regain their attention. Similarly, if they are being fidgety, it can mean that they are bored by your speech or even that the temperature of the room is uncomfortable. This is one of the most telling signs of how an audience is receiving your speech, assuming that it doesn't have to do with the temperature.

If your audience members are murmuring amongst themselves, it can mean that they are offended by the sentiment of your speech, or disagreeing with your message and voicing that disagreement to each other. One of the most obvious signals given by audience members, and in some cases one of the only ones that may be given consciously, is sighing and checking watches or phones for the time. It doesn't take a behavioral psychologist to know that this means your speech is running a little long. If your audience responds to your humor, it means that you did a good job of establishing the speaker to audience connection early on. If they do not respond, it means the opposite. Lastly, your audience's facial expressions can say something about what's going through their heads. If you are painting a picture or describing an event that they find frustrating, they can grimace; a sign that they have good rapport established with you and are in agreement with your message. You should be concerned if you are indignantly relaying a frustrating situation and your audience is not grimacing. Similarly, you should be concerned if you are *not* relaying a frustrating situation and they *are* grimacing.

All of these signs are very subtle and to have the presence of mind to focus on them while also delivering your speech effectively is a challenge that requires practice. It will, however, pay dividends in your ability to ensure every speech you give is a success by allowing you to adapt to different circumstances when they arise. It's obviously important not only to notice these signs, but to respond to them.

Noticing these signs and reacting to them is a prerequisite to exceptional speaking. A mindset that will help you notice these signs is always focusing on your audience. By placing your attention towards your audience instead of yourself, which can understandably be difficult, it will become much easier to spot the signs they are giving off. Additionally, now that you know what they are, it won't be quite as difficult to observe them when they occur. A good practice to get into is to do periodic scans of the audience, in an imperceptible way, to receive the feedback they are giving you through these subtle indicators.

Typically, speakers tend to pay very close attention to themselves and every little action they take on the stage; every single intonation and shift in their body language. They are very conscious of themselves. To be a truly great public speaker, however, you must actively shift your attention away from yourself and develop a sense of audience consciousness.

READING THE OCCASION

You just learned about audience interaction: now, you'll learn how to read the occasion. Remember the different opportunities to speak publicly presented early on in the book? If not, I'll remind you of them. They were: speaking at social gatherings, career driven speaking, public speaking-oriented events, and non-public-speaking oriented events. You can't read your audience until you actually see them and they begin giving you signals. You can, however, make some educated guesses about your audience based on the occasion you are speaking at. Regardless of which of the four types of occasions you are speaking at, ask yourself these questions and try to find the answers to them before actually getting up to deliver your speech: What purpose is the occasion for? Do I know none, a small number, most, or all of the people in the audience? How large is my audience, how fancy is my venue, and am I getting paid to give the speech? Am I similar to my audience members or am I an authority on a given subject?

The purpose of the occasion is especially important to keep in mind. Whenever you need to speak to a group of people and you want to figure out the best approach, ask yourself this: "why are they all here?" If you know your speech doesn't suit the purpose for your audience being there, then don't give it. If you know it doesn't, but you feel confident that you can alter it accordingly, then do that. A big part of giving successful speeches is serving your audience. In other words, fulfilling the purpose of your audience actually being there. Make sure you align your purpose with your audience's purpose. Think back to the different public speaking triads, and make sure your tone fits the triad you are trying to build. Not only that, but make sure that the triad you are trying to build is exactly the triad your audience will be receptive to, and that it is what they want.

The number of people in the audience that you know is also very important to find out, if you can. It will be much easier to give a confident speech to people that you know. Additionally, you'll know what type of humor works on them, and for many reasons the entire speech will be a much smoother process. Generally, people tend to like listening to their friends or acquaintances give a speech more than a stranger. If you know none of the audience members, then you can do a much more substantial introduction of yourself. If you know a small number, what you can do is say "I don't know most of you, but is that [insert friend's name here] I see? And [insert another friend's name here] in the second row?" This is effective because while you may not know everyone, the people you do know might. Suddenly, you'll go from being a complete stranger to a friend of a friend. Of course, don't use this strategy if it's unlikely that your friends in the audience will have other friends in the audience. You can safely assume that if you are giving a speech to a company of 100 people, and you know about 20 of them, that those 20 you do know likely know some of the 80 you don't. In other situations, it's not quite as likely. And, lastly, if you do know most or all of your audience, then use that as an advantage. Make jokes you know they like, take political stances you know they all agree with, and use a friendly approach because you are, after all, friends or at the very least friendly acquaintances.

The size of your audience, how fancy your venue is, and whether or not you are getting paid are three factors associated with how much officiality should go into your speech. If your audience is twenty people, your venue is a local pub, and you aren't getting paid, then the speech can be more relaxed. In fact, that's exactly what your audience is expecting. A relaxed, easy-going, and conversational speech. On the other hand, if your audience is one thousand people, your venue is a massive auditorium with Roman moldings and gold chandeliers, and you are getting paid for the speech, then the speech demands a higher level of officiality, a less easy-going approach, and more formality. Find out what you can about the size of your audience, the venue, and what kind of direct compensation you're getting. These factors will help you determine what type of approach is best.

The final question, that of where you stand in relation to your audience, is also very crucial. You can find yourself giving a speech to subordinates in your company, to equals, or to superiors. Of course, I mean that strictly in the hierarchical sense.

Nonetheless, each of these different situations demands a different approach. If you are a mid-level manager giving a speech to a group of higher-up executives, be more respectful and less familiar. However, be confident, assertive, and don't be reverent: just be respectful. It's a tough balance to strike sometimes, but you never want to sound like you are gawking in awe of your audience. That's psychologically off-putting. If you are speaking to equals, then do not patronize. Do not make it seem to them that you see yourself as superior just because you are giving a speech to them. Be very, very careful of this. A mid-level manager giving a speech to other mid-level managers must be very careful to ensure that no feeling of self-superiority is perceptible, and indeed, that no such feeling exists in the first place. Do not explain things that they might already know just for the sake of explaining them. Lastly, if you are speaking to subordinates, again only in a hierarchical sense, then show humility but also demand respect. If you are an authority on a given subject, and you have valuable knowledge that your audience wants, that is a very different situation then when speaking to equals and speaking to superiors.

AUDIENCE INTERACTION

Reading your audience is based on seeing public speaking as a form of two-way communication in which one of the channels of communication is simply much subtler than the other one. What if you deliberately make that second channel of communication less subtle? Well, that can make for a very engaging speech. There are many ways to interact with your audience and develop a dialogue with them.

You can ask for a show of hands: "by a show of hands, how many people in this room believe in climate change?" You can even do a sort of pre-test post-test poll by asking for a show of hands at the beginning of your speech and then asking the same question at the end. Our climatologist would ask "now that I've finished my presentation to you all, I'd once again like to ask how many of you believe in climate change?" This sort of audience interaction serves a practical purpose because it gives you feedback on whether you were able to persuade your audience members.

Another form of audience interaction is not asking for responses by a show of hand, but by calling on specific audience members and asking them specific questions. For example: "the gentleman in the second row in a nice suit... do you know how many degrees Celsius our planet has warmed up over the past ten years?" There's a certain power that comes with implying that you're going to call on random people to answer your questions. Nobody will resist that, and they will all immediately pay extremely close attention. Why? They fear being called on and not knowing the question or the context of the question. Calling on random people for answers is a true power-move.

When you're doing this, the goal isn't necessarily to get an accurate response. The goal is to get your audience sitting on the edge of their seats. If you get an accurate response, great. If not, everyone will chuckle and the speaker to audience connection will be bolstered by that. The truly important goal of getting your audience to sit on the edge of their seats and be fully engaged will still have been accomplished. It's not expected that you'll get an accurate answer: it's expected that you won't. However, at this point, everyone in the audience will be thinking: "what if I get asked the next question? I better pay attention."

Don't ask the same question to a different audience member over and over again until it's answered. Ask it to one person, and if they get it wrong simply say "very close, but not quite," and then ask if anyone knows the answer. If nobody raises their hand or shouts it out, then answer it yourself. The ultimate goal of engaging your audience will still have been achieved.

There's an even more sophisticated way of using audience interaction. Remember the persuasive principle of likability? People are more willing to help those they like, and people like those who have established similarity, presented common goals, and complimented them. Use this when interacting with your audience. Ask them what goals their working towards, and say "Me too. That's exactly what I want." Ask them where they like to vacation and say "Me too. I've been there a few times, it's great." Tell them that you like their ties, watches, or eyeglasses. They will appreciate these little things and like you more because of them. These techniques aren't always applicable if your audience is very large, but for smaller, more personal audiences, they are highly effective.

Keep in mind when interacting with your audience that if you intend to call on a specific person, make it clear who you are referring to by saying things like "the gentlemen with the red tie in row four," or "the young lady in row two with the pink dress." This will avoid the awkward situation of your audience members not knowing who you are trying to call on.

QUESTION AND ANSWER

A very special public speaking paradigm occurs during question-and-answer segments. In the previous section, we discussed asking the audience questions. Now, we'll discuss answering their questions.

It's very rare to have a successful informational or persuasive speech that doesn't allow a substantial question and answer period afterwards. Why should you take the time to answer questions? Well, it's as simple as this: your audience will almost always have questions!

Think about the learning process as you've experienced it in your life. Typically, when you learn some information, doesn't the information you learn seem to raise more questions? That's exactly what it's like for your audience. Even if you think you covered everything about a topic, which is very hard to do in the first place and isn't something you should try, I promise you that your audience still has questions.

When you're giving a persuasive speech, you are trying to get your audience to give up one or more of their essential resources: either time, energy, or money. If someone is considering doing so, of course they will want to ask more questions just to ensure that they are making the right decision. Clearly, question and answer segments of your speech are highly valuable for achieving your purpose.

Another advantage of question-and-answer segments is that during your speech, some of your audience members might be forming a few doubts in their mind as they listen. A question-and-answer period allows these doubts to be put out into the open, where you can address them head on. You can't address an issue, doubt, or concern if you don't know what it is or that it even exists. As a salesman or saleswoman, a question-and-answer period allows you to see what obstructions to buying your audience might be feeling.

Consider this: as a public speaker, you are a resource to your audience. If you are a resource for persuasion (by being a potential provider of a solution to one of their problems), or for information, then your audience will want to use you to your fullest potential by asking the questions that they haven't yet found an answer to in your speech.

Make sure that when initiating a question-and-answer period you leave a longer pause between it and the end of your speech, and make sure that it's clear to your audience what is happening. Definitely say something. Don't expect your audience to just know that they can ask you questions. Not only that, but definitely say more than this: "I will now be taking questions." That's better than nothing, but to provide a more jarring signal to your audience that they can ask you questions, a longer statement is more appropriate. Something along the lines of "At this point, I will be taking questions for ten minutes. If you want to ask a question about the content of my speech or about me, please do so. I'm open to any and all questions: I want to make sure you all get the most out of this presentation. Just raise your hands and I'll call on you." It's even better to tell your audience at the beginning of your speech that you will be taking questions after your speech, so that they can consider and prepare questions as you speak.

Don't be thrown off by skeptical, even hostile questions. Let's imagine that our climatologist opens it up for questions, and an audience member says: "Alright, I think this whole presentation was just quite frankly ridiculous. How do you expect that to be sufficient evidence that the climate is actually getting warmer? Just look outside. How do you respond to the fact that we've had the coldest Thanksgiving in the past century?" Indeed, a natural human reaction would be to retort something like: "Have you listened to a word I've said? How can you deny the clear evidence? You are only belittling my work because you don't understand it." However, as a public speaker, much of what you do involves avoiding natural human reactions. A response like that makes it seem that you and your audience are hostile to each other. Even if other audience members agree that the initial question was foolish, there's no need to fire back at your audience member. The rest of your audience will find it incredibly admirable if you respond assertively, but kindly to a very hostile question. A response like this is much better: "Thank you, that's a good question. So, I'll just say that I'm sorry you found the presentation ridiculous. I still hope that you got something out of it, even if you disagree. Now, to answer your first question about how I can expect that evidence to be enough, I think that's a question a lot of people are asking themselves about climate change. It's not just you. And my response is this: even if you don't believe in my work, there's a massive body of scientific literature on climate change. 97% of it supports my conclusion. And to answer the second question, about the fact that we've had the coldest Thanksgiving in history, I think that's a fair question. Here's the answer: yes, we have. But climate change creates a broad trend. There will be outliers. Additionally, climate change increases the volatility of the climate, meaning that as the overall climate, on a big picture level, is getting warmer, the less and less cold days we do have might actually be colder than before. Does that answer your question? Let me know if there's any other question you have, I'm always happy to answer. Thanks again."

Just remain calm and respectful. Your knowledge will do the rest. Never condescend onto an audience member who asks a question with an obvious answer, and never lash out at them. As you can probably see by our climatologist's response, a response to an audience question should be fairly long. Up to two minutes. Oftentimes, when an audience member asks you a question, they aren't just looking for a one-word answer. They certainly want that, but they still want more. They are prompting you to make a type of "mini-speech" right then and there in response to their question. If someone asks "when was climate change first identified?" the climatologist shouldn't just name a time and place. They should expand on that, provide context, and describe interesting details.

Always turn the question around. This will make sure that your audience members all understand what you're responding to, because they may have missed the question being asked. Turning the question around is briefly restating the question in your answer. For example, if the question is "Why do many people deny climate change?" a climatologist should begin the answer with "The reasons many people deny climate change are [reasons]."

Sometimes, a question-and-answer period involves a back and forth. It could be an argumentative back and forth, or a back and forth of questions. Be prepared to handle that gracefully. Also, keep in mind that while you should direct your response to the audience member who asked the question, it's very possible, indeed likely, that other audience members had the same question. Don't think of it as just a response to the one person who asked the question, but a response for the entire audience. Lastly, when you finish your response, ask the person who asked you the question if they have any additional questions and if you fully answered the first one.

Question and answer sections are, quite frequently, almost as important as the actual speech. Never overlook the importance of a question-and-answer segment.

ASPECTS OF DELIVERY CONCLUSION

Now you know it all. You've officially learned just about everything there is to learn about public speaking with power, influence, and persuasion. The last thing left for you to do is to take the knowledge of these skills and to put them into practice. Remember what Anton Chekhov said? "Knowledge is of no value unless you put it into practice." You're ready. You've read the most comprehensive resource on public speaking available. Time to put it to work in as many ways as you possibly can.

KEY INSIGHT:

No Great Speaker Does Everything According to the Textbook.

Public Speaking is Part Art, Part Science. Balance Structure and Strategy with Spontaneity.

PUTTING IT ALL TOGETHER

An exemplary speaker will spend 5 minutes in silence after committing to a speech, simply developing the proper mental frame. They will then consider the public speaking triad for the type of speech they are giving, and whether it is to inform, persuade, inspire, entertain, or a combination. They will be confident in themselves, and if not, they will acknowledge any anxiety they may be feeling instead of repressing it, and then compartmentalize it. If they are still feeling anxious, they will perform a relaxation technique. They will carefully consider how to use each part of their speaker's toolbox as best as they can, making sure not to forget any specific technique. If they have this book, perhaps they will read through the "takeaways" section for some key reminders (this section is coming shortly).

They will either choose to write a complete manuscript, or speak freely around a set of ideas. Upon choosing their method, they will prepare according to what is best suited to their chosen method. They will prepare a simple visual aid, such as a small notecard, if they feel it is necessary. They will have smoothed out their speech by practicing impromptu speeches at least once a day. They will choose an outfit that is slightly more formal than what their audience will wear, but still similar. They will prepare their presentation tools if they choose to use them, and they will keep the words on the slides brief and include many pictures to provide the audience with visual accompaniment to the speaker's voice. They will use a slide clicker to change slides from anywhere in the room, and they will blank slides instead of leaving a slide on display that is no longer important.

The speaker will ensure that their speech is structured well, and they will write an engaging hook. They will also write a meaningful call to action for the end of their speech. They will integrate pathos, ethos, and logos in their speech and use the six methods of persuasion if they want to persuade or inspire. They will tie their speech to the core human desires, and they will take advantage of kairos if applicable. They will use statistics with influence and avoid logical fallacies, all the while using particularly powerful sentence structure. Metaphors, similes, and analogies will be abundant in their speech, and they will choose a diction and word choice befitting of their situation, audience, and subject matter. They will speak with high substance by giving more information in less words, and they will also provide novelty to their audience by moving at a fast but thorough pace through the material. They will use positive and inclusive language to connect to their audiences. They will decide if their topic has saliency, intensity, and stability. If it doesn't, they will either have a connection to make that does, or they will acknowledge that their topic is permissive. Because their topic is permissive, they will then focus on creating saliency, intensity, and stability in whatever direction they want. They will understand if their subject is divisive, or if it has consensus, and prepare themselves and their speech accordingly. They will choose one main theme that synergizes very well with their subject. They will provide mental model shifts to their audience through reframing techniques, and they will use frame presentation in order to use the other reframing techniques. They will make their speech simple, to the relief of themselves and their audience. They will include a priming statement at the start of their speech. They will include one or two personal anecdotes to connect with their audience.

As soon as they get on stage and begin speaking, they will project their voice and emphasize particular words to deliver a stronger message. They will use dramatic pausing to build suspense and strategically choose their talking pace. The tone they use will be deliberately matched to the content of their speech, and throughout their speech they will use breaking rapport tonality. They will modulate their volume, pitch, and speed in a way that mirrors the words they are saying, and if not, they will at least modulate it to create variety. In doing so, they will avoid a boring verbal pattern. The vocal exercises they will have done prior to their speech will help them and give their voice a much better timbre.

They will stand with confident posture, make eye contact with audience members, and use powerful gestures. They will pace across the room once or twice throughout their speech to create movement on the stage, and they will use facial expressions to illustrate their message.

They will speak conversationally or formally based on the situation, and they will choose wisely between the two. They will master the approach suited to their purpose, whether it is to inform, persuade, inspire, or entertain. They will be cognizant of timing and not run on too long. They will avoid almost all conversation fillers and fumbles, and also have a distinct and memorable individual style. If they do interject a conversation filler or accidentally fumble, they will not panic and they will gracefully proceed. They will also respond gracefully to challenges and challenge others just as gracefully if the situation calls for it. They will inject pleasantries into their speech to bolster the speaker to audience connection. They will use emotion, intensity, and conviction, but they will focus on one of the three in particular: whichever one is best suited to their message. Nonetheless, they will abundantly use all three if they feel it will help their speech. They will strategically accept or deny use of a podium, and they will use props in a way that contributes positively to their speech. They will also strategically use or not use a microphone, and also strategically choose whether or not to have a PowerPoint. Throughout the entire speech, they will be reading the audience and reacting to what they see. They will not hesitate to interact with the audience. They will allocate a significant amount of time to a question-and-answer segment. They will carefully consider the occasion for their speech, and deliver it accordingly. They will experience success because they took time learning how to speak publicly.

Who is this phenomenal, polished public speaker? Who could it be? Well, it's you. Honestly, it's *anyone* who has something to say. It's anyone who has something to say and pursues public speaking with dedication, passion, and determination. So, if you're willing to do that, it will be you. And eventually, you'll come to realize something. It is effortless.

MY LAST PIECES OF ADVICE

I'm going to give you my last few pieces of advice here. First and foremost, don't be a perfectionist. Never count yourself a failed speaker if you made one little mistake. I have seen nationally recognized speakers, and I have competed in countless final rounds between the top six competitors in groups of 100 competitors. Let me tell you one thing that has happened time and time again: I have made mistakes, and my competitors have made mistakes. It does not matter all that much. Little mistakes are overlooked quickly and emphatically by an audience which is learning from you, connecting to you, and appreciating you.

My next advice is to detach yourself from the outcome. A salesman trying to sell to an audience will be more likely to fail if they stake their self-worth on the outcome. Be willing to accept any outcome, and by virtue of your willingness to accept defeat, you are less likely to experience it. A speaker which needs a specific outcome will subconsciously allow that neediness to seep into their voice. It's happened to me, and I've seen it happen to countless others.

Now, let me tell you something else: you have a unique, interesting, and wonderful personality. You should be willing to let your personality shine through when you speak. Your audience will be appreciative of it. One of the events I competed in when I was in high school and attended Massachusetts Speech and Debate League tournaments was essentially a political round-table debate. I absolutely loved it. In fact, it was my main event. Finals rounds were incredibly tense. The stakes were high, there was an audience of up to 50 people, and each of the six finalists was in it to win it. Shouting matches were as common in this event as they are on televised political round-tables (there were basically no rules preventing this). Competitors put on very stark, professional veneers, much like lawyers. On the other hand, I made jokes here and there. I let my personality shine through instead of masking it. The judges appreciated it, the laughing audience appreciated it, and it even lightened the mood for the other five competitors who were all out to get me. Always let your personality shine through. It shows confidence and control.

Now, my last piece of advice as you continue along the public speaking journey, and a piece of advice that applies if you are just beginning and if you have already mastered it, is this: enjoy it. Public speaking really is a keystone skill, and it will make your life more enjoyable in several important ways. As you progress, don't lose sight of that and you will retain your motivation to keep moving forward.

To summarize: don't be a perfectionist, detach yourself from the outcome, let your personality shine through, and enjoy the process.

FINAL WORDS

Public Speaking is not important for its own sake. It is as important as this book suggests only because *you* are important. It is important because it gives someone important an outlet. It is important because it is a merchant dealing priceless merchandise: your ideas.

An incalculable number of brilliant ideas have lived and died inside one mind: the mind of someone who needed to be heard, but wasn't. Instead of spreading from person to person, and mind to mind, these ideas were trapped. I consider this an age-old tragedy that has gone undetected for centuries: the death of ideas that could have saved lives and prevented disasters. Do not let this be you. Let your ideas see the light of day and use what this book taught you to make the world a better place.

That's what it's all about: using your voice and making yourself heard so that you can live up to your fullest potential and hopefully make the world a better place in doing so. Therein lies the true importance of public speaking. It is not an inherently valuable activity. It is valuable because you are. So, use it for you. Harness your voice, collect your ideas, and be heard by mastering the power of public speaking.

..............................Chapter Summary................................

- There are multiple aspects of delivery that allow you to speak with poise, impact, and confidence.
- Pay attention to the audience: They are communicating essential meaning to you.
- Read the occasion: Ensure that what you have planned for your message fits the context of your delivery.
- Challenge others and receive challenges gracefully and tactfully, showing respect for your interlocuter.
- Apply the different possible styles of delivery: modulate your intensity, emotion, and conviction as needed.
- Consider the crucial choices you will have to make: Podium or no podium? Mic or no mic? Props or no props?

HOW TO MASTER PUBLIC SPEAKING (PART SIX)

1	Background
1.1	Many Public Speaking Books Fail to Teach the Subject Optimally
1.2	This Book Is Designed to Correct Their Mistakes
1.3	Public Speaking is Part of the Foundation of Success
1.4	Public Speaking Will Massively Improve Your Career and Life
1.5	You Will Be More Likely to Get Hired, Promoted, and Paid More
1.6	Starting the Public Speaking Journey Demands Beating Anxiety
1.7	Public Speaking Means to Speak to 10-1,000,000,000 People
1.8	Adopting a Mental Frame of Abundance Will Improve Your Results
1.9	Multiple Opportunities Arise for Practicing the Skill: Seize Them
1.10	Vastly Different Speeches Are Similar at Their Fundamental Level
1.11	The First Type of Speech is Speaking to Inform
1.12	The Second Type of Speech is Speaking to Persuade
1.13	The Third Type of Speech is Speaking to Inspire
1.14	The Fourth Type of Speech is Speaking to Entertain
1.15	All Speeches Share Some Common Fundamentals
1.16	Most Speeches Fulfill More Than One of the Four Purposes
1.17	A Speaker Uses His Words, Body, and Voice to Convey His Message
2	Preparation
2.1	The First Determinant of Speaking Success is Confidence
2.2	Public Speaking Anxiety is Normal, Natural, and Beatable
2.3	There Are Multiple Powerful Strategies For Defeating the Anxiety

Email Peter D. Andrei, the author of the Speak for Success collection and the President of Speak Truth Well LLC directly.

pandreibusiness@gmail.com

SOMETHING WAS MISSING. THIS IS IT.

D ECEMBER OF 2021, I COMPLETED the new editions of the 15 books in the Speak for Success collection, after months of work, and many 16-hour-long writing marathons. The collection is over 1,000,000 words long and includes over 1,700 handcrafted diagrams. It is *the* complete communication encyclopedia. But instead of feeling relieved and excited, I felt uneasy and anxious. Why? Well, I know now. After writing over 1,000,000 words on communication across 15 books, it slowly dawned on me that I had missed the most important set of ideas about good communication. What does it *really* mean to be a good speaker? This is my answer.

THERE ARE THREE DIMENSIONS OF SUCCESS

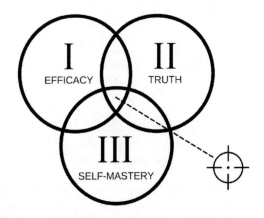

FIGURE I: A good speaker is not only rhetorically effective. They speak the truth, and they are students of self-mastery who experience peace, calm, and deep equanimity as they speak. These three domains are mutually reinforcing.

THE THREE AXES, IN DIFFERENT WORDS

Domain One	Domain Two	Domain Three
Efficacy	Truth	Self-Mastery
Rhetoric	Research	Inner-Peace
Master of Words	Seeker of Truth	Captain of Your Soul
Aristotle's "Pathos"	Aristotle's "Logos"	Aristotle's "Ethos"
Impact	Insight	Integrity
Presence of Power	Proper Perspective	Power of Presence
Inter-Subjective	Objective	Subjective
Competency	Credibility	Character
External-Internal	External	Internal
Verbal Mastery	Subject Mastery	Mental Mastery
Behavioral	Cognitive	Emotional

I realized I left out much about truth and self-mastery, focusing instead on the first domain. On page 27, the practical guide is devoted to domain I. On page 34, the ethical guide is devoted to domain II. We will shortly turn to domain III with an internal guide.

WHAT A GOOD SPEAKER LOOKS LIKE

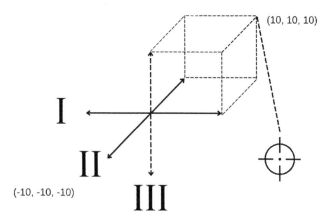

FIGURE II: We can conceptualize the three domains of success as an (X, Y, Z) coordinate plane, with each axis extending between -10 and 10. Your job is to become a (10, 10, 10). A (-10, 10, 10) speaks the truth and has attained self-mastery, but is deeply ineffective. A (10, -10, 10), speaks brilliantly and is at peace, but is somehow severely misleading others. A (10, 10, -10), speaks the truth well, but lives in an extremely negative inner state.

THE THREE AXES VIEWED DIFFERENTLY

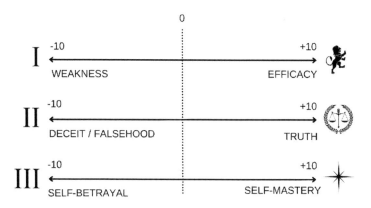

FIGURE III: We can also untangle the dimensions of improvement from representation as a coordinate plane, and instead lay them out flat, as spectrums of progress. A (+10, -10, -10) is a true monster, eloquent but evil. A (10, 10, 10) is a Martin Luther King. A more realistic example is (4, -3, 0): This person is moderately persuasive, bends truth a little too much for comfort (but not horribly), and is mildly anxious about speaking but far from falling apart. Every speaker exists at some point along these axes.

THE EXTERNAL MASTERY PROCESS IS INTERNAL TOO

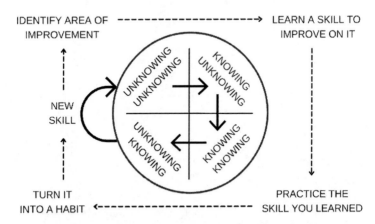

FIGURE IV: The same process presented earlier as a way to achieve rhetorical mastery will also help you achieve self-mastery. Just replace the word "skill" with "thought" or "thought-pattern," and the same cyclical method works.

THE POWER OF LANGUAGE

Language has generative power. This is why many creation stories include language as a primordial agent playing a crucial role in crafting reality. "In the beginning was the Word, and the Word was with God (John 1:1)."

Every problem we face has a story written about its future, whether explicit or implicit, conscious or subconscious. Generative language can rewrite a story that leads downward, turning it into one that aims us toward heaven, and then it can inspire us to realize this story. It can remove the cloud of ignorance from noble possibilities.

And this is good. You can orient your own future upward. That's certainly good for you. You can orient the future upward for yourself and for your family. That's better. And for your friends. That's better. And for your organization, your community, your city, and your country. That's better still. And for your enemies, and for people yet unborn; for all people, at all times, from now until the end of time.

And it doesn't get better than that.

Sound daunting? It is. It is the burden of human life. It is also the mechanism of moral progress. But start wherever you can, wherever you are. Start by acing your upcoming presentation.

But above all, remember this: all progress begins with truth.

Convey truth beautifully. And know thyself, so you can guard against your own proclivity for malevolence, and so you can strive toward self-mastery. Without self-mastery, it's hard, if not nearly impossible, to do the first part; to convey truth beautifully.

Truth, so you do good, not bad; impact, so people believe you; and self-mastery, as an essential precondition for truth and impact. Imagine what the world would be like if everyone were a triple-ten on our three axes. Imagine what good, what beauty, what bliss would define our existence. Imagine what good, what beauty, what bliss *could* define our existence, here and now.

It's up to you.

THE INNER GAME OF SPEAKING

REFER BACK TO THIS INTERNAL GUIDE as needed. These humble suggestions have helped me deliver high-stakes speeches with inner peace, calm, and equanimity. They are foundational, and the most important words I ever put to paper. I hope these ideas help you as much as they helped me.

MASTER BOTH GAMES. Seek to master the outer game, but also the inner game. The self-mastery game comes before the word-mastery game, and even the world-mastery game. In fact, if you treat *any* game as a way to further your self-mastery, setting this as your "game above all games," you can never lose.

ADOPT THREE FOUNDATIONS. Humility: "The other people here probably know something I don't. They could probably teach me something. I could be overlooking something. I could be wrong. They have something to contribute." Passion: "Conveying truth accurately and convincingly is one of the most important things I'll ever do." Objectivity: "If I'm wrong, I change course. I am open to reason. I want to *be* right; I don't just want to seem right or convince others I am."

STRIVE FOR THESE SUPERLATIVES. Be the kindest, most compassionate, most honest, most attentive, most well-researched, and most confident in the room. Be the one who cares most, who most seeks to uplift others, who is most prepared, and who is most thoughtful about the reason and logic and evidence behind the claims.

START BY CULTIVATING THE HIGHEST VIRTUES IN YOURSELF: love for your audience, love for truth, humility, a deep and abiding desire to make the world a better place, the desire to both be heard and to hear, and the desire to both teach and learn. You will find peace, purpose, clarity, confidence, and persuasive power.

START BY AVOIDING THESE TEMPTING MOTIVES. Avoid the desire to "outsmart" people, to overwhelm and dominate with your rhetorical strength, to embarrass your detractors, to win on the basis of cleverness alone, and to use words to attain power for its own sake. Don't set personal victory as your goal. Strive to achieve a victory for truth. And if you discover you are wrong, change course.

LISTEN TO YOURSELF TALK. (Peterson, 2018). See if what you are saying makes you feel stronger, physically, or weaker. If it makes you feel weaker, stop saying it. Reformulate your speech until you feel the ground under you solidifying.

SPEAK FROM A PLACE OF LOVE. It beats speaking from a desire to dominate. Our motivation and purpose in persuasion must be love. It's ethical *and* effective.

LOVE YOUR ENEMIES (OR HAVE NONE). If people stand against you, do not inflame the situation with resentment or anger. It does no good, least of all for you.

AVOID THESE CORRUPTING EMOTIONS: resistance, resentment, and anger. Against them, set acceptance, forgiveness, and love for all, even your enemies.

PLACE YOUR ATTENTION HERE, NOW. Be where you are. Attend to the moment. Forget the past. Forget the future. Nothing is more important than this.

FOCUS ON YOURSELF, BUT NOW. Speaking gurus will tell you to focus solely on your audience. Yes, that works. But so does focusing on yourself, as long as you focus on yourself *now*. Let this focus root you in the present. Don't pursue a mental commentary on what you see. Instead, just watch. Here. Now. No judgment.

ACCEPT YOUR FEAR. Everyone fears something. If you fear speaking, don't fear your fear of speaking too. Don't reprimand yourself for it. Accept it. Embrace it, even. Courage isn't action without fear. Courage is action despite fear.

STARE DOWN YOUR FEAR. To diminish your fear, stare at the object of your fear (and the fear itself), the way a boxer faces off with his opponent before the fight. Hold it in your mind, signaling to your own psyche that you can face your fear.

CHIP AWAY AT YOUR FEAR. The path out of fear is to take small, voluntary steps toward what you fear. Gradual exposure dissolves fear as rain carves stone.

LET THE OUTER SHAPE THE INNER. Your thoughts impact your actions. But your actions also impact your thoughts. To control fear, seek to manage its outward manifestations, and your calm exterior will shape your interior accordingly.

KNOW THAT EGO IS THE ENEMY. Ego is a black storm cloud blocking the warm sunlight of your true self. Ego is the creation of a false self that masquerades as your true self and demands gratification (which often manifests as the destruction of something good). The allure of arrogance is the siren-song of every good speaker. With it comes pride and the pursuit of power; a placing of the outer game before the inner. Don't fall for the empty promises of ego-gratification. Humility is power.

DON'T IDENTIFY WITH YOUR POSITIONS. Don't turn your positions into your psychological possessions. Don't imbue them with a sense of self.

NOTICE TOXIC AVATARS. When person A speaks to person B, they often craft a false idea, a false avatar, of both themselves and their interlocuter: A1 and B1. So does person B: B2 and A2. The resulting communication is a dance of false avatars; A1, B1, B2, and A2 communicate, but not person A and B. A false idea of one's self speaks to a false idea of someone else, who then does the same. This may be why George Bernard Shaw said "the greatest problem in communication is the illusion that it has been accomplished." How do you avoid this dance of false avatars? This conversation between concepts but not people?

Be present. Don't prematurely judge. Let go of your *sense* of self, for just a moment, so your real self can shine forth.

MINE THE RICHES OF YOUR MIND. Look for what you need within yourself; your strengths and virtues. But also acknowledge and make peace with your own capacity for malevolence. Don't zealously assume the purity of your own motives.

RISE ABOVE YOUR MIND. The ability to think critically, reason, self-analyze, and self-criticize is far more important than being able to communicate, write, and speak. Introspect before you extrospect. Do not identify as your mind, but as the awareness eternally watching your mind. Do not be in your mind, but above it.

CLEAR THE FOG FROM YOUR PSYCHE. Know what you believe. Know your failures. Know your successes. Know your weaknesses. Know your strengths. Know what you fear. Know what you seek. Know your mind. Know yourself. Know your capacity for malevolence and evil. Know your capacity for goodness and greatness. Don't hide any part of yourself from yourself. Don't even try.

KNOW YOUR LOGOS. In 500 B.C. Heraclitus defined Logos as "that universal principle which animates and rules the world." What is your Logos? Meditate on it. Sit with it. Hold it up to the light, as a jeweler does with a gem, examining all angles.

KNOW YOUR LIMITS. The more you delineate and define the actions you consider unethical, the more likely you are to resist when they seem expedient.

REMEMBER THAT EVERYTHING MATTERS. There is no insignificant job, duty, role, mission, or speech. Everything matters. Everything seeks to beat back chaos in some way and create order. A laundromat doesn't deal in clean clothes, nor a trash disposal contractor in clean streets. They deal in order. In civilization. In human dignity. Don't ignore the reservoir of meaning and mattering upon which you stand. And remember that it is there, no matter where you stand.

GIVE THE GIFT OF MEANING. The greatest gift you can give to an audience is the gift of meaning; the knowledge that they matter, that they are irreplaceable.

HONOR YOUR INHERITANCE. You are the heir to thousands of years of human moralizing. Our world is shaped by the words of long-dead philosophers, and the gifts they gave us: gems of wisdom, which strengthen us against the dread and chaos of the world. We stand atop the pillars of 4,000 years of myth and meaning. Our arguments and moral compasses are not like planks of driftwood in a raging sea, but branches nourished by an inestimably old tree. Don't forget it.

BE THE PERSON YOU WANT TO BE SEEN AS. How do you want to be seen by your audience? How can you actually be that way, rather than just seeming to be?

HAVE TRUE ETHOS. Ethos is the audience's perception that the speaker has their best interests at heart. It's your job to make sure this perception is accurate.

CHANGE PLACES WITH YOUR AUDIENCE. Put yourself in their shoes, and then be the speaker you would want to listen to, the speaker worthy of your trust.

ACT AS THOUGH THE WHOLE WORLD IS WATCHING. Or as though a newspaper will publish a record of your actions. Or as though you're writing your autobiography with every action, every word, and even every thought. (You are).

ACT WITH AUDACIOUS HONOR. As did John McCain when he called Obama, his political opponent, "a decent family man, [and] citizen, that I just happen to have disagreements with." As did Socrates and Galileo when they refused to betray truth.

ADOPT A MECHANIC'S MENTALITY. Face your challenges the way a mechanic faces a broken engine; not drowning in emotion, but with objectivity and clarity. Identify the problem. Analyze the problem. Determine the solution. Execute the solution. If it works, celebrate. If not, repeat the cycle. This is true for both your inner and outer worlds: your fear of speaking, for example, is a specific problem with a specific fix, as are your destructive external rhetorical habits.

APPLY THE MASTERY PROCESS INTERNALLY. The four-step mastery process is not only for mastering your rhetoric, but also for striving toward internal mastery.

MARSHAL YOURSELF ALONG THE THREE AXES. To marshal means to place in proper rank or position – as in marshaling the troops – and to bring together and order in the most effective way. It is a sort of preparation. It begins with taking complete stock of what is available. Then, you order it. So, marshal yourself along three axes: the rhetorical axis (your points, arguments, rhetorical techniques, key phrases, etc.), the internal axis (your peace of mind, your internal principles, your mental climate, etc.), and the truth axis (your research, your facts, your logic, etc.).

PRACTICE ONE PUNCH 10,000 TIMES. As the martial arts adage says, "I fear not the man who practiced 10,000 punches once, but the man who practiced one punch 10,000 times." So it is with speaking skills and rhetorical techniques.

MULTIPLY YOUR PREPARATION BY TEN. Do you need to read a manuscript ten times to memorize it? Aim to read it 100 times. Do you need to research for one hour to grasp the subject of your speech? Aim to research for ten.

REMEMBER THE HIGHEST PRINCIPLE OF COMMUNICATION: the connection between speaker and audience – here, now – in this moment, in this place.

KNOW THERE'S NO SUCH THING AS A "SPEECH." All good communication is just conversation, with varying degrees of formality heaped on top. It's all just connection between consciousnesses. Every "difference" is merely superficial.

SEE YOURSELF IN OTHERS. What are you, truly? Rene Descartes came close to an answer in 1637, when he said "cogito, ego sum," I think therefore I am. The answer this seems to suggest is that your thoughts are most truly you. But your thoughts (and your character) change all the time. Something that never changes, arguably even during deep sleep, is awareness. Awareness is also the precondition for thought. A computer performs operations on information, but we don't say the computer "thinks." Why? Because it lacks awareness. So, I believe what makes you "you," most fundamentally, is your awareness, your consciousness. And if you accept this claim – which is by no means a mystical or religious one – then you must also see yourself in others. Because while the contents of everyone's consciousness is different, the consciousness itself is identical. How could it be otherwise?

FORGIVE. Yourself. Your mistakes. Your detractors. The past. The future. All.

FREE YOUR MIND. Many of the most challenging obstacles we face are thoughts living in our own minds. Identify these thoughts, and treat them like weeds in a garden. Restore the pristine poise of your mind, and return to equanimity.

LET. Let what has been be and what will be be. Most importantly, let what is be what is. Work to do what good you can do, and accept the outcome.

FLOW. Wikipedia defines a flow state as such: "a flow state, also known colloquially as being in the zone, is the mental state in which a person performing some activity is fully immersed in a feeling of energized focus, full involvement, and enjoyment in the process of the activity. In essence, flow is characterized by the complete absorption in what one does, and a resulting transformation in one's sense of time." Speaking in a flow state transports you and your audience outside of space and time. When I entered deep flow states during my speeches and debates, audience members would tell me that "it felt like time stopped." It felt that way for me too. Speaking in a flow state is a form of meditation. And it both leads to and results from these guidelines. Adhering to them leads to flow, and flow helps you adhere to them.

MEDITATE. Meditation brings your attention to the "here and now." It creates flow. Practice silence meditation, sitting in still silence and focusing on the motions of your mind, but knowing yourself as the entity watching the mind, not the mind itself. Practice aiming meditation, centering your noble aim in your mind, and focusing on the resulting feelings. (Also, speaking in flow is its own meditation).

EMBARK ON THE GRAND ADVENTURE. Take a place wherever you are. Develop influence and impact. Improve your status. Take on responsibility. Develop capacity and ability. Do scary things. Dare to leap into a high-stakes speech with no preparation if you must. Dare to trust your instincts. Dare to strive. Dare to lead. Dare to speak the truth freely, no matter how brutal it is. Be bold. Risk failure. Throw out your notes. The greatest human actions – those that capture our hearts and minds – occur on the border between chaos and order, where someone is daring to act and taking a chance when they know they could fall off the tightrope with no net below. Training wheels kill the sense of adventure. Use them if you need to, but only to lose them as soon as you can. Speak from the heart and trust yourself. Put yourself out there. Let people see the gears turning in your mind, let them see you grappling with your message in real time, taking an exploration in the moment. This is not an automaton doing a routine. It's not robotic or mechanical. That's too much order. It's also not unstructured nonsense. That's too much chaos. There is a risk of failure, mitigated not by training wheels, but by preparation. It is not a perfectly practiced routine, but someone pushing themselves just beyond their comfort zone, right at the cutting-edge of what they are capable of. It's not prescriptive. It's not safe either. The possibility that you could falter and fall in real-time calls out the best from you, and is gripping for the audience. It is also a thrilling adventure. Have faith in yourself, faith that you will say the right words when you need to. Don't think ahead, or backward. Simply experience the moment.

BREAK THE SEVEN LAWS OF WEAKNESS. If your goal is weakness, follow these rules. Seek to control what you can't control. Seek praise and admiration from others. Bend the truth to achieve your goals. Treat people as instruments in your game. Only commit to outer goals, not inner goals. Seek power for its own sake. Let anger and dissatisfaction fuel you in your pursuits, and pursue them frantically.

FAIL. Losses lead to lessons. Lessons lead to wins. If there's no chance of failure in your present task, you aren't challenging yourself. And if you aren't challenging yourself, you aren't growing. And that's the deepest and most enduring failure.

DON'T BETRAY YOURSELF. To know the truth and not say the truth is to betray the truth and to betray yourself. To know the truth, seek the truth, love the truth, and to speak the truth and speak it well, with poise and precision and power… this is to honor the truth, and to honor yourself. The choice is yours.

FOLLOW YOUR INNER LIGHT. As the Roman emperor and stoic philosopher Marcus Aurelius wrote in his private journal, "If thou findest in human life anything better than justice, truth, temperance, fortitude, and, in a word, anything better than thy own mind's self-satisfaction in the things which it enables thee to do according to right reason, and in the condition that is assigned to thee without thy own choice; if, I say, thou seest anything better than this, turn to it with all thy soul, and enjoy that which thou hast found to be the best. But if nothing appears to be better than [this], give place to nothing else." And as Kant said, treat humans as ends, not means.

JUDGE THEIR JUDGMENT. People *are* thinking of you. They *are* judging you. But what is their judgment to you? Nothing. (Compared to your self-judgment).

BREAK LESSER RULES IN THE NAME OF HIGHER RULES. Our values and moral priorities nest in a hierarchy, where they exist in relation to one another. Some are more important than others. If life compels a tradeoff between two moral principles, as it often does, this means there is a right choice. Let go the lesser of the two.

DON'T AVOID CONFLICT. Necessary conflict avoided is an impending conflict exacerbated. Slay the hydra when it has two heads, not twenty.

SEE THE WHOLE BOARD. Become wise in the ways of the world, and learned in the games of power and privilege people have been playing for tens of thousands of years. See the status-struggles and dominance-shuffling around you. See the chess board. But then opt to play a different game; a more noble game. The game of self-mastery. The game that transcends all other games. The worthiest game.

SERVE SOMETHING. Everyone has a master. Everyone serves something. Freedom is not the absence of service. Freedom is the ability to choose your service. What, to you, is worth serving? With your work and with your words?

TAKE RESPONSIBILITY FOR YOUR RIPPLE EFFECT. If you interact with 1,000 people, and they each interact with 1,000 more who also do the same, you are three degrees away from one billion people. Remember that compassion is contagious.

ONLY SPEAK WHEN YOUR WORDS ARE BETTER THAN SILENCE. And only write when your words are better than a blank page.

KNOW THERE IS THAT WHICH YOU DON'T KNOW YOU DON'T KNOW. Of course, there's that you know you don't know too. Recognize the existence of both of these domains of knowledge, which are inaccessible to you in your present state.

REMEMBER THAT AS WITHIN, SO (IT APPEARS) WITHOUT. If you orient your aim toward goals fueled by emotions like insecurity, jealousy, or vengeance, the world manifests itself as a difficult warzone. If you orient your aim toward goals fueled by emotions like universal compassion and positive ambition, the beneficence of the world manifests itself to you. Your aim and your values alter your perception.

ORIENT YOUR AIM PROPERLY. Actions flow from thought. Actions flow from *motives*. If you orient your aim properly – if you aim at the greatest good for the greatest number, at acting forthrightly and honorably – then this motive will fuel right actions, subconsciously, automatically, and without any forethought.

STOP TRYING TO USE SPEECH TO GET WHAT YOU WANT. Try to articulate what you believe to be true as carefully as possible, and then accept the outcome.

USE THE MOST POWERFUL "RHETORICAL" TACTIC. There is no rhetorical tool more powerful than the overwhelming moral force of the unvarnished truth.

INJECT YOUR EXPERIENCE INTO YOUR SPEECH. Speak of what you know and testify of what you have seen. Attach your philosophizing and persuading and arguing to something real, some story you lived through, something you've seen.

DETACH FROM OUTCOME. As Stoic philosopher Epictetus said: "There is only one way to happiness and that is to cease worrying about things which are beyond the power of our will. Make the best use of what is in your power, and take the rest as it happens. The essence of philosophy is that a man should so live that his happiness shall depend as little as possible on external things. Remember to conduct yourself in life as if at a banquet. As something being passed around comes to you, reach out your hand and take a moderate helping. Does it pass you? Don't stop it. It hasn't yet come? Don't burn in desire for it, but wait until it arrives in front of you."

FOCUS ON WHAT YOU CONTROL. As Epictetus said, "It's not what happens to you, but how you react to it that matters. You may be always victorious if you will never enter into any contest where the issue does not wholly depend upon yourself. Some things are in our control and others not. Things in our control are opinion, pursuit, desire, aversion, and, in a word, whatever are our own actions. Things not in our control are body, property, reputation, command, and, in one word, whatever are not our own actions. Men are disturbed not by things, but by the view which they take of them. God has entrusted me with myself. Do not with that all things will go well with you, but that you will go well with all things." Before a high-stakes speech or event, I always tell myself this: "All I want from this, all I aim at, is to conduct what I control, my thoughts and actions, to the best of my ability. Any external benefit I earn is merely a bonus."

VIEW YOURSELF AS A VESSEL. Conduct yourself as something through which truth, brilliantly articulated, flows into the world; not as a self-serving entity, but a conduit for something higher. Speak not for your glory, but for the glory of good.

Email Peter D. Andrei, the author of the Speak for Success collection and the President of Speak for Success LLC directly.

pandreibusiness@gmail.com

Made in United States
Troutdale, OR
12/06/2023

15459232R00184